A Practical Approach to Animal Welfare Law

A Practical Approach to Animal Welfare Law
2nd Edition

Noël Sweeney

 5m Publishing

First published 2013
Second edition 2017

Published by
5M Publishing Ltd,
Benchmark House,
8 Smithy Wood Drive,
Sheffield, S35 1QN, UK
Tel: +44 (0) 1234 81 81 80
www.5mpublishing.com

A Catalogue record for this book is available from the British Library

ISBN 9781910455807

Book layout by Servis Filmsetting Ltd, Stockport, Cheshire
Printed by Replika Press Pvt Ltd, India

CONTENTS

INTRODUCTION

'Animals' is a term of abuse often used by humans to describe violent football fans and drunken thugs who run amok during demonstrations that were planned to be peaceful. 'Animals' as a pejorative term has become so widespread it was used in 2016 to describe a convicted paedophile who had slyly groomed and coy-duck style indecently assaulted a child. However, notwithstanding the history of our universal practice of putting animals on trial as common criminals for more than 1,000 years, it is humans who commit crimes against other humans and animals. Few, if any, violent, crapulent animal criminals invade a football pitch when their team is losing or hunt humans to death for fun. In 2016 a purblind American politician branded protesting arsonists as 'animals'.

Indeed, rather than the reverse, animals are classified as our *'property'* so they can and do become victims within our legal system. Much as a shuttlecock child who can be moved from parent to parent and care home to foster home within our system, so can animals be subject to rules designed by us to take advantage of their lack of legal status.

When we consider 'welfare' as a concept, we are generally dealing with someone who is vulnerable and in need of assistance lest they are exploited by other less scrupulous individuals. The vulnerability is respected and accounted for within our social services. Conversely, where animals are concerned we have no representative save for indirectly by some lacklustre government departments and worthy charities.

The first major animal welfare legislation was introduced in England in 1822 by an Irish barrister, Richard 'Humanity Dick' Martin. The statute, titled An Act to prevent the cruel and improper Treatment of Cattle, known colloquially as 'Martin's Act', was the benchmark used by the SPCA when it was formed in 1824. As a group and social movement it knew that, while fine words butter no parsnips, the law is the only way to protect animals and lessen their suffering at human hands. Martin explained the aim of that change was that: 'If legislation to protect animals is to be effective, it must be adequately enforced.'

How far-sighted some people have been can be seen by the Puritans introducing protection for animals in America in 1641. Richard Ryder, the scientist who coined the word *'speciesism'*, cites an Irish law with the same aim in 1635. Yet earlier laws were enacted in Scotland: the first statutes were the Horses Act 1587, the Killing and Maiming of Cattle Act 1581 and the Horse Shoeing Act 1478, which controlled 'ignorant and drunken smiths'. Those statutes were controlling humans rather than showing care for the animal's welfare. Martin's Act was the most important one given its aspirant aim and moral purpose.

Law is more important in relation to animals than it might at first glance appear to be. Ultimately law is a social tool that can be used on their behalf to rescue a 'rescued' dog who is wrongly sentenced to death or an abandoned horse starving in a mud-ridden field when the departing caravans leave the village green. The law can reach the dark recesses of an abattoir when whistle-blowers reveal animal abuse that is concealed as there are no cameras there.

A Practical Approach to Animal Welfare Law is not intended to be a Delphic legal treatise. Instead it is intended to be equally for those with no legal experience as well as practising vets and lawyers who are new to this field. It is aimed at and hoped to be of value to people who are involved in working with animals on a daily basis, whether for a living or as a volunteer. At best it might provide a practical guide for those who wish to know what they can do to assist animals who rely upon them in relation to their daily needs. For in law, as in life, animals may well be our friends and neighbours.

There are well over 100 Acts and 1,000 statutory instruments that affect animals within criminal law. Seeking to address many of those would result in a tome so unwieldy as to be unmanageable for the average person working with animals on a farm, in a pet shop, in a sanctuary, at a vet's surgery, for a charity and in court. As a result, this book concentrates on analysing the two main statutes that affect people who own or work with animals, the Animal Welfare Act 2006 [AWA] and the Dangerous Dogs Act 1991 [DDA].

In different ways those two statutes have the same aim, namely the care and welfare of animals. Though the Acts are separate in form and procedure, they can interact when irresponsible owners fail in their duty towards their charges.

The advantage for the reader is that the AWA and the DDA are concerned with all aspects of criminal law as it affects animals. Together they are the two most important statutes that are used by the authorities to prosecute people who fail to fulfil their legal duty and responsibility towards animals that they own or have to care for regarding their welfare. Together those two Acts are the main ones that are used to protect animals from harm and unnecessary suffering. Those Acts can impinge upon owners and workers whose daily lives are intertwined with domestic cats and horses and sheep and imported exotic creatures. Legal protection relates to all 'protected' animals, including abandoned cats, circus acts, farm animals, those in laboratories, held in zoos and the increasing statistics of misery that are animals in distress. That protection extends to dangerous dogs unleashed by dangerous owners.

Animals are so much part of the fabric of our lives that they affect the highest and the lowest within society. Some people take their dogs to the office as an additional member of staff. In America in 2015 they started a project of introducing child-friendly 'pat' dogs in court where children were witnesses, usually involving them as victims of sexual offences. The dogs help to put the children at ease and enable them to give evidence against the perpetrators who abused them. Given the connection between abuse to children and animals, it is a symbiotic relationship borne of a basic unspoken mutual understanding.

Yet when a defendant, *Devon D*, was convicted in the USA of sexual assault and risk of injury to his three children, he appealed on the basis that the dog was prejudicial to his defence. He claimed that the dog's presence would 'improperly influence the jury by making it appear the child was someone with whom they should sympathise.' He went further by claiming that rather than having a real dog, Summer, she could have clung to a stuffed teddy bear. Somewhat strangely his claim succeeded in the Connecticut Appeal Court. Fortunately the Connecticut Supreme Court rejected his appeal and reversed that dubious decision.

In its judgment the court said: 'We conclude that the pivotal question is not whether the special procedure is necessary but whether it will aid the witness in testifying truthfully and reliably. We further conclude that the record in the present case demonstrates that the trial court expressly found that Summer would help [the child] to testify more reliably and completely and that Summer's presence would not violate the defendant's right to a fair trial. Finally, the record indicates that the trial court took extensive measures to ensure that the jurors never saw Summer.' [See: The Link Letter: *National Link Coalition*: July/August 2016]

That decision echoed one in the Michigan Appeals Court in May 2016, where the court ruled that 'the presence of a dog did not adversely prejudice the jury in convicting a man of sexually abusing his niece'. Each decision was the right one for the child and the community.

We should adopt the same approach in our courts as vulnerable children can be assisted in giving their evidence. That in turn can assist the judge and jury in making their respective decisions. It is underlined by the recurring fact that most child victims of sexual abuse will know their abusers. The comfort of an animal can evoke empathy and sympathy.

A project in Scotland is bridging that gap in a positive way between people and animals: prisoners are training dogs that are later used as 'assistance' companions for disabled people.

An anecdote of compassion in action with a raw example of empathy happened in the UK when Doctor David Nott received the MBE from the Queen. He is a medical war hero who suffered from post-traumatic stress syndrome [P-TSD]. At dinner he sat next to the Queen. Dr Nott was not merely tongue-tied, he could not engage in conversation at all. He was so stricken with the effects of P-TSD that words literally failed him. The Queen immediately sensed his acute embarrassment and the reason for his taciturnity. She gestured to a courtier, who brought her corgis to their table. Then the courtier brought some dog food. Then together the doctor and the Queen passed a pleasurable evening feeding the corgis. Without words she put him at ease by her humanity, which was expressed through her corgis.

It was proof, if proof were needed, that a pet is no less than a member of the family and our society. The law should reflect and respect that elemental point.

Yet while Article 8 of the European Convention for the Protection of Human Rights [1950] protects 'the right to respect for his private and family life', it does not include an individual's right to keep a pet. Indeed, keeping a pet does not even fall within the sphere of 'private or family life'. That indicates a lack of understanding of the importance of an animal to the owner and within a family. Holding that a pet is not worthy as a member of the 'family' is an example of the prejudice against animals innate within our legal system.

More than merely being part of the family, animals can often be part of the creative process. When Bobby Zimmy took Hamlet, not the depressed Shakespearian loner but a huge poodle, into the studio in Woodstock in America as part of The Band, the result was the wildly wonderful album *Music from Big Pink*. In the UK, an animal enhanced the growling blues of Rod 'the Mod' Stewart. The late great drummer, Mickey Waller, who made pragmatic use of his law degree to claim unpaid royalties, was always accompanied by his loyal pooch Zak, a boxer. Zak usually sat quietly in the corner. However, obviously taken by the mood of the music, he can be heard howling in time to the wailing harmonica on *Sweet Little Rock 'n' Roller* on the stylish *Smiler*. The legendary Dave Swarbrick ['Swarb'], a virtuosic player blessed with a talent so fine he could outplay the devil to win a gold fiddle. Swarb started to take Ruby, his canine companion, on tour with him. Their friendship had a visible mutuality that lifted the music to a level that was so supreme the top notes could only be heard by angels and dogs.

That is the reason the brilliant cutting cartoonist, Michael Heath, asked if he could take his dog as his 'Desert Island Disc' request for a 'luxury'. It was the single item he wished to accompany him when he was marooned on that island. The choice was not only a grand gesture, it was one borne of an irresistible plea that could not be refused given the sad saxophone sound that would never end as at feeding time he called out the name of his faithful friend: Charlie Parker.

As in 2016 there are about nine million dog owners and eight million cat owners in the UK, the scope for fallout in terms of the criminal law is unavoidable. It is beyond the prosaic practice of violent thugs with trophy dogs who train them to be a live weapon. Now the incidents can range from your dog biting a burglar on his buttocks to a swarm of bees that stings your neighbour, and a cock that disturbs your sleep by crowing thrice before dawn.

In May 2016 Sir David Attenborough made a statement honed on his years of experience of being with gorillas, in such close contact he was almost a member of their family: 'Gorillas are just like us.' In America in the same month a 17-year-old silver-backed 400lb gorilla, Harambe, was shot in a Connecticut zoo to 'save' a four-year-old boy who had wandered away from his mother and somehow fallen into the gorilla's cage. Harambe had been born in a Texas zoo and lived in one until his death. The child was unharmed.

Then again, in Ireland in August 2016 a young boy climbed into the rhino enclosure at Dublin Zoo. The adult holding the boy's hand from the safe viewing side shared the adventure with the world on social media. So it was a bit of family fun as if the child was in any danger they could always kill the rhino.

Normally we rely on the judiciary to protect animals and punish transgressors by remaining neutral and stoic. However, even judges have emotions that can surface where their pets are concerned. His Honour Judge [HHJ] Simon Newell was angry after being barred from taking his dog, Marley, into a wine bar rather than remain in the garden. Therefore 'in apparent retaliation' the judge parked his car near the bar, Barrique, in Lytham with 'a series of bizarre notes taped to the windscreen'. One note described the ban as 'woof justice' for Marley. That sparked a brief feud between the judge and the owner of the bar. The feud was concluded after the police spoke to both parties and confirmed no offence in the legal sense was committed. A final note of conciliation was tendered by the judge wishing the owner 'a dog-free future' and signed 'A very chastened Marley'.

We often judge people by how altruistic they are towards others less fortunate than themselves or who help someone in need while others walk on by. A major study of whales identified humpback whales intervening to counter 'attacks by killer whales on seals, sea lions, sunfish and juvenile whales of other species'. Whatever may have been their mixed reasons of instinct and survival, significantly the 'humpbacks … gained no obvious benefits for their time and energy [they] spent'. The humpbacks had travelled more than a mile and spent up to seven hours around killer whales seeking to 'protect' the potential prey from death.

Animals and law are connected as they are valued and undervalued according to their status and worth to us much as any other item of property. The Theft Act 1968 defines products that can be stolen as 'Property includes money and all other property, real or personal …Wild creatures, tamed or untamed, shall be regarded as property …' A mongrel may be the only friend a person has so the bond between them would be as rare as love and the theft rawer than truth. When Troya, a Spanish presa canario, was stolen on Christmas Eve 2015 and later found floating in a Manchester canal having been cruelly killed, she was the first animal to be featured on the BBC flagship programme, *Crimewatch*. An autopsy proved that Troya had been hanged or strangled. For the owner, given the theft and the suffering in the mode of her death, as a victim she was similar to a child that had been abducted and tortured and killed.

Animals have a certain undeniable claim within society to be treated as sentient living creatures deserving of being protected by law. That is not a grudging concession granted by some self-ordained superior being, but the recognition that law is the universal language that speaks for the vulnerable and the weak. Isonomy guarantees the principle of equality within law that cannot be fudged or judged to exclude some people. There is a reason to believe that treating other beings as subject to the same noble ideals we seek enhances humanity and society. By lessening their suffering we can become kinder and pursue our ideal of justice. That concept is contained within the aim of the AWA and the DDA. Each Act attempts to control us in our treatment of animals as otherwise we can harm other people and them. Regardless of whether our acts are intentional or reckless, the result is the same.

Whether the ideas within those Acts have been achieved in practice depends upon how we have interpreted and used the law. This analysis will show to the reader if we have failed or succeeded in that search for justice. Even if justice is blind, we cannot conceal the truth.

Those who work with animals are the fulcrum on which the mechanism of our law functions. Above all aspects of their activities, they are instrumental in upholding those legal principles. *A Practical Approach to Animal Welfare Law* takes account of our relationship with animals. By applying the standards of the AWA and the DDA regarding 'duty' and 'responsibility', the owners and workers can positively change the potential plight of their animals. Their pledge feeds the future of animals, which can shape the law to meet the needs of an enlightened society.

TABLE OF CASES

TABLE OF STATUTES

TABLE OF STATUTORY INSTRUMENTS

Animal Welfare Act 2006

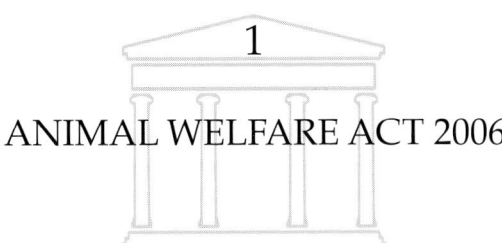

1

ANIMAL WELFARE ACT 2006

1.1 Value

The Protection of Animals Act 1911 [POA] belied and denied its name. It was deliberately drafted with limited protection for animals in mind. That Act concentrated on the concept of cruelty and allowed animal abusers to escape their just deserts by a combination of legal loopholes and judicial fudges. Each deficiency in that Act was drafted and thereafter interpreted narrowly in favour of defendants to the detriment of animals. Domestic animals were barely protected while wild animals were used and abused at will. The POA purposely exempted hunting and vivisection from its terms to protect people practising those interests. An accurate impression can be deduced from the expression that defined a domestic animal as one 'which is tame or which has been or is sufficiently tamed to serve some purpose for the use of man'. Their value was assessed by us on their 'use' to us.

After almost a century the POA was finally replaced by the AWA. In approach, content and spirit the AWA is a radical departure from the POA. The AWA swept away the cobweb ideas and ushered in a new way of thinking about animals in relation to ownership and harm and society. No advocate with a sense of purpose would now be able to rely on the old ideas within the POA to persuade any court in the future.

While the POA was primarily concerned with cruelty, the AWA is concerned with welfare. The words 'cruel' and 'cruelty' are not used in the AWA at all. Instead, the word 'suffering' is used throughout. That is consistent with the twin limbs of 'duty' and 'responsibility' that are imposed upon people for the treatment of their animals. Those legal inconsistencies that riddled the POA, especially in the treatment of farm animals and wild animals in captivity, were addressed by the AWA. The AWA places a duty of care on the person responsible for the animal's welfare. That stance is a change of principle that aims to protect animals from their natural predators: humans.

A pivotal point that is repeated in sections 4 and 9, dealing with the 'prevention of harm' and the 'promotion of welfare' states the principle without prevarication: *Nothing in this section applies to the destruction of an animal in an appropriate and humane manner.*

That underlines the value of an animal's life now as unless the manner of their death is 'appropriate' and 'humane', it is unlawful. The AWA restricts an owner's right to treat an animal in a way that harms its welfare. Therefore, the owner has a primary duty to care for his animals rather than choose to destroy his property. As death is the result of a final act or omission, that clause places an onus on the owner of animals to take account of their welfare. In his choice of the form of their life and death, he is liable for the manner of it if that is inappropriate or inhumane. After all, pleasure and pain is shared by all living beings.

That concept of 'welfare' underpins the whole of the AWA. It is the cornerstone of the principles within it. While the idea of welfare was of concern to Henry S. Salt more than a century ago, it has only had legal significance since the 1960s. Salt, a visionary teacher, markedly noted in *Animals Rights Considered in Relation to Social Progress* [1892]: 'to live one's life – to realise one's true self – is the highest moral purpose of man and animal alike.'

1.2   Thing

Salt's view applies to Marshall Rosenberg, the American psychologist, too. Rosenberg was a pioneer of non-violent communication. He used a giraffe as a model to aid his patients and assist their recovery. His approach centred on the belief that a giraffe was such a graceful creature that people empathised with the feeling they gained in his company, and this helped to assuage their pain. Although the giraffe was a huge animal, he was gentle and calm, which proved to be a balm for Rosenberg's perturbed patients.

In 2016 Aryanna Gourdin travelled from Utah in America to South Africa for a hunting safari. She killed a giraffe. Gourdin posed beside the dead giraffe, holding her rifle and smiling for the camera. She posted photos on social media of her trophy plus other animals she had shot. Gourdin, who was accompanied by her father, is 12 years old.

The going rate to kill a giraffe is £2,500. Africa is a microcosm of our value of all animals. Their net worth to us is measured by the premise and assessed on the basis that they have no legal '*personality*'. [See: **Chapter 20**]

Our legal system classes a furry striped animal activated by a ventriloquist's arm as being no different than the real thing. Each one, be it a toy or a tiger, is a different form of the same item, though each one is no different in law. 'Property' is a concept that permeates our law. As a matter of law an animal is just a '*thing*'. That is why the AWA is concerned with welfare not 'rights'. Therefore, while there are criminal sanctions for abuse of animals and a prohibition on causing them 'unnecessary suffering', their fate and fortune and future rests in our hands. Whether we care for their welfare or not, we control their daily lives in many ways because it is our calculated choice to deny them a legal voice.

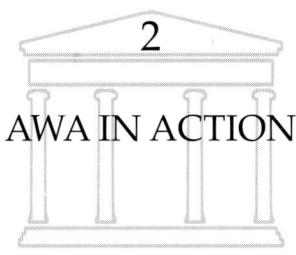

2

AWA IN ACTION

2.1   Aim

The UK's AWA balances the benefit of controlling animals with a burden on people who choose to look after and live and work with them. It is a criminal Act whose purpose is to protect those animals from *'unnecessary suffering'* by ensuring we adopt a *'good practice'* when dealing with them during our collective daily lives.

While wild animals are still largely denied protection, in certain limited circumstances the AWA can apply to them. The protection extends to an animal that is owned by a person or there is someone who is responsible for them. Yet the offences relating to 'animal fighting' have a much wider application and catches those who are directly and indirectly involved in that criminal activity. Although animal experiments and vivisection are outside the scope of this book, the AWA is so wide in effect that it relates to that area too. In general the Act extends the mantle of law to cover domestic and farm animals as each are often used and abused by us. The AWA seeks to protect those animals' interests against their abusers.

2.2   Freedom

The AWA incorporates the principles outlined by the Brambell Committee in its *Report of the Technical Committee to Enquire into the Welfare of Animals Kept Under Intensive Livestock Husbandry Systems*

[1965]. As a result, the term 'welfare' was adopted in the legislation to protect animals. By relying on 'welfare' it was positively and purposely using a term that was usually applied to children.

That concept of welfare from the Brambell Report was endorsed by the Farm Animal Welfare Council [FAWC], which was formed in 1979. The FAWC concluded that all animals should have the 'five freedoms', which are:

1. Freedom from hunger and thirst – by ready access to water and a diet to maintain health and vigour.
2. Freedom from discomfort – by providing an appropriate environment.
3. Freedom from pain, injury and disease – by prevention or rapid diagnosis and treatment.
4. Freedom to express normal behaviour – by providing sufficient space, proper facilities and appropriate company of the animal's own kind.
5. Freedom from fear and distress – by ensuring conditions and treatment, which avoid mental suffering.

Although those 'Freedoms' are less than ideal, they are the minimum requirements to ensure animals are properly treated by people who have a duty of care towards them, are responsible for them, intend to kill them, or engage in all those matters. Those 'Freedoms' are the core of the AWA.

The AWA is based on and adopts the principle that the welfare of the animal is paramount. During the trial of *Gray v. RSPCA* [2010] A20090060 some of the defence counsel relied on the POA in their submissions. That approach was misconceived as if it had any validity the AWA would be a legal paper tiger without bite or teeth. HHJ Tyrer took the opportunity to fix the court's judgment on the principles that formed the AWA. The judge declared the irrelevance of the POA to their decision: 'Before the passing of this new Act [AWA], there was a great deal of case law on the meaning of the previous provisions of section 1 of the Protection of Animals Act 1911. In our judgment the old jurisprudence is no longer relevant.'

HHJ Tyrer confirmed the supremacy of the AWA. Gray appealed to the High Court. Oddly, one counsel relied on authorities relating to the POA again. He tried to revive the dead law of the POA.

Lord Justice Toulson [LJ] dismissed his submission: 'That Act [POA] was the corner piece of animal welfare legislation prior to its repeal and replacement by the 2006 Act. The judge took the view that the language of section 1 of the 1911 Act, and authorities as to its construction, were irrelevant to the construction of section 4 of the 2006 Act. The judge was right.'

That attempt by the defence to rely on the POA was pointless as the AWA swept away all the old ideas and replaced them with new concepts that were hitherto unknown within animal law. Both judges were forthright and right. If either of the judges had decided otherwise the result would have cast the AWA into a lasting legal limbo. [See: **2.7**]

Animals to which the Act applies

2.3   Animal Welfare Act 2006 s.1

(1) In this Act, except subsections (4) and (5), 'animal' means a vertebrate other than man.

With a knowing nod to the idea we are all Darwin's cousins, the AWA defines animals it applies to as 'a vertebrate other than man'.

The AWA does not apply to an animal while it is in a foetal or embryonic form. That is a questionable omission as causing 'suffering' to a pregnant animal would be an aggravating feature. Human foetuses have legal protection for that reason. If an animal is pregnant its needs and welfare are affected because of its condition. The unborn progeny can have their pending birth terminated and their welfare affected as a result of any abuse directed at their prospective parent.

Nevertheless, the AWA allows for changes in legal protection according to the advancement of knowledge and science. The 'appropriate national authority' that governs the regulations is the Secretary of State for England and the National Assembly for Wales. They have power to extend and make and amend the regulations. In 2015 the International Institute for Species Exploration confirmed the existence of many new animals and plants. They include such a variety as a cart-wheeling spider, a feathered dinosaur and a bone-house wasp. This provision would allow the authorities to include such creatures within the protection of the AWA.

Though the Act can be amended, it must relate to the promotion of animal welfare. The power may only be exercised if it is satisfied 'on the basis of scientific evidence' that animals of the kind concerned are ones capable of experiencing 'pain or suffering'.

'Pain' is not defined directly in the Act. 'Suffering' is defined as 'physical or mental suffering and related expressions shall be construed accordingly'. Animals can feel mental suffering and in extreme cases even post-traumatic stress disorder. The resonance between a human reaction to conditions and animals' behaviour are related and shared. Prisoners can become mentally disturbed, known colloquially as 'cabin fever' or 'stir crazy', which is a condition that can be reflected by animals in war zone and a zoo. Bad dog breeders can induce such a state by confining dogs in boxes, making them breeding machines as a means of creating a profit. Those conditions manifestly affect their actions, causing the dogs high levels of stereotypical stress.

Hence, on balance the cogent conclusion confirms the size of the cell and the bars on a cage can induce negative stress regardless of whether the one incarcerated is a human or an animal. For each one the suffering is a similar strain.

Even so, 'pain' should be accurately defined in the AWA. The definition should be amended to include all forms of physical ill-treatment and psychological pain. Whether or not there was any proven 'fear' involved in the killing of an animal should be defined to remove any lurking doubt. An animal's life has value because they are alive. Moreover, like the soldiers they serve beside, the dogs of war can and do suffer from psychological stress: each of our heroes can be affected by P-TSD.

A continuing problem within the POA, which resulted in many bad decisions, was the concentration by judges on whether the animal that was abused suffered 'cruelty' or not. As that Act has rightly been confined to a legal graveyard, so should those ideas. An animal's 'suffering' should be defined to include every form of mental and physical pain that is similar to the suffering of a child. That approach would take account of the particular vulnerability of each respective victim. Indeed, in a reverse situation that proves the point, the High Court of New Zealand confirmed that the cruelty offence in the Animal Welfare Act 1999 is derived from the Court of Appeal decision in *R. v. Hende* [1996] 1 NZLR 153, which dealt with the offence of wilfully ill-treating a child in a manner likely to cause unnecessary suffering. That progressive decision accentuates that children and animals share the core condition of welfare that is the pivot upon which the law balances to protect the weak.

'Protected animal'

2.4   Animal Welfare Act 2006 s.2

An animal is a 'protected animal' for the purposes of this Act if:

(a) it is of a kind which is commonly domesticated in the British Islands,

(b) it is under the control of man whether on a permanent or temporary basis, or

(c) it is not living in a wild state.

In general, only a protected animal has legal protection in respect of its welfare. A 'protected' animal is one 'commonly domesticated', under our 'control' or not living in a 'wild state'. That theme runs throughout the AWA in relation to the principal offences.

An animal that is commonly domesticated would include stray dogs and feral cats. It covers animals whose conduct and life-cycle have been conditioned by being under human control. That affects their breed and physiology as normally they would have been subject to living conditions dictated by us that can determine their behaviour. A relationship between the kind of animal and the human control would exist as it has to be one we have *'commonly'* domesticated. Besides wandering hedgehogs, it would include wild Dartmoor ponies and visiting Canada geese if people become involved in their feeding and living conditions.

If it is a wild animal that has been captured by a person, whether on a *'permanent or temporary'* basis, the Act would provide protection. The urban fox that occasionally becomes a pet could not be hunted on the high street or killed at will if it suffered in the process. As the urban fox is not now so rare, to extend care to them is natural as we have been instrumental in causing them to move towards us in order to survive. Forty per cent of gardeners see foxes on a regular basis. Therefore a pet fox would be no less protected than an ordinary domestic cat. In London the locals have adopted Cyril the squirrel and feed him nuts on a daily basis. If Cyril becomes a 'pet' so he relies on them for food then he too could be protected.

Fox hunters following a 'trail' hunt or engaged in an illegal one have a duty and responsibility under the AWA towards their domesticated hound dogs. The term 'captive animal' used in the POA often confused the courts and prosecutors. In comparison, the term *under the control* is much wider. Now even if an animal was not handled by a human, given the new technology for tracking and tracing and trapping animals used by baiters and poachers, an animal could be under the *control of man* if it cannot escape. That is underlined by the fact the animal can be controlled on a 'permanent or temporary basis'.

It would not matter if the animal was still underground as a badger may equally suffer from a terrier attack as suffocate if its sett is blocked. The baiter and the hunter is intent on getting as well as keeping an animal under 'control' until it is killed by his dogs, just him, or both. Similarly, a captive bird would be caught within the AWA. The deciding factor is that the animal lacks the freedom to live without control within its own environment.

The purpose of the term is to include animals that are not presently under our control, but have been and are not yet living independently in the wild. It would apply to Nellie the Elephant when she ran away from the circus. Or to a 'stir-crazy' tiger who escaped from the zoo. Their status is dependent on the fact that prior to their bid for freedom the elephant and tiger were controlled by us and thus are 'not living in a wild state'.

That acknowledges that the animal may have been wild initially, but has been changed and conditioned by us. A wild animal not normally within the AWA would become subject to it if it is captured or rescued by a person. Our duty and responsibility under the Act then flows from the fact of our act. The animal remains protected unless and until its status changes upon being released, whether by human choice or its own escape.

An animal that is adopted as a pet, whatever its origin, becomes a 'protected animal'. While a rat may invoke strong feelings of the bubonic plague and is generally wild, a pet rat would be within the AWA no less than any other cherished pet.

Responsibility for animals

2.5   Animal Welfare Act 2006 s.3

(1) In this Act, references to a person responsible for an animal are to a person responsible for an animal whether on a permanent or temporary basis.

Responsibility for an animal runs through the sinews of the AWA. Once the responsibility attaches to a person, the duty towards that animal and consequences of care for its welfare flows from that status. 'Duty' and 'Responsibility' towards an animal are the two sides of the same condition. You cannot possess one without possessing the other.

The responsibility for an animal does not shift with control or possession, but lasts as long as the ownership itself. When a person has that responsibility, the liability attaches to that status. The responsibility includes being 'in charge' of an animal and for any person under 16 years old for whom he has 'care and control'.

People do not escape liability by claiming, whether falsely or otherwise, that they do not 'own' the animal. If they have responsibility for an animal on a 'permanent or temporary basis', that is enough for a duty to ensue. That is why it includes being in 'charge' of one. So if the owner is on holiday or in hospital, whoever has accepted the temporary care of the animal equally accepts and assumes the legal responsibility. All the duties follow from that joint role and status.

That duty would extend to a vet caring for an animal overnight in his surgery, staff at a cattery and kennels, as well as volunteers at an animal sanctuary. It would apply to a police officer who seizes a dog, be it a pit bull terrier or poodle, as his or her responsibility attaches to that decision. Even if it is illegal to own an animal, the responsibility for its welfare is on the person who has control. That includes caring for an animal while the owner is in prison. [See: **11.4**]

An adult is responsible for any animal that his or her child owns. The care and control of the animal is shared by the adult in respect of both child and animal. So the owner is not free from responsibility merely because the child causes the animal to suffer. In that event they are both liable.

In *Gray v. RSPCA* the recorder, HHJ Tyrer, dealt with the issue head-on as counsel for James Gray Senior argued that James Gray Junior, his 14-year-old son, could not be 'responsible' in law for an omission in his treatment of animals. The Recorder rejected that idea out of hand: 'It does not mean that the fifth appellant [Gray Junior] cannot be responsible in law. What other purpose can section 3 have? If the fifth appellant cannot be responsible in law for an animal because of his age why did Parliament deal with the position of those who have actual care and control of him?'

HHJ Tyrer held it extended responsibility for any animal looked after by someone under 16 years old to those who have care and control of that child. Therefore if a person, usually a parent, has had some responsibility for any animal during the period covered by the charge in question, be it temporary or permanent custody or control, then he is liable in law. The liability arises because the parent has vicarious ownership or is in charge of the animal. It would equally apply to anyone who had 'actual' parental care and control of the child in a care home or detention centre.

The recorder was right. The attempt by the defence to use the POA was perverse as the AWA introduced new ideas that abolished those anachronistic ones. [See: **2.8**]

Unnecessary suffering

2.6   Animal Welfare Act 2006 s.4

(1) A person commits an offence if
   (a)   an act of his, or a failure of his to act, causes an animal to suffer,

(b) he knew, or ought reasonably to have known, that the act, or failure to act, would have that effect or be likely to do so,

(c) the animal is a protected animal, and

(d) the suffering is unnecessary.

The avoidance of and liability for causing *'unnecessary suffering'* to an animal beats at the heart of the AWA. The liability of the offender extends to active and passive harm, whether it is caused by an act or a failure to act. That term includes that the person knew the result of his action or omission would cause such suffering *'or be likely to do so'*. That avoids a narrow construction and simplifies the wider interpretation for the court in relation to what is expected and forbidden.

The prevention of 'unnecessary suffering' is the duty imposed on the owner that makes him liable for harm that could and should have been avoided. So it does not require a state of mind involving a *'specific'* intent to commit a crime such as wounding with intent or murder. Those offences require that the offender had a specific intent to commit that actual offence. In comparison this is a *'basic'* intent offence for which the *mens rea* [guilty mind] is an intentional or reckless one. Hence the offence can be committed by a reckless state of mind. That mental condition of the offender is much wider in form and effect and includes acting recklessly or being reckless in failing to act with the result the animal is harmed and suffers.

2.7   Spindles

In *Gray v. RSPCA* the importance of the AWA can be seen in operation. *Gray* was an appeal from Bicester Magistrates' Court by five of the Gray family, namely the husband and wife, two daughters and a son. All five had been convicted of animal abuse under the AWA.

A horse business was run by the appellants at Spindles Farm in Speen, Buckinghamshire, between 2007 and 2008. The RSPCA inspectors attended the farm and seized and removed more than 100 animals, mainly horses, ponies and donkeys, and discovered the bodies of 32 equines. Given the conditions found there, the investigators gave it a name that reflected their discovery: 'More than 30 animals were also found dead at what became known as "Hell Farm" ...'

The animals had numerous health problems, including strangles, salmonella infections, anaemia, parasite infections, impaired liver functions and internal organ damage. Kirsty Hampton, the RSPCA inspector, said, 'The stench of decomposition and urine was over-powering. The sight of horses left in such a miserable state will stay with me forever and I hope I never have to see animals treated with such little care and compassion again.'

The recorder took the opportunity to concentrate on the principles of the AWA. He said: 'What has to be established is either subjective knowledge namely personal knowledge, or objective knowledge namely that the individual ought reasonably to have known that his or her act or failure to act would cause an animal to suffer unnecessarily.'

There are two alternative offences: (i) the act of 'omission' that causes the unnecessary suffering to an animal; (ii) being responsible for an animal that he 'permitted' or 'failed' to prevent another person causing unnecessary suffering to that animal.

The owner has to consider the welfare of the animal from each perspective, the subjective and objective view. There are a set of relevant *'considerations'* that the court can take into account in order to determine whether any suffering is unnecessary. Those considerations include all aspects of the animal's welfare ranging from:

(a)   whether the suffering could 'reasonably have been avoided or reduced'; to
(b)   whether the conduct concerned was that of 'a reasonably competent and humane person'.

A person is liable if his act or omission was intentional. That is a 'subjective' test as his knowledge and act coincides with the cause. However, it is much wider than that as otherwise the potential offence would easily be defeated by the defence. A person would also be liable if he acted recklessly as he 'ought reasonably to have known' of the actual or potential effect. As it is 'likely to do so' that is an 'objective' test.

The liability extends to a person who is in a supervisory capacity as well as one who fails to supervise the offender. Each person commits an offence if he acts or fails to act in a way that was 'reasonable in all the circumstances' to protect the animal from the suffering.

2.8   Spindles revisited

Gray was convicted of 11 offences. He was sentenced to 24 weeks' imprisonment and disqualified for an unlimited time from dealing in, owning or keeping equines, with a further stipulation he could not apply for a termination of his disqualification for a period of ten years. Additional orders were made for deprivation and seizure of animals to which the various charges related. Gray was ordered to pay £200,000 towards the prosecution's costs of the appeal in addition to the £400,000 costs ordered by the district judge.

In *Gray v. Crown Court Aylesbury and CPS* [2012] EWHC 25 he appealed against the convictions and the costs. Defence counsel claimed that the 'offence requires either actual knowledge or a form of constructive knowledge that the animal was showing signs of unnecessary suffering, and that negligence is not sufficient'. He relied on the POA again, even though that point had been dismissed by the recorder.

In the High Court, Toulson LJ rejected that notion: 'The language of the provisions is significantly different. It would be wrong in principle to construe the provisions of the 2006 Act by reference to differently worded provisions of the repealed legislation.'

He confirmed that the defendant's conduct is judged by what a reasonable person in his position would have known about the consequences of his conduct. The aim was to consider whether the animal had suffered unnecessarily, not the mental state of the person concerned. So the recorder 'was right to construe section 9 as setting a purely objective standard of care which a person responsible for an animal is required to provide.' The offence did not relate to the defendant's state of mind, but to the animal's suffering.

The notion of defence counsel was misplaced as if it was accepted the AWA would have no purpose. If the defendant's liability depended upon a 'specific' intent the AWA would have been as pointless as the POA.

Toulson LJ concluded Gray had been rightly convicted.

Mr Justice Silber [J] considered the issue of costs. Counsel for Gray argued the maximum fine that could be imposed for the respective offences was the yardstick for the related costs. That would have limited the potential maximum sum to £140,000. He also claimed the costs should be paid out of income as opposed to capital. Silber J dismissed the notion saying: 'Indeed if Mr Fullerton [defence counsel] was right and costs orders could only be made which would be payable out of income and not capital, it is difficult to see how costs orders could be made against serving prisoners as they would have no income but might have substantial capital in the form of a house.'

That defence submission would make it impossible to relieve drug dealers and professional criminals of their illicit rewards. Silber J considered and dismissed Gray's appeal on costs.

2.9   Conduct

If the conduct that caused the suffering was a breach of a code of practice or a licence it is 'evidence' that would count against a defendant. That is an advantage for the prosecution as it allows it to rely on any breach to show the suffering caused was 'unnecessary'. However, if it was an inevitable consequence of complying with those practices then it would be unlikely to be an offence. Therefore if a person is charged, that fact would provide a defence; if the case was borderline it could lead to a submission of 'no case to answer' or, on conviction, be mitigation towards a more lenient sentence.

If the conduct was for the benefit of the animal, then the suffering could or would be necessary. An operation performed by a vet could be properly performed, yet would cause the animal to suffer. Nevertheless, that would be for a legitimate purpose and necessary providing the vet was competent and acted humanely.

The relevant circumstances are also taken into account. If the person was genuinely doing his best, the fact it turns out wrong would not make him liable. In an emergency a person may make a mistake yet act as a 'reasonably competent and humane person'. That would apply if an animal was seriously injured in a road traffic accident and was in severe pain. Then, if the person causing the suffering had been incompetent or inhumane the liability would remain.

The advantage of those considerations for the animal is it allows the court to consider whether the suffering was unnecessary from their victimized position. An animal has the protection from being a victim of unnecessary suffering before or during its death. That coincides with the ethos of the AWA. A significant change introduced by the AWA is the owner's duty to care for the animal's welfare. As a consequence, that includes the animal being entitled as a matter of law not to be killed at will.

A person has no legal duty to help a stranger in danger of drowning or being burned alive. The same principle applies to animals. However, if the person is 'responsible' for the animal he would have a concomitant duty to assist the animal and try to abate any suffering. His duty is to do so as otherwise his failure to act would be an offence.

In 2016 Jonathan Theobald allowed his three staffie-type dogs, Daisy and Mitch and Rascal, to be fried alive. He locked the dogs in his car without air or water or ventilation and went off to the gym for five hours. Meanwhile, the temperature outside soared from 19C to 40C. The prosecutor said, 'These animals would have suffered immensely. They would have gone through stages of panic, heat stress and likely seizures and injury in attempt to escape before dying. This case is unforgivable.' He was seen at his home with the bodies of the dogs in his car. When he was questioned by the police about the death of the three 'rescued' dogs, Theobald said: 'I left them in the car too long. It is a fair cop.' Theobald received a suspended sentence.

Mutilation

2.10   Animal Welfare Act 2006 s.5

(1) A person commits an offence if
   (a)   he carries out a prohibited procedure on a protected animal;
   (b)   he causes such a procedure to be carried out on such an animal.

The use of the word *'mutilation'* in the AWA is deliberate. It indicates a physical change by a procedure that is inimical to an animal. That is why the prohibited procedure is so wide. A person commits an offence if the mutilation is performed on a protected animal.

A person commits an offence if he 'permitted' a prohibited procedure to be performed on a protected animal. Permitting includes having knowledge and being negligent via a Nelsonian eye. If the procedure is something he could or should prevent, he is liable. Hence it can be committed intentionally or recklessly by the owner failing to care for his animal's welfare by allowing any mutilation of them.

This section creates three offences:

1. Carrying out a prohibited procedure.
2. Causing such a procedure to be carried out.
3. Permitting or failing to prevent another person doing so.

A prohibited procedure involves interference with 'the sensitive tissues or bone structure of the animal, otherwise than for the purpose of its medical treatment.' The interference alters the animal's condition by some form of mutilation which is not for their benefit. A physical change could also affect the animal's mental condition.

The kind of alteration aimed at includes cutting a dog's ears to add fierceness for fighting or botched medical operations that border on butchery. Sometimes an owner will treat an animal himself in order to save on vet's fees. Those actions may be performed by an amateur or a quack, although a qualified person would not be excused from liability if the procedure was prohibited. The aim is to prevent those duty-bound to protect an animal from mutilating them.

An exemption from the offences can be introduced by the appropriate national authority specifying by regulations that they 'do not apply' in particular circumstances. As that would legalise what would otherwise be illegal, 'before' making any such regulations the authority *'shall'* consult persons that appear to them to represent any interest as the authority considers 'appropriate'.

That mandatory duty has the advantage it gives an opportunity for any interested party opposed to the intended exemption to voice his or her view, which then has to be taken into account.

To comply with that duty, the authorities would have to seek out such interested persons. Moreover, if they failed to take account of such interests and wrongly considered them to be inappropriate, any regulations they introduced could be challenged. While the authorities have discretion as to whom they consult, if they fail to consult some relevant bodies they could be subject to judicial review. If they consulted irrelevant persons, that could be challenged too. Failure to consult anyone would be grounds for an appeal. Their duty is to be fair and open. Then the decision and the reason it was made is known to those whom the AWA is meant to protect. An 'interested' person is much wider than the owner as it could include a body that wishes to oversee the exemption and tender opposition to protect the animals that it affects. The community could raise an objection that the victim's vulnerability would prevent it raising it in its own right, by virtue of having no actual or legal voice. [See: **2.17**]

The importance of this provision is plain from the fact it is repeated in a similar form in five other sections [6, 13, 15, 16 and 17] in the AWA. They refer to both regulations and codes of practice. Indeed, the effect of the duty on the authorities and how it affects those who oppose their power can be seen in sharp focus in the landmark case, *R (on the application of Petsafe Ltd and another) v. Welsh Ministers* [2010] EWHC 2908, where the introduction of a ban on dog collars administering an electric shock by a regulation was challenged in the High Court by a commercial business. An animal's welfare was balanced against a company's profit. [See: **2.18**]

In 2016 Christopher Griffiths fed cocaine to his Staffordshire bull terrier, Victor. Griffiths then cut Murphy's ears off using a pair of pliers and scissors. He was convicted. His appeal against conviction failed. Griffiths was sentenced to 24 weeks' imprisonment. The RSPCA inspector, Glen Murphy, said Victor 'suffered heart-breaking injuries, but survived.'

Docking of Dogs' Tails

2.11   Animal Welfare Act 2006 s.6

(1) A person commits an offence if
  (a) he removes the whole or any part of a dog's tail, otherwise than for the purpose of its medical treatment;
  (b) he causes the whole or any part of a dog's tail to be removed by another person, otherwise than for the purpose of its medical treatment.

For many years people have gained a peculiar personal pleasure from docking the tails of their dogs. Often it is the result of misguided anecdotal bar-room wisdom. Sometimes it is the owner's vanity or the fashion of myopic people who parade their egos at dog shows. The result is a dog will suffer for the simple reason it has been born with a particular tail because that is as nature intended. Be it long or short, straight or curly, the tail has a distinct purpose for a dog, including showing emotion and assisting balance. A tail enables it to swish and wag it, and run and act defensively when it is attacked by other animals.

This section was introduced to protect dogs from the perversity of their owners. So unless the reason was for medical treatment, tail docking is prohibited and an offence.

When a dog has just been born its tail can be docked without it being as painful as it is at a later stage, although it is still sensitive. As a result there is a condition that provides a defence to these offences if the dog is a 'certified working dog that is not more than five days old'. This has become known as a *'subsection (3) dog'* because it allows docking that would otherwise be unlawful. As being 'a working dog' has advantages for the owner it must be certified by a vet that two conditions are met:

  (i)   evidence was produced to a vet that complies with regulations made by the appropriate national authority; and
  (ii) the dog is of a type specified by those regulations.

A regulation may be made allowing an inspector the power to check there is no contravention of the AWA. That would entail him or her being able to read a microchip on a dog or inspect any vet's certificate in relation to the animal. From 1 April 2016 it is compulsory for owners to microchip their dogs under the Microchipping of Dogs [England] Regulations 2015.

In 2011 it was confirmed in a case that docking the tails of five Jack Russell pups when they were one day old does cause 'pain and they can be permanently sensitised to pain by trauma'. The defendant got another person to do the deeds. He was convicted and fined.

In summary this section creates *five* different offences, which are if a person:

1. Removes any part of a dog's tail other than for their medical treatment.
2. Permits it to be removed other than for their medical treatment.
3. Fails to identify the 'subsection (3) dog' as required by the regulations.
4. Shows a docked dog to the public for a fee.
5. Gives false information to a vet about a 'subsection (3) dog'.

Prior to the AWA it was still practised on a wide scale. Now it has to be borne in mind that a vet can only carry out the procedure if he complies with the AWA. So, unless he had a reasonable belief that the dog was only four days old, if he carried out docking on a seven day old dog he would commit an offence. That would require evidence from another vet or expert rather than relying on the shape of the dog's tail.

More than a century ago the practice of docking animals' tails was recognised and condemned in the classic animal welfare case *Ford v. Wiley* [1889] 23 QBD 203, where Hawkins said, 'Docking is another painful operation, which, no doubt, can occasionally be justified; but I hold a very strong opinion against allowing fashion, or the whim of an individual, or any number of individuals, to afford a justification for such painful mutilation and disfigurement.'

Acute caudal myopathy is a painful condition known as 'limber tail' that stops a dog's tail from supporting its own weight. It stops, sometimes only temporarily, over-excited dogs from wagging their tails. So they are denied showing the metronomic signs of pleasure they want to convey to their owners.

Docking was criticised by the Royal College of Veterinary Surgeons [RCVS] as 'unethical'. While it only took 100 odd years, that moral objection is now encompassed within the AWA.

Administration of poisons

2.12   Animal Welfare Act 2006 s.7

(1) A person commits an offence if, without lawful authority or reasonable excuse, he
   (a) administers any poisonous or injurious drug or substance to a protected animal, knowing it to be poisonous or injurious, or
   (b) causes any poisonous or injurious drug or substance to be taken by a protected animal, knowing it to be poisonous or injurious.

Some people think it is hilarious to feed their pets anything from alcohol to drugs. Given their anatomy and digestive systems and size, any such substances and others, can be harmful to an animal. All animals can be affected adversely by a substance that is not a food they naturally eat. At best it can induce a deleterious effect on their organs while at worst it can be fatal. Therefore this section prohibits a person feeding an animal a poisonous substance.

Primarily it is aimed at those taking advantage of animals by making them take drugs to run faster, fight harder or grow fatter. While it is aimed at curbing how the animal is affected by the substance, it would apply to anyone using a substance in horse racing, dog fighting, bestiality and pornography.

There are few prosecutions of this offence because as the abused animal is rarely discovered at the time, the injurious drugs naturally disappear within their system. Or the animal just dies. In 2011 a defendant was being routinely interviewed by the police when he admitted abusing his greyhound, Jake, by giving him cannabis resin, sleeping tablets and sildenafil. He did so 'to either suppress or enhance the dog's performance at the race track so he could bet on the outcome of the race'. So he won whether the dog ran fast or slow. The Hartlepool Magistrates held the offence was 'aggravated by the defendant's desire for commercial gain'. Typically, they imposed a suspended prison sentence.

In *R. v. Wilson* [2009] Andrew Wilson beat his pet dog, Bronx, and fed him Stella lager. Wilson hit his dog, a bull mastiff, over the head. Bronx was taken to the RSPCA Dogs and Cats Home and seen by the vet, Mandy Stone. She said: 'Bronx had a nasty cut to his head and was staggering around, looking confused and generally depressed, it wasn't until Wilson was questioned and admitted that he gave Bronx alcohol that I realised why. He had a dangerous amount in his body and had Bronx been a smaller dog, may not have survived.'

The person would commit an offence unless he had 'lawful authority or reasonable excuse' for doing so. The act of 'administering' indicates an intention to do the act as opposed to accidentally poisoning an animal. That is supported by the fact the person must know it is 'poisonous or injurious'. However if, as in *Wilson*, the defendant was drunk or drugged, it would not be a defence. The two offences are administering the drug or causing it to be taken by the animal. That would be dependent on his knowledge as if he was sober. A drunken person cannot use his self-induced state as a 'reasonable excuse'.

The offence extends liability to (a) a person who is in a supervisory capacity and (b) one who is not supervising the one who commits the offence. The idea of 'permits' puts an onus on the person who is responsible to ensure his animal is not abused by another person. The circumstances such as *Wilson*, be it an intentional or reckless state of mind, would suffice. That relates to the state of the owner and any other person, whether they are drunk or drugged or both. Indeed, a drunken dog could be more dangerous than a sober one. So the owner's intoxication would not provide a defence or mitigation, but would be an aggravating factor in terms of his sentence. It could also lead to an offence under the DDA. [See: **9.1**]

The animal does not have to actually suffer as a result of a person administering a drug. As the liability springs from the illegal deed: the 'quantity or manner' of the substance being administered is the prohibited act. Therefore, even a harmless substance could be harmful if it is given in a way that is injurious to the animal. A substance that is harmless in small amounts could be harmful if the dose is too high.

Apart from a genuine accidental dose or accidental poisoning, based on evidence adduced by the defendant, a person would be liable for a reckless state of mind. If it were otherwise, a man who was like *Wilson* could claim he thought he was beating a carpet not his dog, or he thought he was giving his dog a drink of water rather than Stella lager. Someone who had taken drugs would not be able to escape from liability by claiming he did not understand what he was doing when he shared his spliff with his dog. Indeed, in 2009 a man in France was liable for feeding his duck 'weed'. Similarly, in 2009 a couple had an emaciated dog tied up outside their premises. A RSPCA inspector said by virtue of the dog's condition it had not been fed for some months. The defendants admitted that was true. Instead of food they had fed it 'potentially lethal doses of tobacco'. The court imposed a suspended sentence.

In 2016 a spaniel was rushed to a vet in Devon after being found to be 'high on drugs'. He was 'twitching a lot' and 'hallucinating' as if he was 'trying to catch something that wasn't there'. It was unclear whether he had ingested amphetamines or cannabis or simply eaten some local 'magic mushrooms' while out on his daily stroll. He recovered after being treated with a legal drug, diazepam. [See: **2.10**]

Fighting

2.13   Animal Welfare Act 2006 s.8

(1) A person commits an offence if he
    (a) causes an animal fight to take place, or attempts to do so;
    (b) knowingly receives money for admission to an animal fight;
    (c) knowingly publicises a proposed animal fight;
    (d) provides information about an animal fight to another with the intention of enabling or encouraging attendance at the fight;
    (e) makes or accepts a bet on the outcome of an animal fight or on the likelihood of anything occurring or not occurring in the course of an animal fight;

(f)　takes part in an animal fight;

(g)　has in his possession anything designed or adapted for use in connection with an animal fight with the intention of its being so used;

(h)　keeps or trains an animal for use for in connection with an animal fight;

(i)　keeps any premises for use for an animal fight.

Animal fighting is justified by participants as a 'sport' no different than badger baiting, fox hunting or hare coursing. Pitting animals against each other intentionally causes a lot of suffering to the animals, which are often dogs; often, as intended, there is severe injury to the victims too. Those trained dogs, whether they win or lose the fight, often live limited lives. Each victim normally has numerous injuries. Depending on their condition, if they can they will be made to fight again. They may die as a result of their injuries. Alternatively, because of their injuries they will be deemed unfit and then killed by their owner.

A fighting dog has a limited life as its value to the owner is its capacity to kill an opponent. The owner would rarely take an injured dog to a vet as if he realised the injuries were the result of dog fighting, he would report the owner to the RCVS and the police. As yet a vet is under a professional duty to do so. It should be a legal one.

The AWA simplified and widened what activity is illegal as it applies to animals and humans. Humans who are directly and indirectly involved in abusing animals by participating or promoting fighting commit an offence. There are more than 20 ways to commit the offence.

Animal fighting is on the increase in the United Kingdom, especially dog fighting. It is common in cities such as Birmingham among immigrants who indulge in it in Pakistan. The authorities in Pakistan rarely prosecute anyone for participating in their sport. It is common amongst gypsies, where it is almost a custom according to an investigation that included bare-knuckle boxing, arranged fighting between children, cock-fighting and dogs attacking deer. Leo Maguire, the director of the film documentary *Gypsy Blood*, said: 'I was attracted by the violence of my two main characters …' As the content concerned the police and RSPCA, each carried out an investigation in relation to any potential offences. [See: *Gypsy Blood*: Channel 4, 19 January 2012]

This section bans all forms of using protected animals to kill other animals. It circumscribes our innate penchant as *'animal fight'* is defined as: An occasion on which a protected animal is placed with an animal, or with a human, for the purpose of fighting, wrestling or baiting.

Videos of animal fights are illegal, but such films find a ready market. There is a prevalence of 'snuff' movies where animals are cruelly killed by provocatively dressed women, so combining the perversion of pornography with cruelty. The videos are mass-produced and sold on a connected secret international network by the producers for profit.

A pest control officer acting within his employment that involved the use of one animal to catch another would not fall within the AWA. The licence would legalise what would otherwise be an unlawful purpose. Then the primary purpose would be to control the activity of the animal designated a 'pest', not to cause the animal to be involved in baiting or fighting. Nevertheless, if he placed a bet on how many rats were killed or indulged in a malpractice that resulted in a 'fight', that would be an offence.

Badger baiting is still enjoyed by people who gain pleasure from inflicting pain on animals, often using dogs they own and parade as family pets. While a badger as a wild animal would not normally have the protection of the AWA, once it is 'under the control of man' it would become a 'protected animal'. Therefore, it would be a double-breach of causing unnecessary suffering to each animal.

The definition of 'premises' is wide as it is normally a skittle alley in the back room of a pub temporarily rearranged with a ring for an animal fight, or a barn on a farm. Betting usually takes place proportionate to how much blood and lust is spent by all those involved, namely the animals, the participants and the spectators. It is often a family affair as many dogs will need to be trained for some considerable time to build up their strength. This can involve pulling a car, on a gym treadmill or attacking kittens swinging suspended from a tyre. It may be a mixture of those activities. As an athlete trains for a marathon or the Olympics, the owners are intent on training their animals to be in the best shape to deliberately maim, wound and kill other animals.

In 2015 three men belonging to an 'organised dog fighting' gang with links to Europe were convicted. The RSPCA and the police carried out the investigation. Six pit bull terrier-types were found along with a 'considerable collection' of dog fighting items. The paraphernalia included a treadmill, numerous books on the subject, hanging scales, a flirt pole, boards and blood-stained carpet. The inspector confirmed 'there was no doubt that this was a dog fighting pit. Scar patterns on four of the dogs examined by a vet were 'caused by fights of significant duration, on multiple occasions.' The defendants received a suspended sentence. [See: **6.3**]

This section is primarily aimed at the main men, the organisers and participants. Those who they inform on the grapevine and are present at the animal fight without 'lawful authority or reasonable excuse' commit an offence. Save for the informer, investigator or underground activist, it would be rare for a person to be lawfully present.

Significantly, an 'animal fight' covers 'an animal', not just a protected one. Therefore, even if no one is responsible for the animal, an offence is still committed. Besides any other legislation, it could cover the killing involved in badger baiting, cock fighting and fox hunting as well as stray dogs and abandoned kittens in the more conventional abuse of them in animal fighting. That would depend upon the arrangement of the actual fight.

The High Court in *RSPCA v. McCormick* [2016] EWHC 928 held that animal fighting would not include standard or traditional fox hunting. The question for the court was:

In order for an offence of animal fighting to be committed contrary to s. 8 … must any 'other' animal, with which a protected animal is placed, be the subject of some control or restraint by some person or persons connected with that activity or some other artificial constraint so that its ability to escape is prevented?

The answer would normally be 'Yes', as Carr J said: 'Taking a dog (or other protected) animal into land or woods where there might or would be wild animals and then letting the dogs go in the hope that they would hunt and then attack those wild animals leading to a fight cannot be said to amount to a "placing" for the purpose of fighting within section 8 of the Act. If a fight or intended fight is to fall within the meaning of section 8, it cannot be the by-product of a chance meeting but rather must be a contrived or artificial creation specifically for the purpose of a fight during which, on the assumed facts, the other animal has no natural means of escape.'

Carr J said: 'This was a most unusual case, in that there was no direct evidence of any of the activity alleged to have taken place, which was the subject of the offences under section 8 of the Act.' The allegation rested on evidence from Facebook, mobile telephone messages and photographs, plus items found following a search warrant. The case was based on *'assumed facts'* of the prosecution allegation that of the five defendants, alleged to be the Devon Destroyers, 'one or more of the Respondents had raised the issue, on social media between them, of potentially digging out from its sett any badger found by the dogs, or roping any such badger and taking it to where the dog or dogs could attack it.'

The point relied upon by the court was that, given the definition of an animal fight, this was not an offence because: 'Thus the release of the dogs on the assumed facts here was not a placing of the dogs with the wild animals being targeted. At best the Respondents were letting the dogs loose in a certain unrestricted area where there might be or were other animals – the dogs were not being *"placed with"* those other animals.'

Nevertheless, this case is neither as narrow nor as confined as it might initially appear to be because, as Carr J confirmed during the judgment: 'As for the example advanced by the RSPCA, namely of two dogs bred for fighting being placed together in an open field to fight, quite different considerations arise. If the dogs were encircled by onlookers so as to prevent escape, there would be no reason why such activity could not fall within section 8 of the Act.'

Further, to be within section 8, rather than a 'by-product of a chance meeting … it must be a contrived or artificial creation specifically for the purpose of a fight during which, on the assumed facts, the other animal has no natural means of escape.'

Carr J confirmed the phrase 'placed with' has to be construed as a 'matter of normal language'.

That is consistent with the contrived or artificial 'creation' when a terrier man places a dog in a hole in the path of a fox to cause a fight as at that time the fox has no natural means of escape. The findings of the Burns Report [2000] confirmed the circumstances and result: 'There are also reports of injuries caused in fights between terriers and foxes underground. There are two main areas of concern about digging out/terrier work from the perspective of the welfare of the fox: the possible distress experienced by the fox as the terrier men dig down – which may take a substantial time – and the possible distress, or even physical injuries, caused by the terrier.

'We are satisfied that fights do occur from time to time and that these would involve some compromise of the welfare of the terrier.

'Their concerns were exacerbated by reports of injuries received by foxes and terriers fighting underground.'

Those findings and the reasoning in *McCormick* are consistent with the American authority, *TJ v. State of Indiana* [2010] 932 N. E. 2d 192, where two young boys were charged with 'knowingly or intentionally' promoting or staging an 'animal fight contest'. They opened the gate of a neighbouring house and allowed their dog to enter. One of the boys said, '*get 'em, get 'em*', to encourage their big dog to attack a small dog in the back yard. Both boys were convicted. Their appeal was dismissed.

While it was opportunistic and spontaneous, 'placing' their dog in the presence of the other dog that had no means of escape from the yard amounted to a 'fight' they had created.

The Hunting Act was introduced in 2004. The AWA was introduced in 2006. Regardless of the Acts dealing with separate areas, there is actually or potentially a crossover as each seek to protect animals from humans. Therefore, the draftsman is bound to have taken that fact into account. Consequently, subject to the circumstances and evidence, illegal hunting is still caught by the AWA. A terrier man's involvement is within the definition of an animal fight as it includes 'with an animal, or with a human'. He would be caught by that fact if he assists in the final act of the fight to kill the trapped fox.

Fighting extends from causing an animal fight to take place to '*attempting*' to do so. Therefore, it catches those who are involved as it applies to all the attendant activities from start to finish of fixing and training that enables a fight to fructify.

Duty of person responsible for animal to ensure welfare

2.14　Animal Welfare Act 2006 s.9

(1) A person commits an offence if he does not take such steps as are reasonable in all the circumstances to ensure that the needs of an animal for which he is responsible are met to the extent required by good practice.

　　The animal's needs 'shall' be taken to include:
　(a)　the need for a suitable environment,
　(b)　the need for a suitable diet,
　(c)　the need to be able to exhibit normal behaviour patterns,
　(d)　the need he has to be housed with, or apart from, other animals, and
　(e)　the need to be protected from pain, suffering, injury and disease.

This introduces the language of tort [a civil wrong] in placing a duty on the person responsible for the animal's welfare. A person charged with such responsibility cannot escape liability by abandoning the animal or acting irresponsibly by claiming ignorance about the 'needs' of their animal.

Abandonment is a constant problem as people routinely abandon their pets. They may move away and leave the animals to fend for themselves. They may leave a house full of cats and dogs starving to death, who then try to survive by eating their former companions. If an animal suffers as a result of being abandoned, usually through lack of food and water, the owner commits an offence under sections 4 and 9. The suffering of the animal by distress and hunger is an aggravating factor that would make it a more serious form of the offence.

A person could be using an animal for a 'lawful purpose' or a 'lawful activity'. A dog may be used by an army officer to help locate people after an explosion or to find a bomb before it has exploded. The police often use horses to control protesting crowds or rioting thugs who attack them with missiles from rocks to

Molotov cocktails. If an officer was charged with an offence, the court would take into account how the 'purpose or activity' hindered his duty in meeting the animal's welfare needs, according to what is reasonable in the circumstances of the case. If the animal is injured it may not be an offence as it would be subject to the balance between the risk to the animal and the need to uphold the law. This does not provide a person with an absolute defence. The animal may have been injured because the officer was negligent or unprofessional in performing the particular activity. That would depend on how the injury happened and whether it could have been avoided. The 'considerations' relating to unnecessary suffering would apply to the circumstances. [See: **2.7**]

That position applies to the police in an off-duty role too. The thugs throwing missiles would be guilty of an injury to the horse. It would be criminal damage as the horse is property. However, it would be arson and not simple criminal damage if the horse was burned.

Though the 'needs' of an animal are wide, they are not limited to those specified. They include the 'five freedoms', which consider the animal in relation to their environment and protection from suffering. An animal might normally be content or better placed among other animals. However, it may need to be with its mother or other similar animals to be healthy. Then separating it from its mother or the others would be a breach of that duty.

The protection from pain may relate to prevention of an injury as well as an existing injury. Where the animal is injured, accidentally, intentionally or even congenitally, its needs include being protected from further injury. '*Suffering*' of an animal would depend on expert evidence. Otherwise there is a danger the condition is assessed on an anthropomorphic basis with the nature of the animal's pain lacking accuracy and reliability. It might not be possible to make an accurate assessment and decide the issue until the animal dies. Then the degree of suffering could be deduced from the animal's organs after a post-mortem examination. [See: **2.3**]

Although 'disease' is not defined, there is the potential for sudden widespread diseases that affect a whole herd instantly, such as BSE [bovine spongiform encephalopathy]. Ideally, animals should not be destroyed without independent evidence rather than from some government department or self-interested body. The person responsible would have to 'ensure' those infected do not affect the others. Equally, the animals affected should not be subject to further avoidable pain. If the condition continues and so affects the animals, it would be a breach of his or her duty and inconsistent with 'good practice'. Action could be taken against anyone, government department or otherwise, acting without independent evidence.

The 'circumstances' that a person has to consider when taking 'steps' to ensure the needs of an animal include any lawful purpose and lawful activity that pertain to the animal. Given that these are included in 'particular', it places a burden on the person so it is not seen merely as a profit-making machine, but as sentient animals with appropriate needs. The purpose and activity is to take account of each animal's needs. For purely personal financial gain, some owners refrain from feeding an animal that is due to be slaughtered. That is a contravention of the AWA and consequently an offence.

An American case in 2005 shows a judicial understanding of the value of the biter being bit. Ms. Murry of Ohio decided to abandon 33 kittens in the woods as she was 'moving and having personal problems'. She was found guilty of abandonment of the animals. The judge, perceiving that the most effective sentence was to make the defendant swallow her own medicine, ordered Murry to spend 'a night in the woods without water, food, or light'.

Improvement notices

2.15   Animal Welfare Act 2006 s.10

(1) If an inspector is of the opinion that a person is failing to comply with section 9(1), he may serve on the person a notice which
   (a)   states that he is of that opinion,
   (b)   specifies the respects in which he considers the person is failing to comply with that provision,
   (c)   specifies the steps he considers need to be taken in order to comply with the provision,
   (d)   specifies a period for the taking of those steps, and
   (e)   explains the effects of subsections (2) and (3).

An inspector has to ensure a person discharges his or her duty towards any animal it is responsible for in terms of its welfare. If in the inspector's opinion a person is failing in his or her duty he can issue an improvement notice. It is an important step for two related reasons. The notice is a direct 'warning' to the person concerned. Once an improvement notice is issued the person is notified he must act or action will be taken against him. If he fails to act, it will be. Then a prosecution will follow.

The improvement notice must be detailed and specific as it has legal implications and consequences. It specifies the reason for the inspector's 'opinion' and how the person nominated has failed to comply with the statutory provision. It states what he must do and when he must do it. The improvement notice is a clear warning the person has to take action as otherwise he is in danger of being prosecuted. That is an interim stage where he has breached his duty and the remedy is in his hands by complying with the notice. After it is served no proceedings can be taken before the end of the 'compliance period'.

If the specified steps are taken within the compliance period no proceedings will be taken in respect of that potential breach. However, it does not bind the inspector in respect of another or a different offence. As all the welfare aspects are concentrating on the animal's benefit, it places a burden on the person responsible for the duties towards his animal. The law favours compliance by the person who has failed in his duty. Therefore the inspector has a discretion to 'extend, or further extend' the compliance period.

The fact a person has ignored an improvement notice is an aggravating factor the court can take into account in any proceedings. In that event it would be relevant and admissible evidence during a trial. His recalcitrance would also be relevant after a trial, for if the person was convicted or pleaded guilty, his failure to comply with the notice would affect the sentence.

A person to whom an improvement notice is issued tends to be irresponsible in his duties towards animals in his care. He has often committed more than one kind of offence regarding his failure to properly discharge his responsibility. Therefore if the improvement notice specified particular animals, such as a failure to feed a group of pigs, he could still be prosecuted for failing to feed a group of sheep. Equally, if the improvement notice specified he did not provide adequate bedding for cattle, he could still be prosecuted for failing to provide water for those same cattle. Each of the considerations for the inspector and consequent duty for the person responsible for the animal are separate.

Thus the inspector is giving the person a chance to change by issuing an improvement notice. He does not have to do so. If the circumstances warrant it, the inspector could take immediate action without issuing a notice. Moreover, if he initially complies with the order and then lapses, the inspector could issue a subsequent improvement notice. Either way it is the inspector's choice. The chance to change and choice to allow him to do so is solely dependent on the inspector's opinion.

An inspector is defined as 'a person appointed to be an inspector for the purposes of that provision by the appropriate national authority, or a local authority'. He is a vital part of the procedure in the functioning of the AWA. As an inspector requires particular experience and knowledge, the person appointed is usually qualified in animal welfare such as an RSPCA inspector or an animal behaviourist. Given the extensive powers they possess, ranging from putting a person out of business to providing evidence that would put him behind bars, the role of the inspector is itself tightly regulated. The inspector is a person with power and responsibility combined with a defined legal immunity from liability. [See: **5.2**]

Transfer of animals by way of sale or prize to persons under 16

2.16   Animal Welfare Act 2006 s.11

(1) A person commits an offence if he sells an animal to a person whom he has reasonable cause to believe to be under the age of 16 years.

Transferring the ownership of an animal is just the same as transferring any tangible thing. It does not matter whether it is a pet tortoiseshell cat or a cartoon character depicting one. The essential difference between them is with one you are dealing with a living creature. So the AWA seeks to make the person responsible for the animal's welfare a responsible person. Therefore there are limits on when a person under 16 years old can be given an animal as a prize or a transfer by sale. Under the Pet Animals Act 1951 it was an offence to sell a pet animal to children under 12. Increasing the age is a positive change that enhances the welfare of animals. The AWA places a value on an animal as a living creature in its own right. It explicitly curbs the idea that animals are toys given away as prizes at a fair or in a competition. That takes a slight account of the repeated resigned phrase of the animal organisations that mop up the Boxing Day detritus of abandoned gifts: 'A dog is for life and not just for Christmas'. Rabbits are similarly synonymous with being cute cuddly toys rather than living creatures with welfare needs of their own. In 2016 the Blue Cross charity stopped selling 'bunnies' a month before Easter for that very reason.

The advantage of this provision is it puts the onus on the vendor to ensure the buyer is over 16 years old. He must have a 'reasonable cause' for such a belief. That applies to a sale that is an otherwise perfectly legal transaction.

It is an offence if he sells an animal to a person whom he has a 'reasonable cause to believe' is under 16 years old. That could be by physical appearance as a child dressed in a school uniform would put him on notice.

It is an offence to enter into an arrangement with a person under 16 years old who has the 'chance' to win an animal as a prize. The offence relates to the potential winner being under 16 years old. A 'transfer' does not have to be completed or be likely to be completed. The mere chance of the prize causes the culpability to arise.

There may be a defence if the child is in the company of an adult. Then a person does not commit an offence if he enters into an arrangement in the presence of the child and he is accompanied by a person who is over 16 years old. The seller has to have a 'reasonable cause to believe' the child is in the company of the older person.

If no one over 16 years old is present when the arrangement is made, but the seller has reasonable cause to believe that a person who has 'actual care and control' of the child has 'consented' to the arrangement, that is not an offence. As the arrangement would be in the absence of the person having the care and control of the child, the seller would need solid evidence to support his belief.

A person could not rely on any potential defence using a vague musing or notion that, 'He looked over 16 to me', or 'His mate said it would be alright.' There would have to be reliable evidence given that the essence of the section is to protect animals at the point of sale and thereafter by ensuring the buyer is a responsible person. The seller has to be too.

This section is aimed at transferring animals to persons under 16 years old, which often happens within families. In that event there is no offence 'if he enters into the arrangement in a family context'. That term is wide enough to cover a parent to a child, step-parents, older siblings and relatives.

Both parties are liable under the AWA. That is the aim of the prohibition. While a child may demand the animal as a pet, they are usually not quite so keen on cleaning cages and seeing to their daily needs. So the liability is shared between the parent and the child. If it were otherwise it would defeat the provision intended to protect an animal against his owner. Indeed the court confirmed that position in *Gray v. RSPCA*. [See: **2.5**]

Regulations to promote welfare

2.17   Animal Welfare Act 2006 s.12

(1) The appropriate national authority may by regulations make such provision as the authority thinks fit for the purpose of promoting the welfare of animals for which a person is responsible, or the progeny of such animals.

This section allows the appropriate national authority to make regulations to 'promote' animal welfare. That is vital as it enables the authority to react to changing circumstances as well as initiating regulations of their own volition.

This provision has the mandatory requirement that the authority '*shall*' consult such persons that represent any interests that the authority considers appropriate. They must do so 'before' making regulations. This power can only be exercised subject to that provision. It is an important balance and check upon an otherwise wide power that could be arbitrary or appear to be. If the authority failed in its duty to be fair in who it did or did not choose to 'consult', its decision would be open to a challenge by judicial review. [See: **2.10**]

Changes in circumstances and the knowledge gained can be reflected in the promotion of animal welfare. If new scientific evidence became available to show some form of protection was necessary, this section would allow the change to be introduced. An unusual positive point is it extends to the progeny of the animal. The appropriate national authority can make provision as it 'thinks fit' for the purpose of 'promoting the welfare' of the progeny of such animals. So the regulations can protect the progeny as well as the parent animal. Given the limit on protection of a foetus under section 1 this power is a positive provision. [See: **2.3**]

The section envisages contact and co-operation with various animal organisations plus bodies that could be introduced to cover areas of animal welfare in a wide context. While the section is general in application, the regulations may in 'particular' promote the *'needs'* of animals. That allows representative bodies to voice their concerns for the welfare of animals.

In 2016 the UK government announced a change in policy that would have had the effect of reversing that positive policy. Liz Truss, the then Secretary of State for the Environment, said she was going to abolish the regulations and introduce a voluntary policy towards poultry. As that was perceived to be detrimental to the 'needs' of the animals, there was understandable concern by many welfare organisations. The Department for Environment, Food and Rural Affairs [Defra] had planned to replace the statutory codes protecting the welfare of poultry with an industry-led guideline. That would have resulted in the British Poultry Council [BPC] taking control over chicken farming practices. Truss intended to introduce further reform of livestock farming including guidelines relating to cattle and pigs and sheep. Many 'interested' bodies raised objections to her proposal. They feared the real objective was so the farmers could earn higher profits as less time would be devoted to their animals so their welfare would be bound to be affected. Philip Lymbery, of the Compassion in World Farming [CWF] said: 'The government's proposal to scrap these statutory codes would have been a major leap backwards for farm animals – allowing industry bodies to set, regulate and inspect welfare standards on UK chickens with no third-party involvement.' Sean Wensley, of the British

Veterinary Association [BVA], also objected, saying, 'we have questioned the way in which the consultation has taken place and raised concerns that public confidence could be undermined by a process that wasn't sufficiently transparent.'

In the wake of food scandals from horsemeat to campylobacter, scrapping government standards risks undermining public confidence in the food people consume. If the industry is checking its own standards, what checks govern the industry? Such a proposal seems potentially rife with ready-made problems that could and should be avoided.

Defra's reflective view was judicious: 'We have given the matter further consideration and believe we can achieve this objection by retaining the existing statutory codes.' Truss recanted and abandoned her proposal. However, the significant point is that had she not changed her mind it would have been feasible to challenge her decision as being 'unreasonable' given that the welfare of the chickens actually or potentially would suffer. That would have been contrary to the purpose of the primary legislation and so could have been *ultra vires* [beyond the power] in relation to the intention of Truss.

The significance of that intervention and recantation is three-fold: (a) it proved that the voice of those speaking on behalf of animals was heard; (b) it avoided other animals being affected in the future; (c) those responding bodies could have taken legal action if the codes of practice were changed to the detriment of the animals they were meant to protect.

2.18   Collars

The Welsh Assembly has been more imaginative than the English authorities by banning collars that cause injuries to dogs. In *R. (on the application of Petsafe Ltd and another) v. Welsh Ministers* they banned the collars despite powerful opposition. The issue in the case was whether the Welsh ministers were entitled to prohibit the use on cats and dogs of any electronic collar that was designed to administer an electric shock. They introduced the Animal Welfare (Electronic Collars) (Wales) Regulations 2010 under the AWA whereby anyone using such a collar commits an offence.

The first claimant was a manufacturer and distributor of pet products. The products it distributes included electronic collars. The second claimant was an unincorporated association of four companies that manufactured and distributed electronic training aids for animals. They sought permission to apply for judicial review of the 2010 Regulations and, if permission was granted, an order quashing the regulations, which they claimed were invalid.

The High Court analysed all the issues in relation to English and European law. Setting the scene Beatson J said: 'The use of electronic collars and similar devices is controversial. A number of groups, including the Kennel Club, have been campaigning for some time to ban them because they have the potential to have adverse consequences for animals, and are cruel and unnecessary. Others maintained that the scientific evidence does not support a ban or regulation, and that the devices help to avoid injury to animals on roads or at the hands of farmers protecting their stock. During 2007 a number of government bodies in the United Kingdom considered the question. In England, the Defra commissioned research to assess the effect of pet training aids on the welfare of domestic dogs. In Scotland and Wales there were consultation exercises to consider whether electronic collars are harmful to dogs and cats and whether they should be banned.'

The court noted the ban was supported by many animal welfare associations including the RSPCA and the People's Dispensary for Sick Animals [PDSA]. The Welsh Association of Chief Police Officers [ACPO] had banned the use of electric-shock collars in 2000 and they are not used by its police service.

Beatson J endorsed the opinion and action of the Welsh ministers: 'It is trite law that, in considering the unreasonableness of legislative acts such as regulations and by-laws made by public authorities, and in particular democratically accountable public authorities, a court should be slow to find that they are … unreasonable or perverse.' After Beatson delivered a penetrating analysis he added: 'This application is dismissed.'

This was a positive interpretation of a positive measure boldly introduced by the Welsh ministers notwithstanding the cost, considerable opposition and substantial legal arguments they had to meet and defeat. That it succeeded on all fronts is a credit to the

vision of those ministers. It also augurs well for the power of the AWA. [See: **3.4**]

The legislation was tested in 2011 by the RSPCA. Inspector de Celis was alerted to a stray collie dog wearing an electric collar in Wales. He removed the collar and checked the dog, Doug, as he was micro-chipped. When the owner collected Doug from the kennels he was confronted about the collar. Initially he denied knowledge of the change, but later admitted he had previously been 'warned' about it. He was convicted at Bridgend Magistrates' Court and fined, with the collar being forfeited. This was the first case under the regulation.

The collars are illegal in several other countries including Austria, Germany, Norway and Switzerland.

Defra confirmed that when it tested these collars on dogs in 2013 the results were: (a) one in four showed signs of stress and (b) one in three yelped at the first use of them.

In 2016 Dr Samantha Gaines, the Head of the Companion Animals Department of the RSPCA, said: 'We support a ban of these collars as scientific research clearly shows that the application of an electric shock can cause both a physiological stress response and behaviours associated with pain, fear and stress in animals, therefore impacting on their welfare.

'Furthermore, as animals trained with these devices can show behaviours associated with pain and fear both during training and some time afterwards, the use of shock collars can have long-term effects.'

Meanwhile, the British government fails to address this issue. Why does an animal welfare body not take legal action against the government to seek a Declaration in the High Court as a prelude to a ban? How many more animals must suffer before the collars are banned?

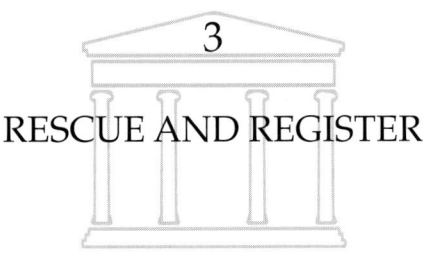

3

RESCUE AND REGISTER

3.1 Distress

There are various procedures relating to persons who control animals or rescue them if they are in *'distress'*. Controlling those who are in control of animals is by licensing and registration of their 'activities'. Codes of practice are common in respect of farm animals. They are used to promote the welfare of protected animals. If aspects of their welfare are breached it can lead to consequent distress to animals. Distress covers the problem and solution as the inspectors and police have extensive powers to deal with an animal including arranging for their death.

Licensing or registration of activities involving animals

3.2 Animal Welfare Act 2006 s.13

(1) No person shall carry on an activity to which this subsection applies except under the authority of a licence for the purposes of this section.

Although an 'activity' is not defined, the powers of the authority cover any that exist that affects the animal's welfare. That allows it to control those persons who control animals by monitoring their movements and operations.

It may be by a licence or registration. Registration has an advantage for the authority as it allows it to control those concerned commercially or charitably with animals. It can check that any activity is properly carried out to ensure compliance with the animal's welfare. The principal point is regulations apply when an animal and its progeny are those for whom someone is 'responsible'. As a consequence, a person who carries out an activity without the licence or registration commits an offence.

The power could be used to control an activity that is legal at present by making it an offence. That power could be used to amend the licence or registration, and even repeal them. There are specific statutes named in the AWA such as the Performing Animals (Regulation) Act 1925 that can be amended. As this is a controversial area that governs animals used in circuses, many of those opposed to it could – and indeed should – be consulted under this section 'before making regulations'. Although there is discretion as to whom the authority should 'consult', it '*shall*' consult such persons that represent relevant 'interests'. As it is a mandatory duty, failure to do so could be challenged by judicial review. [See: **2.10**]

During 2011 the welfare group Animal Defenders International visited the Bobby Roberts Circus over a number of weeks and videoed the treatment of Annie, a 58-year-old elephant. As a result of its underground activity, the owner, Roberts, was charged with causing unnecessary suffering to a performing elephant. The court was shown secretly filmed footage of Annie being beaten with a pitchfork by a groom. It was believed that he returned home to Romania. Roberts was convicted and sentenced to a three-year conditional discharge.

In 2011 after a public protest, politicians initially claimed that they could not outlaw the use of animals in circuses because it would contravene the Human Rights Act 1998 [HRA]. They relied upon the HRA on numerous occasions, including a 'reply' in Parliament. However, that was untrue. The politicians' promise to change the law remains unfulfilled.

Under these provisions the authority introduced the Welfare of Racing Greyhounds Regulations 2010. The power should be used to regulate the use of a whip in horse racing. There is no reason why a jockey should be allowed to whip their horse. All the feeble reasons put forward do not justify their actions. The primary duty on the authority is not commercial interests or profit, but to consider the effect of the 'activity' on the animals' welfare. If that were properly considered by a court the use of the whip would probably be abolished. As the 'activity' is contrary to the ethos of the AWA, it is no different than electric-shock collars. [See: **2.18**]

The licence and the register for the related activity can be inspected by an inspector. The regulations allow for entry and inspection as well as ensuring that those being monitored have insurance in respect of the activity.

Supplementary provisions relating to the regulations specify a licence cannot run for more than three years. A duty relating to the issue and monitoring of a licence includes:

(a) a licensing authority must inspect premises before granting a licence;

(b) regulations may allow an authority to impose conditions or require it to do so.

In 2016 Scotland announced 'its intention to ban the use of wild animals in travelling circuses'. Campaigning groups have urged the other United Kingdom governments to endorse and follow that course.

Codes of practice

3.3   Animal Welfare Act 2006 s.14

(1) The appropriate national authority may issue, and may from time to time revise, codes of practice for the purpose of providing practical guidance in respect of any provision made by or under this Act.

A code of practice can be issued and amended and revoked. It provides guidance for people involved with the welfare of animals. The codes are introduced after detailed consultation and agreement by Parliament. They can be relied upon as 'evidence' in court by a prosecutor if he is seeking to enforce the breach of any particular code. Although such a breach is not an offence, it can be taken into account by the court when considering the evidence adduced to support the charge.

A code of practice can take account of changing conditions within society, which can then be reflected in the best practice to promote animals' welfare. When new scientific knowledge is gained it could be used for the benefit of animals. Farm animals have been protected for many years by various codes of practice that promote their welfare. They follow from the principles of the 'five freedoms' and associated recommendations by the FAWC. In due course codes were introduced to cover areas that protected cows, horses, pigs and sheep. The AWA extends the protection to non-farm animals too. [See: **2.2**]

The powers granted are extensive as the authority may issue codes that offer 'practical guidance'. It may revise existing codes. As it relates to any provision made 'by or under this Act', it could affect an existing section as well as a provision introduced by a regulation.

As the codes '*shall*' be published in a manner the authority considers 'appropriate', it would have to be brought to the attention of those who could or would be affected, whether within the industry or the general public. A failure to comply with a code 'shall not of itself', make that person liable to prosecution. Nevertheless, such a failure has evidential weight. Therefore it is important for the prosecutor in respect of an offence. Equally, it is important for the person charged lest it can be used to establish a defence.

Essentially the code provides guidance on how to care for an animal's welfare and guard against avoidable bad practice. The value of a breach of a code to an inspector is he can use that to consider any potential proceedings, for an intentional breach indicates a lack of care. Thereafter a court can take any breach into account when considering the welfare standards within the AWA. The prosecution can rely on non-compliance as evidence that tends to 'establish liability' if the codes are breached. Where an allegation is denied, the defence may rely on compliance with the code to prove 'negative liability'. In each event the strength of the code is that it is as persuasive as evidence for the prosecution or defence.

The leading regulation to protect farm animals is The Welfare of Farmed Animals (England) Regulations 2007. As that was introduced by the AWA it is often used by the prosecution for a breach either in its own right or in conjunction with other offences within the Act, especially under sections 4 and 9. [See: **2.6**; **2.14**]

The strength and weakness of the prosecution and defence case centres on the evidence that underlines or undermines their respective positions. That depends on how the animals were affected by any breach of the code. It has to be remembered that the codes are meant to protect animals' welfare and not increase profits at their expense. [See: **2.17**]

Making and approval of codes of practice: England

3.4   Animal Welfare Act 2006 s.15

(1)   Where the Secretary of State proposes to issue (or revise) a code of practice under section 14, he shall:
  (a)   prepare a draft of the code (or revised code),
  (b)   consult about the draft such persons appearing to him to represent any interests concerned as he considers appropriate, and
  (c)   consider any representations made by them.

A code is issued following a draft and consultation with interested persons and the approval of Parliament. Those persons who have such 'interests' would be able to challenge the draft if they had not been consulted. Even if they were and their views were unreasonably disregarded, such a decision could still be subject to an appeal. [See: **2.10**]

If the draft is disapproved by Parliament within a 40-day period then it cannot be introduced in that form. If the draft is approved by Parliament within that period it can be introduced. However, even where the draft has been 'approved' by Parliament, that is not the end of the matter. The Secretary of State can produce a 'new' draft of the proposed or revised code, which is then laid before Parliament.

Under section 16 there are similar provisions for the National Assembly in Wales. It has been proactive in outlawing the use of electronic dog collars that were deemed to be cruel and contrary to the welfare of dogs. [See: **2.18**]

Under section 17 there are powers for a revocation of the codes of practice. The idea of a code of practice is to allow for changing circumstances and offer guidance to those concerned with the welfare of animals. Therefore it is important that a new code could replace the existing one rather than a mere revision. Before making an order to revoke a code the authority *'shall'* consult such persons that appear to them to represent any relevant 'interests'.

That shows the importance of the regulatory body 'consulting' the interested persons and taking account of their views. Consistent with the similar provision throughout the AWA, if they are not consulted they could challenge a code if they should have been. Equally if they had been consulted, but their concerns were ignored they could challenge the code. The burden would be on them to show they or their concerns were 'appropriate'. A body who had views relevant to the code, yet were ignored, could apply for judicial review as the purpose of the provision would itself be being ignored. [See: **2.10**]

That detailed process enhances the evidential weight of the code if and when a case comes before the court. It is why a judge will examine the consultation and views as part of the process and prior to the introduction of a code. Any failure by the politicians to respect that approach will reflect on the fairness of the process and hence validity of the code.

Powers in relation to animals in distress

3.5 Animal Welfare Act 2006 s.18

(1) If an inspector or a constable reasonably believes that a protected animal is suffering, he may take, or arrange for the taking of, such steps as appear to him to be immediately necessary to alleviate the animal's suffering.

   If a veterinary surgeon certifies that the condition of a 'protected' animal is such that it should in their own interests be destroyed, an inspector or a constable may:
   (a) destroy the animal where he is or take him to another place and destroy him there, or
   (b) arrange for the doing of any of those things.

An inspector or a constable may without the certificate of a veterinary surgeon if it appears to him:

(a) that the condition of the animal is such that there is no reasonable alternative to destroying him, and

(b) that the need for action is such that it is not reasonably practicable to wait for a veterinary surgeon.

This section incorporates the underlying philosophy of the AWA. It allows those in power to monitor the animal's welfare and then take immediate action to remedy an urgent situation that threatens its welfare, up to and including death. As 'distress' is not defined, that allows for an assessment of the animal's condition by an inspector or a constable. If either party 'reasonably believes that a protected animal is suffering' he may take such steps as appear to him to be *'immediately necessary'* to alleviate the animal's suffering.

There is added protection for *'animals in distress'* under sections 19 and 20. Those powers allow an entry to premises and orders made by a court. That is essential to deal with the pressing problem of an animal in distress. The subjective opinion of the inspector or constable relates to a situation presenting a sense of urgency.

This section is wide in three important ways, namely:

1. Action can be taken to protect an animal even if no proceedings have been issued.
2. It is not restricted to animals that are kept for a commercial purpose.
3. It allows an inspector or a constable to take into possession an animal that is already suffering and one that is likely to suffer if he does not take action.

That grants protection for animals who are presently suffering as well as those who are at risk in the future unless they are rescued at that time.

The power to take an animal into 'possession' includes a power to take its dependent offspring as well. The inspector may remove the animals and arrange for their care at a suitable place. When he does so he may 'mark' the animal for identification purposes. That could be significant for the owner and the police if the animal becomes an exhibit in any subsequent proceedings or action is taken by either party in due course. Once an animal is taken into possession the person exercising the power has a duty to look after its welfare.

As it is a continuing duty the inspector remains responsible for the animal's welfare by ensuring it receives any treatment that is necessary. That includes arranging for its care and removal to a place of safety. If he decides to care for the animal on the premises, he can make use of any equipment there. The power of the inspector or constable means he could use any of the apparatus on a farm without the farmer's permission or consent.

Where a vet certifies the 'condition' of an animal is such it is in their 'own interests' to be 'destroyed', an inspector or constable may destroy the animal or arrange for that destruction.

A degree of urgency may arise where an animal is involved in a road traffic accident and is in severe pain on the highway. If there is an emergency the position of the animal is paramount. The intervention by an inspector or a constable is permissible if he has acted with a 'reasonable belief'. Any urgent action taken by him would be judged according to the circumstances of the crisis.

It may be the area or weather conditions, or simply the time such that an emergency has arisen and no vet is available. While that places a responsibility for the animal's welfare on the inspector or constable, it applies a duty to release its misery by death if the suffering is such that it is in animal's *'own interests'*. If either of those persons reasonably believes a protected animal is suffering he may take steps that appear to him to be immediately necessary to alleviate the animal's suffering. On any level it is an urgent situation. Indeed then, even without the certificate of a vet, he may destroy the animal if it 'appears to him' there is no reasonable alternative to that final act.

If the animal's suffering is certified by a vet, but does not need to be destroyed, then an inspector or constable may take possession of the animal. The vet must certify that the suffering will be likely to continue if the circumstances do not change. That would then allow them to seize the animal regardless of any opposition by the owner.

Given it is an emergency, the inspector or constable can act without a vet's certificate to take an animal into possession for the same reasons, namely the animal is suffering and will continue to do so if its circumstances do not change. The additional condition before they can act is that there is a need for action and it is not 'reasonably practicable' to wait for a vet.

As these powers are really relating to an urgent situation or an emergency, it is quite feasible that the owner or person 'responsible' in law for the animal is not at the scene. If the inspector or constable takes the action without the knowledge of that responsible person, he must as soon as 'reasonably practicable' after exercising the power take such reasonable steps to notify that person.

It is one thing for a person to question or perhaps disagree with the person exercising the power under this section. That is acceptable as long as it is in a spirit of inquiry. However, if he 'intentionally obstructs' the person exercising the power, he commits an offence.

When this kind of emergency arises there may be attendant expenses in rescuing and transporting and treating the animals. As the animal will require care and comfort via the constable and veterinary treatment, any attendant expenses can be reimbursed on application to a Magistrates' Court. The court may make such an order as it thinks fit. The person ordered to pay those expenses has a right of appeal to the Crown Court.

The position may move from an urgent one to an emergency. In that event the inspector or constable can take the animal into possession without waiting for a vet. That extends to the dependent offspring. A forced separation could make the progeny suffer, mentally and physically. The progeny would then become protected animals in their own right.

A vet could examine and take samples from the animal, usually blood or urine, in order to satisfy him- or herself as to whether the animal should be taken into possession or, depending on their condition, killed. A sample would also be relevant evidence to support any charge against the potential defendant. Further samples could be taken on a post-mortem examination. All of them would be potential evidence in any subsequent proceedings.

3.6 Words

Animals in need of varying degrees of urgent treatment equally need to be protected. As a person has the right to kill an animal, the law requires evidence to sanction that act. Whether the certificate of a vet has to be in writing or is an oral opinion sufficient is the vital question.

It was considered in the High Court in *James v. RSPCA* [2011] EWHC 1642. Yvonne James pleaded guilty at Goole Magistrates' Court to three charges of causing unnecessary suffering to protected animals. The charges related to three horses found to be 'living in atrocious conditions'. James appealed against a 'costs' order for £38,644.56. She claimed it should have been reduced because the seizure and detention of the horses was 'unlawful' as the vet's 'certificate' was not in *writing*.

At the request of the RSPCA the vet went to the stables, where she examined the horses. The vet found they were suffering and in need of treatment. As a result, the police officer, who also had been requested to attend by the RSPCA, assumed responsibility for the horses. They were later cared for by the RSPCA.

Keith J said: 'The critical point is that the veterinary surgeon's certificate that the horses were suffering was not in writing. It was just what she said, and the first ground of appeal is that only a certification in writing amounts to a sufficient certification …'

The question for the opinion of the High Court was:

Is it lawful under section 18(5) of the AWA for an inspector or constable to take a protected animal into his possession if a veterinary surgeon present at the scene states *orally* that the animal is suffering?

The court held that although the word 'certifies' is not defined in the Act it connotes a degree of formality that means it is necessary that the certification has to be in writing. If 'a certificate' is to be issued it should be in writing because a document tends to be issued rather than an expression of opinion.

Keith J considered the contention of the RSPCA that an animal might be subjected to further suffering if a vet called to the scene is not in a position to immediately produce a written certificate of the animal's condition. That might happen if there are a large number of animals, some of whose seizure is necessary because they need urgent treatment; while others do not and there is not sufficient time to produce a written certificate covering only those animals whose seizure is necessary. It might also happen if the circumstances at the time made production of a written certificate impracticable, for example, if the weather was too bad for the appropriate documentation to be raised on site, or if the site was dangerous and the veterinary surgeon as well as the animal had to leave the site as soon as possible.

Keith J concluded: 'It would, I think, be very surprising if section 18(5) were to be construed in a way which permits a police officer to act so as to put an animal out of its distress before the veterinary surgeon arrives, but does not permit the animal to be relieved of its suffering after the veterinary surgeon arrives, even though the veterinary surgeon thinks that the animal is suffering, but for one reason or another does not put that into writing.'

For those reasons, the judge concluded that section 18 does not require the certification to be in writing. So the seizure and detention of the defendant's horses were lawful.

The issue was revisited in *Gray v. Crown Court Aylesbury*. Gray claimed the seizure of numerous animals was unlawful. Toulson LJ outlined the issue: The animals were seized in purported pursuance of section 18 by police officers acting on *oral* statements made by veterinary surgeons that they considered it necessary in order to protect the animals from likely suffering. After the animals were seized, they underwent examination and samples were taken for analysis. The results formed part of the evidence for the prosecution. [See **2.8**]

HHJ Tyrer in the Crown Court found the unprecedented scale of the situation discovered on the visits resulted in pressure of circumstances such that 'oral certifications were the only viable course to adopt'. Even if the seizures were unlawful, the illegality did not make the evidence inadmissible as a matter of principle: therefore it was *fair* to admit the evidence.

Defence counsel submitted that the Crown Court erred in law in rejecting his submission about (a) the lawfulness of the seizures and (b) the admissibility of the resulting evidence.

Toulson LJ referred to the Oxford English Dictionary definition of 'certificate' as: 'A formal document attesting a fact, esp birth, marriage, or death, a medical condition, a level of achievement, a fulfilment of requirements, ownership of shares, etc.'

He concluded: 'In my judgment, to be within section 18(5) the certifying must be in writing. However, it does not follow that the seizures in the present case were unlawful. As I have noted, the court found that the action taken in the present case was the only viable way to proceed. On that factual finding, it appears to me that the constable who seized the animals acted lawfully under section 18.

'The court was entitled to conclude that the probative value of the relevant evidence justified its admission and that no significant prejudice was caused to Mr Gray by the fact that the veterinary surgeons' assessment of the animals' condition was not put in writing.'

Therefore Gray's application for judicial review was dismissed.

Both judgments were right. The evidence was relevant and admissible and it was fair to admit it. Crucially, the defendant was the one who abused the animals. Gray was attempting to use the law as a defence when he had broken it. If the court had decided in Gray's favour it would have made the AWA unworkable. The AWA and the role of a vet in alleviating an animal's suffering when it was a life-and-death situation would have been rendered nugatory.

Power of entry for section 18 purposes

3.7 Animal Welfare Act 2006 s.19

(1) An inspector or a constable may enter premises for the purpose of searching for a protected animal and of exercising any power under section 18 in relation to it if he reasonably believes:
   (a) that there is a protected animal on the premises, and
   (b) that the animal is suffering or, if the circumstances of the animal do not change, he is likely to suffer.

To counter problems of entry to premises where animals are in '*distress*', the AWA grants the inspector or constable powers of entry to perform their duty. They may enter premises for the purpose of 'searching' for a protected animal. The person exercising the power can do so if he 'reasonably believes' a protected animal is on the premises and is suffering. He can take action if the animal is '*likely to suffer*', if he fails to do so. That power covers any potential and actual suffering of the protected animal.

The position is stronger if he enters under that power or with a warrant as then he may take the animal away and arrange for a post-mortem examination of any carcass. Any obstruction of a person exercising such a power is itself an offence. If he takes another person with him in exercising the power of entry or executing a warrant, each of them possess those powers. Any obstruction of either person would be an offence.

There is a potential flaw in the law as it does not authorise entry to any 'part of premises' that is used as a private dwelling. If a person simply transfers the suffering animal from the farm to his lounge, how is the animal going to be discovered and saved from suffering? In the growing animal abuse practice of dog fighting and badger baiting, the offenders usually take their dogs back home to recover.

He could enter part of the premises used as an office, but could not go into the residential part unless he has obtained a warrant. By then it could be too late. [See: **4.3**]

As an inspector or a constable may find some resistance when they try to enter premises to search for an animal they can use 'reasonable force' to gain entry. That only applies if it is necessary and he has to enter before a warrant can be obtained and executed. That would be the case if an animal is suffering and it is imperative he acts immediately as otherwise the suffering would be more severe. An obstruction by the householder would be an offence. [See: **5.5**]

If force is necessary to gain entry without a degree of urgency, a warrant has to be obtained. A justice of the peace may issue one that authorises an inspector to enter the premises and to use reasonable force. The warrant can only be issued if the justice of the peace is satisfied the animal is suffering or is likely to if there is no change in its circumstances. A vital additional requirement to the condition is that a justice of the peace must be satisfied in relation to section 52. Then a warrant can be granted without notice to the occupier if the specified strict condition is satisfied. Notice would defeat the reason for the investigation. Without that condition any animal abuser would be a snook-cocker towards the victims. [See: **4.3**]

Orders in relation to animals taken under section 18(5)

3.8   Animal Welfare Act 2006 s.20

(1) A Magistrates' Court may order any of the following in relation to an animal taken into possession under section 18(5)
  (a) that specified treatment be administered to the animal;
  (b) that possession of the animal be given up to a specified person;
  (c) that the animal be sold;
  (d) that the animal be disposed of otherwise than by way of sale;
  (e) that the animal be destroyed.

As live animals are property in law they can be bought and sold, used and abused just like any other property. However, if an inspector or constable has acted on a vet's certificate or of his own accord and taken an animal 'into possession' under this section, it may be retained. There could also be dependent offspring of the parent animal. The person exercising the power can apply to the Magistrates' Court for an order relating to him. The magistrates can make an order for matters affecting the animal's future, including veterinary treatment, and sale or disposal by death.

If the animal is pregnant when she is taken into possession, these powers extend to any offspring of the pregnancy. So if the parent animal and any offspring required 'treatment' of a straightforward veterinary nature that would be covered by 'caring' for the animal. If they were in need of more serious surgery, then the magistrates could make an order.

As the animal may have been taken against the wishes of the owner or, depending on the circumstances, even without his knowledge, he has a right to apply to the Magistrates' Court in respect of his property. The owner could apply for the magistrates to order any of those powers including the return of the animal to him. Depending on the circumstances, he may apply for the disposal or death of his animal.

The Magistrates' Court may hear an application by 'any other person appearing to the court to have any sufficient interest in the animal'. There could be a conflict between the owner and another person as one may want to sell him, while the other may want to kill him. Whether it is a single or dual application, the decision is balanced by what is best for the animal. If there were conflicting applications the court could decide in favour of one or other or make a completely different decision. To make the right decision in protecting the court and the animal, and to avoid a challenge on appeal, the judicious course would be to seek the opinion of a vet. That course would endorse the principles within the AWA. He should also give evidence in court that could then be subject to cross-examination by all the parties.

Ownership is important as a legal concept, so those powers of the court cannot be exercised unless it has given the owner an opportunity to be heard. Sometimes animals are abandoned in muddy fields, especially when travellers move on from a site, or the owner is the defendant, who absconds before or during the proceedings to avoid being convicted or sentenced. In the event of the Magistrates' Court being unable to contact the owner, it can carry out any of those powers if it is satisfied it is not reasonably practical to communicate with him. When the court makes any of those orders, it can enforce them by appointing a person to do so. Then the court gives directions for the procedure to be followed. [See: **3.9**]

A rather unusual provision indicates how the court should exercise its powers. It *'shall'* have regard to, 'amongst other things', the desirability of protecting the animal's 'value' and avoiding increasing any expenses that a person may be ordered to reimburse. That appears to allow the court to place a mongrel or a stray at a lower premium than a pedigree poodle. There is no reason to specify an animal's value in monetary terms when that could collide with its welfare now and in the future. If the decision is made to limit the expenses it could lead to the choice between a lower debt and immediate death. That is contrary to the principles of the AWA. The better course is that the abuser should be the loser and bear the burden of the cost, as happens under the American system. The

UK should adopt their system within The Costs of Care of Seized Animals Act 2013 [CCSAA], which protects the animal not the abuser.

There are occasions when the owner or another person takes exception to one of those orders. He may still have the animal on his premises as a 'place of safety'. If he 'intentionally obstructs' the person carrying out the court's order he commits an offence.

Orders under section 20: appeals

3.9   Animal Welfare Act 2006 s.21

(1) Where a court makes an order under section 20(1), the owner of the animal to which the order relates may appeal against the order to the Crown Court.

As the consequences of these powers are serious, the 'owner' has a right of appeal to the Crown Court. While the appeal is pending, none of the orders made by the court can be enforced. They are suspended until the time for an appeal has expired or the appeal has been determined or withdrawn.

There may be a conflict between the owner's application and the court's order, especially where an animal requires treatment. Then, where on appeal the orders are suspended, the court may give *'directions'* about how any animal subject to an order is dealt with during the suspension. Those directions enable the court to protect the animal's welfare pending the result of the appeal.

These provisions are essential as the animal may be suffering and need veterinary treatment, notwithstanding any appeal. The owner's position is subject to the court's decision to minimise the animal's distress.

There could be a conflict of interest between the owner and any other interested person if an application is made by the former to sell the animal and the latter to have it returned to him. In that event the court has a discretionary power to grant either application or to reject them both. It has to make an order that is appropriate to the interests of the animal as compared to the human claimant.

While costs are payable by a convicted defendant it is important the claim is properly made. A defendant was convicted of causing unnecessary suffering to 12 horses and ordered to pay £11,888 towards the cost of their upkeep to the Hillside Animal Sanctuary. On appeal the High Court held that was wrong as 'the mere boarding costs of maintaining the horses' was not 'an investigation cost'. Plainly it was not for the predominant purpose of investigating the case. However, an application can be made to the court for 'directions' as to the 'expenses' in relation to an appeal: *R (Donovan) v. Burnley Crown Court* [2014] EWHC 742.

This section concentrates on the rights of the owner, who is usually the abuser. His re-possession is contrary to the ethos of the AWA. An intermediary body should be appointed with a 'sufficient interest' in the animal's condition and future. An Animals' Ombudsman would protect the interests of victims who cannot complain in their own right. That is after all the purpose of law.

4

EVIDENCE FOR THE PROSECUTION

4.1   Enforce

This chapter analyses the mechanics of the AWA. It is concerned with enforcement, prosecution and sentences upon conviction. The AWA takes account of the fact the victims are animals. As they cannot provide the evidence directly the AWA grants that power to the authorities. That includes the method and place to obtain evidence to mount a prosecution.

Section 52 is considered out of chronological order because it is relevant to the investigation. Sections 22 and 23 relate to the application for and granting of a warrant while section 52 controls the *conditions* upon which a warrant is considered and granted or refused.

Seizure of animals involved in fighting offences

4.2   Animal Welfare Act 2006 s.22

(1) A constable may seize an animal if it appears to him that it is one in relation to which an offence under section 8(1) or (2) has been committed.

Animal fighting 'rings' are arranged, yet are often opportunistic and spontaneous. As the rings commit offences that are being tracked by the authorities and informants, they usually operate by a series of secret meetings on a need-to-know basis by the cloaked cohorts. An area where the ordinary activity it is used for may be a game of skittles can be swiftly transformed into a dog fighting ring. The aim is to feel the thrill of the kill and the prize money that is won and lost by betting on which dog dies. Another form where bloodlust alone is enough is when a terrier is 'placed' in a hole to face a trapped fox with no means of escape, which then becomes a directed 'fight'.

Sometimes an animal fight can be arranged by chance rather than design. The aim would be the same: a literal and legal dog-eat-dog. It would be dangerous for the owners to take a heavily marked mauled dog to a vet, who would recognise the origin of the wounds and inform the police; so they remain licking their wounds. [See: **2.13**]

Consequently, the police need power to enter premises to ensure they can act on 'intelligence' where there is, prior to their visit, little or no proof of the activity. The 'information received' is usually the result of intelligence gained undercover or by an underground animal rights activist who has infiltrated the secret network. That information will filter through to the police and form the basis of his 'belief' to effect an investigation. Everything depends on taking the miscreants by surprise, for once the police announce their presence at a raid the participants scatter and vanish into the night. Allied to that the police have to arrest the main men and seize their animals as evidence. [See: **4.5**]

A constable may enter and search premises to seize an animal if he *'reasonably believes'* an 'animal fight' has been committed. Once the animal has been seized it can lead to a deprivation order or a disqualification order against the owner. There is a simple solution in respect of his dog, which could then be legally killed.

However, the power does not authorise entry to any 'part of premises' that is used as a 'private dwelling'. That could be a serious lacuna in the AWA as the definition of a private dwelling includes 'any yard, garden, garage or outhouse which is used for purposes in connection with it'. That would hamper any investigation as those areas are precisely where the fight is likely to be in full flight. Alternatively those areas are disguised after the event with the bones and blood scrubbed clean from the scene. The yard then resembles a cobbled alley, not a killing pit.

The purpose of this power is to capture the perpetrators and participants and spectators while the fight is in motion. Therefore the major potential problem can be solved by the police executing a warrant. A justice of the peace may issue a warrant to a constable to enter and search premises to seize an animal. As there can be no lawful reason for the activity, there is often obstruction, resistance and assault by the perpetrators. Following a raid, those present equally seek to or do make a hasty escape. The officer, armed with a warrant, can use 'reasonable force' if it is necessary for him to make an arrest.

Only a constable can apply for a warrant under this section. A warrant can be granted if a justice of the peace is satisfied of two conditions:

(i)   there must be 'reasonable grounds' for believing an animal fight has been committed;

(ii) section 52 must be satisfied in relation to the premises.

The necessity could arise as a result of the occupier refusing entry to the officer. The 'occupier' is defined as 'the person who appears to be in charge' of the premises.

Section 52 is strict in its terms as it respects the privacy that attaches to a person's home. Although it may hinder the police in their investigation, it is balanced with the right of a person to restrict those who can lawfully enter his home. Nevertheless, if the onus placed upon the police is discharged, then the warrant can be issued even without advance notice to the occupier.

Conditions for grant of warrant

4.3   Animal Welfare Act 2006 s.52

(1) This section is satisfied in relation to premises if any of the following four conditions is met.

The 'four conditions' specified are:

1.   The *first* condition is that the whole of the premises is used as a private dwelling and the occupier has been informed of the decision to apply for a warrant.

2. The *second* condition is that any part of the premises is not used as a private dwelling. Then the occupier of the premises:
    (a) has been informed of the decision to seek entry to the premises and of the reason;
    (b) has failed to allow entry to the premises on being requested do so by an inspector or a constable;
    (c) has been informed of the decision to apply for a warrant.
3. The *third* condition is that:
    (a) the premises are unoccupied or the occupier is absent, and
    (b) notice of intention to apply for a warrant has been left in a conspicuous place on the premises.
4. The *fourth* condition is that it is inappropriate to inform the occupier of the decision to apply for a warrant because:
    (a) it would defeat the object of entering the premises, or
    (b) entry is required as a matter of urgency.

The first three conditions hinder any potential investigation as once the occupier knows the police intend to apply for a warrant, the evidence will be disposed of or destroyed, especially if it is a dog. After all, the dog could help to prove the offence, particularly if it is wounded as a bite could be positive evidence for the prosecution of the illegal activity that produced it.

Hence the fourth condition counteracts that negative position by allowing the grant of a warrant if it is 'inappropriate' to inform the occupier of the decision to apply for a warrant. There are two alternative limbs, either of which can be met: (a) it would 'defeat the object' of the entry; or (b) the entry is 'a matter of urgency'.

That fourth condition is essential as without it an investigation could end before it began. Every criminal naturally destroys any evidence if he is aware of a pending police visit. The last thing a criminal would want is to allow the police to use his own dog to put the bite on him.

Depending on the condition of the animal, it is likely the occupier would have him at home to recuperate so he can be used to fight again in the future. This section would include a dead dog as sometimes the most potent evidence is provided by a post-mortem examination. It can verify the nature of the wounds and the likely suffering as a result while the animal was still alive. Indeed, it could prove the injuries led to his death.

A vet can examine the animal and provide expert evidence of what caused his condition. A 'fight' could affect an animal's heart and organs as well as telltale bites over their face and body. An orthodontist could match the gnash.

If the owner seeks the return of a seized animal, he could apply to the court under the Police (Property) Act 1897 [PPA]. The application is similar to one under the AWA, but stronger for the owner if the evidence is weak as the PPA places a burden on the police to justify their possession of personal property, whether it is a spurred cock or a ceramic chicken. [See: **1.2**]

As a warrant is an intrusion to the citizen, the court is particularly vigilant to ensure compliance with the terms of it. In *R (on the application of the RSPCA) v. Colchester Magistrates' Court* [2015] EWHC 1418, the validity of a warrant was analysed. The RSPCA charged Deborah Fuller and Philip Sheldrake with three offences of unnecessary suffering and ten offences of failure to meet the needs of 44 dogs at their premises.

District Judge Sheraton [DJ] at Colchester Magistrates' Court excluded the evidence of the search gained under the warrant and dismissed all the charges. The RSPCA appealed against that decision.

A warrant was issued to Tendring District Council under the Environmental Protection Act 1990 [EPA]. Although it also applied for a warrant under the AWA, that was refused because 'the qualifying criteria … were not present at the time of the application'. The search was authorised for 'noise from excessive barking, odour emanating from the premises and the accumulations of dog faeces within the premises'. That related only to the EPA. It would not have been lawful to extend the search beyond those terms.

A police officer saw dogs in 'various states of appearing underfed, some were pitifully thin. … and unclean conditions in which the dogs were kept with no bedding'. The RSPCA charged the defendants, relying on that evidence to support its case.

Beatson LJ analysed the importance of a warrant and why the courts are vigilant: 'The consequences of the gathering of evidence in support of a prosecution under the Animal Welfare Act was severe. The animals would be taken away from the individual. The individual would have to meet the costs of caring for the animals as part of the costs of resisting a prosecution the liability for as well as the legal costs.' This was an example of the 'officers of the State, aided by officers of a large, well-funded charity, which does excellent work in many cases, using the power of the State compulsorily to enter land. It is incumbent that the officers of the State and those who assist them in this way take care that the principle of legality which has protected us so well over many centuries is observed.'

He concluded: 'For these reasons I refuse the application.'

It is axiomatic the RSPCA should have practised the *'principle of legality'*. If not, as here, the animals will suffer in vain.

Entry and search under warrant in connection with offences

4.4   Animal Welfare Act 2006 s.23

(1) Subject to subsection (2), a justice of the peace may, on the application of an inspector or a constable, issue a warrant authorising an inspector or a constable to enter premises, if necessary using reasonable force, in order to search for evidence of the commission of a relevant offence.

   The power to issue a warrant under this section is exercisable only if the justice of the peace is satisfied:
   (a) that there are reasonable grounds for believing (i) that a relevant offence has been committed on the premises, or (ii) that evidence of the commission of a relevant offence is to be found on the premises and
   (b) that section 52 is satisfied in relation to the premises.

Once a warrant has been issued it is vital it is executed with speed. There are limits on the issue of a warrant in order to search for 'evidence' because of the power attached to its use. The warrant will authorise the use of reasonable force, if necessary, for the entry and search.

A warrant is subject to a justice of the peace being satisfied on two grounds. First that there are reasonable grounds for believing a 'relevant offence' has been committed on the premises or evidence of it will be found there. Secondly, section 52 has to be satisfied in relation to the premises. Therefore one of the four specified conditions must be met. [See: **4.3**]

A *'relevant offence'* means any offence within 'sections 4 to 9, 13(6) and 34(9)', which are the core sections of the AWA. Therefore it covers all the serious offences including those relating to 'unnecessary suffering' and 'duty of care'. The licence or registration of the activities involving animals includes where a person breaches a disqualification. Often in cases involving animal abuse, there is a huge whiff of suspicion without proof. Then the abuse would remain undiscovered as usually these offences are committed behind closed doors where they are hidden to most, except the perpetrators themselves as well as silent conspirators among the staff. That is the underlying reason this provision is the key to a detailed investigation of the abuse.

The conditions governing a warrant are set out in detail in Schedule 2 under the heading, *Safeguards etc. in connection with powers of entry conferred by warrant*. There are strict conditions relating to an inspector and a constable in respect of the application and its execution. As a warrant is not easily granted, once it is issued its execution has to be controlled and effective. So Schedule 2 confers additional powers on the person executing it, including inspection of an animal, taking samples and seizing evidence. It confirms the person is authorised to use 'reasonable force' in exercising those additional powers.

None of that would be effective unless there was a sanction against those subject to the warrant. A criminal will tend to show some resistance and is likely to be unco-operative. Therefore if someone intentionally 'obstructs' anyone exercising any of the powers 'conferred by this Schedule', he commits an offence. [See: **5.5**]

Entry for purposes of arrest

4.5   Animal Welfare Act 2006 s.24

The Police and Criminal Evidence Act 1984 section 17 [PACE] gives power to a constable to enter and search premises for the purpose of arresting a person for an offence under various specified Acts and enactments. That section is amended to allow a power of arrest to be extended for certain offences within sections 4 to 8 of the AWA. The officer has that power for all those sections that relate to the 'prevention of harm' to animals, namely suffering, mutilation, tail docking, poisons and fighting. Without that power the AWA would be considerably weakened in practice and effect. The power under PACE of 'entry and arrest' enables the officer to find and arrest the animal abuser as well as protecting the animal. Within that power it allows the officer the opportunity to obtain and preserve the evidence.

Inspection of records required to be kept by holder of licence

4.6   Animal Welfare Act 2006 s.25

(1) An inspector may require the holder of a licence to produce for inspection any records which he is required to keep by a condition of the licence.

When a person owns animals for which he has a licence it is vital that he keeps records that are accurate, reliable and true. Those records have to be available to an inspector. That is essential as otherwise there would be no official way to track and trace any case in which he had breached his duty or failed to fulfil the conditions upon which the licence was granted. So an inspector may 'require' the licensee to produce any records he has to keep as a condition of his licence. Usually they would be in a paper form and signed by the owner. If they are in electronic form, the inspector has the power to require the records to be made available in a visible and legible form. That puts an onus on the licensee. If it is on a computer he can require the person to give him it on a dongle rather than take the computer away. Although the inspector 'may' require production of the records, if he does so the request is an authoritative one. The inspector has power to seize the equipment and could do so if the licensee was unco-operative. Both the equipment and any lack of co-operation would be used in evidence if the licensee is charged with an offence.

If the licensee has inadequate records it would be difficult, if not impossible, to know and check if he has complied with the conditions attached to it. Moreover, it would not be feasible to ensure any diseased animals do not enter – or have not already entered – the food chain intended for humans. Given the repercussions of such a disease it could be serious if it spread to people through the mass consumption of beef burgers or poached eggs.

A person commits an offence if he carries out an activity that requires a licence without possessing one. If he has one and breaches a condition of it, that is an offence. If he carries out an activity involving animals after the expiration of the licence period he commits an offence.

The grant of a licence can be for a limited period. In any event it cannot be for more than three years. That allows the authorities to have control over the licensee during the period it is used and more particularly when an application is made for renewal of the licence. How far the licensee has complied with the conditions would be considered and become decisive. Accordingly, his licence could then be either renewed or amended or refused. Stricter conditions would be likely to be added rather than the existing ones removed. That approach would be consistent with the reason for imposing conditions in the licence.

Inspection in connection with licences

4.7   Animal Welfare Act 2006 s.26

(1) An inspector may carry out an inspection in order to check compliance with
   (a) the conditions subject to which a licence is granted;
   (b) provision made by or under this Act which is relevant to the carrying on of an activity to which a licence relates.

The protection of the animals' welfare is the reason the licensee has to keep records as they go some way to ensure the owner is acting properly and responsibly in relation to his animals. Therefore there has to be co-operation between the inspector and the owner to ensure he complies with the licence 'conditions'. An inspector can then check the licensee has complied with both the reason it was granted and all the activities it covers. As the conditions are attached to the use of the licence, if he breaches a condition during the period it covers or on expiration, he commits an offence.

The inspector may enter any premises specified in the licence as where the activity is authorised in order to carry out his duties. However, as that could be problematic, the power is wider in that he may also enter premises where he 'reasonably believes' such an activity is carried on. Without that wider subjective power it would be difficult in practice for the inspector to control the licensee as well as detect any breaches of the activity by him.

The limitation on the balance between privacy of the person and the potential breach remains. If the activity is being carried on in part of the premises that are being used as a 'private dwelling' the inspector must give 24 hours' notice of his intention to enter to the occupier.

The 24 hours' notice is a balance between the privacy of the occupier against the power of an inspector. The reason that such 'notice' has to be given is it is not within the serious offences ['relevant offence'] of the AWA. There is no power to apply for a warrant under this section. The exclusion of notice when applying for a warrant is reserved for the serious offences. [See: **4.3**]

Nevertheless, the power is wider than it at first appears as it includes the inspector being able to check any provision made '*by or under*' the AWA that is relevant to the licence. If the licensee contravenes the conditions of the licence, he commits an offence. That position is endorsed by conferring a 'power of entry' to the inspector. Then if the licensee intentionally obstructs the inspector he commits an offence. Besides being charged with a criminal offence, any refractory person could have his licence revoked if he prevents the inspector from fulfilling his statutory duty.

Although a warrant cannot be obtained under this section, an inspector could apply for entry with a warrant under sections 19 if there is an *'animal in distress'* and 23 if he *'reasonably believes'* an offence has been committed on the premises. Then there would no need for the inspector to give notice to the occupier. That practical advantage would enable the inspector to limit the suffering of and rescue the respective animal. Equally, it would allow him to catch the criminal in the act. [See: **3.7**; **4.4**]

Inspection in connection with registration

4.8   Animal Welfare Act 2006 s.27

(1) An inspector may carry out an inspection in order to check compliance with provision made by or under this Act which is relevant to the carrying on of an activity to which a registration for the purposes of section 13 relates.

Registration of an activity is closely connected with conditions within the licensing system as each relates to an activity that needs to be monitored by the authorities. Allowing an inspection of the licence alone would be ineffectual to identify and investigate any area of concern. Consequently, an inspector has the power to check compliance with an activity that is registered within the wide-ranging provision of section 13. That power allows an inspector to enter premises where he 'reasonably believes' a person is carrying on a regulated activity. If registration was required but had not been granted, the person carrying out the unauthorised activity would commit an offence. [See: **3.2**]

It would be an invasion of privacy for an inspector to enter a person's home without authority. As with the proposed inspection in connection with the conditions of a licence, similarly 24 hours' notice of the intended entry has to be given to the occupier to any part of the premises that is used as a 'private dwelling'. Notice has to be given to maintain a balance between the powers of the inspector to protect animals with the privacy of the occupier to quiet enjoyment of his home. [See: **4.7**]

Inspection of farm premises

4.9   Animal Welfare Act 2006 s.28

(1) An inspector may carry out an inspection in order to
  (a) check compliance with regulations under section 12 which relate to animals bred or kept for farming purposes;
  (b) ascertain whether any offence under or by virtue of this Act has been or is being committed in relation to such animals.

Before the introduction of the AWA the main statute relating to farms was the Agriculture (Miscellaneous Provisions) Act 1968. While that Act is still partly in existence, Part 2 of it was repealed by the AWA. That has given the authorities additional powers as it extends the monitoring of animal welfare from a domestic setting to the inspection of farm premises.

The inspector may enter premises that he 'reasonably believes' to be premises on which animals are 'bred or kept' for farming purposes in order to carry out an inspection. However, as with other sections, this does not allow entry to part of the premises used as a 'private dwelling'. Nevertheless, a justice of the peace may issue a warrant authorising him to enter any part of the farm to carry out an inspection. The power to issue a warrant is limited. It can only be issued if the justice of the peace is satisfied of two conditions, namely (a) that an inspection is reasonable and (b) section 52 is satisfied in respect of the premises.

Therefore, as the four conditions specified in section 52 apply, the inspector could rely on any one of them. The first three conditions apply on the basis of giving 'notice' to the occupier. It is self evident that such notice could be self-defeating as the animals the inspection is intended to protect could be secretly disposed of or destroyed by the abuser. So the fourth condition can be met and a warrant issued if it would be *'inappropriate'* to inform the occupier of an intention because it would defeat the object or there is an urgency regarding the inspection. As those two limbs are separate, either (i) defeating the object or (ii) the urgency of the situation would be sufficient for an application. [See: **4.3**]

An advantage of using the AWA is that the regulations made under it can be applied within the Act and amended, if necessary, to suit the different conditions. So the Welfare of Farmed Animals (England) Regulations 2007 was introduced to cover the general position of animals on a farm as well as regulations relating to individual animals. Those regulations cover all such animals while they are on the farm as well as travelling to and from it. [See: **2.17**]

An important point in relation to an application for a warrant is it may be made by an inspector under this section, rather than by a constable. That is of practical value as an inspector may have to act in changing circumstances. Moreover, it has to be contrasted with section 22, which is the reverse and only applies to a police officer. [See: **4.5**]

There are additional powers conferred under Schedule 2 that apply to a person executing a warrant to enter the premises. However, there are '*safeguards*' as if a warrant is granted under this section it is subject to conditions in relation to the application and the execution of it. That specifies strict conditions relating to the form, the method and the procedure. It must be executed within three months of the date of its issue. Such conditions apply to protect the privacy of the occupier while ensuring entry is only gained to his premises on valid grounds. Indeed, if the warrant does not strictly comply with the conditions then the entry to the premises 'is unlawful'. Given the consequences of that position for the inspector and the licensee and the animals it is vital the one with the warrant acts within the law. [See: **4.3; 5.5**]

Inspection relating to community obligations

4.10   Animal Welfare Act 2006 s.29

(1) An inspector may carry out an inspection in order to check compliance with regulations under section 12 which implement a Community obligation.

Numerous statutory instruments flow from the European Union that relate to animals in all aspects of their lives and death. An inspector may carry out an inspection to ensure compliance with section 12, which implements a European Community obligation.

An inspector may enter 'any' premises in order to carry out an inspection. However, that does not authorise entry to any part of premises that are used as a 'private dwelling'. [See: **2.17**]

This provision is to check compliance with the European Community obligations. Essentially it is a similar provision to a power in the Animal Health Act 1981 that has effect on an international level. It has the advantage of allowing for any changing circumstances in Europe to be taken into account by present or pending regulations made under the AWA.

Generally Europe, including the United Kingdom, does not have a high standard in relation to the regulations that govern animal welfare. The real progress has been made by and as a result of protest by organisations such as 30 Million Friends on behalf of animals in 2014. While that has led to an advanced definition of animals in France by recognising they are 'sentient beings', we in the United Kingdom have yet to respect that self-evident truth.

Power of local authority to prosecute offences

4.11   Animal Welfare Act 2006 s.30

A local authority in England or Wales may prosecute proceedings for any offence under this Act.

Whilst in appropriate cases there is nothing to stop an animal organisation or an individual taking a private prosecution, generally the power is given to the local authorities in England and Wales. That includes a county council, district council and the county borough council.

Nevertheless, it must be appreciated that lodging a private prosecution is a cherished right derived from the common law. Sometimes it is the only way forward, especially when action is taken on behalf of those hamstrung by the lack of a human tongue. Sometimes it happens for the best or worst of reasons that the police or other authority refuse to prosecute a person. Then a private prosecution can always be lodged. That may be the only negative way to effect a positive change in the law. A case that was initially lost later gained a real change to the ban on veal. [See: *Roberts v Ruggiero*: Unreported: 3/4/85]

While there are sound organisations such as CWF, which took action in *Roberts,* most private prosecutions are undertaken in England and Wales by the RSPCA. The position in Scotland is that the SPCA does not prosecute cases. It collects, informs and provides evidence for the Procurator Fiscal, who then, if he decides to prosecute, undertakes the proceedings in court. Conversely, there would be very few prosecutions of animal abusers without the RSPCA. The police and CPS have limited interest and resources in prosecuting such cases. It is one of the reasons there is opposition to the RSPCA policy by those with vested interests.

The problem of prosecuting cases of animal abuse is that often they are not discovered for some considerable time. An offence may be a continuing one with regard to the animal's welfare. Even when a complaint is made or the offence is discovered, the investigation may take some time as it could be dependent on expert evidence from a vet, including a post-mortem examination. Normally, as they are 'summary' offences, the time limit for prosecutions once a summons is issued is six months. That would defeat the authorities in this case as there could be an Improvement Notice that is ignored, or it may be necessary to trace the perpetrators, who have since moved on, and any progeny who are also affected, perhaps being born during the period of the abuse. Meanwhile, the suffering might continue. Therefore the right to prosecute is more than a legal one; it also serves an important social and community role.

4.12   Prosecutor

The power to prosecute on behalf of those unable to resist or alleviate their own suffering is a significant one. Then the plight of those who are otherwise helpless can be addressed so the abuse is prevented and the abuser is subject to justice. The position was considered in *Lamont-Perkins v. RSPCA* [2012] EWHC 1002, an appeal against two rulings made by HHJ Ambrose at Gloucester Crown Court. Each ruling was made in an appeal by Margaret Lamont-Perkins against her convictions by the Coleford Justices for offences of causing 'unnecessary suffering' to a number of dogs.

HHJ Ambrose ruled the 'information' laid by the RSPCA against Mrs Lamont-Perkins was lodged within the statutory time limit. If the ruling was wrong the case against her would fail.

Wyn Williams J in the High Court said counsel for the appellant submitted that the respondent, the RSPCA, is not and can never be *'the prosecutor'* within the AWA. It claimed it meant a body authorised by statute to initiate prosecutions, not a private body that initiates a private prosecution.

The appellant relied upon the fact the AWA expressly empowers a local authority to prosecute for any offence under the Act. Parliament had 'in mind a restricted class of prosecutor'. Therefore it did not include a private person or body.

Wyn Williams J agreed with the Crown Court judge and said it was important to stress that the power to prosecute must be interpreted in the context of the complete AWA. After analysing the AWA, he said, 'there is nothing in the Act, read as a whole' that leads to the conclusion that 'the prosecutor' should be interpreted narrowly. A narrow construction, as the defence contended, would have excluded the RSPCA.

Yet Wyn Williams J went further and added: 'It is not a power lightly to be conferred upon any prosecuting authority … I am not persuaded, however, that the power … is intended to be available only to a prosecutor which derives its authority to prosecute from statute.'

That was definitely the right decision for two reasons. There are many cases where an existing prosecuting body such as the CPS or Defra fail to be proactive in initiating a prosecution, notwithstanding the state of the evidence. Without bodies such as the RSPCA there would be no prosecution at all in such cases. It is also in the interests of justice that animal abusers are punished. If not it would do more than merely ensure such abusers escape their just deserts. Given that animal abusers graduate to be violent to other vulnerable targets such as children and women, it would put other people and animals at risk of being victims in the future.

The position of the RSPCA is somewhat unusual as it is perhaps the best-known animal charity in the world. Although it has no extra powers over the ordinary citizen, like the police its inspectors are subject to the procedure of PACE. In *RSPCA v. Chester Crown Court* [2006] EWHC 1273 Sedley LJ said: 'You are in a curious position. You are not a public authority in constitution; you are a charity. But, of course, you do have a statutory position as a prosecutor, which others do not have.'

Beatson J added with admirable insight: 'You are like the NSPCC in relation to children.'

Animal abuse, which is increasingly rife in our society, would go unpunished without the RSPCA. It was started in 1824 by a group including the Reverend Arthur Broome, Lewis Gompertz, Richard Martin and William Wilberforce. It was granted royal patronage in 1840 by Queen Victoria. In 2015 alone it prosecuted more than 1,781 people, with a prosecution success rate of 92.4%. Without it more animals would suffer more than they already do at our hands. The RSPCA was instrumental in setting up the NSPCC.

This means the local authority '*may*' prosecute under the AWA. It clarifies it can take action rather than limiting the power only to it. As the right regarding a private prosecution is steeped in the history of our common law the application was misconceived.

Time limits for prosecutions

4.13   Animal Welfare Act 2006 s.31

(1) Notwithstanding anything in section 127(1) of the Magistrates' Court Act 1980, a Magistrates' Court may try an information relating to an offence under this Act if the information is laid
   (a) before the end of the period of three years beginning with the date of the commission of the offence, and
   (b) before the end of the period of six months beginning with the date on which evidence which the prosecutor thinks is sufficient to justify the proceedings comes to his knowledge.

   The '*evidence*' upon which the prosecutor relies is subject to two stringent conditions:
   1. A certificate signed by or on behalf of the prosecutor and stating the date on which such evidence came to his knowledge shall be conclusive evidence of that fact.

2. A certificate stating that matter and purporting to be so signed shall be treated as so signed unless the contrary is proved.

This is one of the most important and contentious provisions in the AWA. The reason is it allows the prosecutor to take proceedings a long time after the offence, subject to his certificate. If the defence can challenge the validity of that certificate the prosecution is likely to fail, either from the start or there may be 'no case to answer'. Thus the certificate has a practical legal use and value for both parties.

The usual period within which a Magistrates' Court may try a case is six months. However, that does not apply if it is:

(a) within three years of the commission of the offence; and
(b) within six months of which time the prosecutor 'thinks' the evidence is sufficient to justify the proceedings comes to his knowledge.

A prosecutor must *sign* the certificate stating his subjective belief as to that 'evidence' and its effect. The certificate is then *'conclusive'* of that fact. As a result, it will be treated as so unless the contrary is proved.

Animal abuse, particularly fights, can often only be prosecuted well after the *six-month* statutory period as the evidence is analysed when the investigation is complete. It may relate to telephone records, a video or items only discovered on a computer because, like a paedophile ring or drug dealers, dog fighting perpetrators equally communicate covertly and in extreme secrecy. However, in relation to those criminal activities of perverts and perpetrators, unlike animal fighting, each could be subject to proceedings in the Crown Court, where the statutory limits do not apply. However, more time is required to gain evidence against animal abusers generally and particularly those involved in fighting rings as they are only summary offences and so held in the Magistrates' Court. [See: **4.18; 6.1**]

4.14   Certify

The certificate is the pulse of a prosecution as animal abuse cases are different from most other criminal offences. They are also similar to sexual offences against children in that they often come to light long after the event. As with children who are very young, the victims are not able to give evidence without the help of an expert who examines the child or animal. The discovery of evidence that is sufficient to mount a case is painstaking and subject to delay. That was at the root of the issue raised in *RSPCA v. Johnson* [2009] EWHC 2702, an appeal by the RSPCA from the decision of the Consett Magistrates' Court. The district judge [DJ] refused to hear an information laid by the RSPCA on the basis it was *'out of time'*.

Paul Johnson was charged with an offence of causing 'unnecessary suffering' to a thoroughbred stallion between 11 May and 11 June 2007 in County Durham. The issue raised by Johnson was whether the information and summons dated 11 June 2008 were out of time. On that document the informant was stated to be 'RSPCA Inspector Jackman 108 (on behalf of the RSPCA)'. The information was laid on 4 June 2008, before the end of the period of six months from the certified date of 21 December 2007, within the statutory period.

Therefore the accuracy of the dates was crucial to the prosecution and defence.

Throughout June to August Johnson made concerted efforts to avoid and hide from Jackman. He did so at the farm and other places. Jackman visited and contacted various bodies for information about Johnson, including the Department of Work and Pensions.

Jackman visited the farm after the December dates that were critical in the appeal; he visited in January and February 2008. Finally he visited a dental practice that he believed was owned and operated by Johnson and saw him there on 27 May. Johnson said: 'I am not interested in talking to you.' Jackman was dogged to the end and visited Johnson again.

In the High Court, Pill LJ said: 'In discharging their duties, Inspectors of the Society clearly need to make inquiries. There is a public interest in prosecutions not being started otherwise than on good grounds and there is a public interest in fairness being shown to those whom it is proposed to prosecute … The judge found that there was, on that basis, sufficient evidence that the respondent owned the horse. The judge found that the Society is a body corporate. He concluded, first, that the Society had sufficient knowledge and evidence to issue a process within the usual six-month time limit that is within six months of 17 June; secondly, he found that the certificate dated 4 June 2008 was a misguided attempt by the Society to extend the time for the issuing of an information. That appears to me to be a finding of bad faith against the Society ...

Pill LJ added this important point: 'If on its face the certificate was conclusive, the judge was still able to investigate whether there had been fraud or an abuse of process.'

Johnson's position was even if the certificate was valid on its face there had been an abuse of process as held by the DJ. Sufficient evidence to justify proceedings had come to the 'knowledge' of the RSPCA as early as the summer of 2007.

Pill LJ reviewed the evidence and said: 'I am unable to accept that any abuse of process is revealed by the conduct of the Society during the period up to the issue of the information. I have already referred to the public interest in careful enquiries being made and the more elusive someone is, the more likely an inspector will want to have the clearest evidence in case some point is taken – an unforeseen point – by the elusive person when charged. Mr Jackman made very considerable efforts to get to the bottom of things.

'There is, however, a degree of judgment involved in bringing a prosecution, and knowledge, in my judgment, involves an opportunity for those with appropriate skills to consider whether there is sufficient information to justify a prosecution.'

Pill LJ then went much further than he needed to and concluded that even a mistake did not invalidate the charge if it was an honest and reasonable one to make: 'I would hold that, mistaken though it was, the stating of the wrong date did not amount to an abuse of process, having regard to the considerable burden upon a defendant seeking to establish that a prosecutor has acted in that way.'

This judgment was no mean triumph for common sense. Johnson had done everything possible to avoid detection. The RSPCA had to be sure it had the right man and had enough evidence to convict him. It had to be sure of that *before* it charged him. If it had acted too soon he might, as he almost did, escape his deserts by an unwise decision in or out of court. If the RSPCA had been at fault then it should have failed. Here the fault lay entirely with the defendant, whose determined efforts to escape justice were foiled. The endeavour of the RSPCA won the day because the delay was engendered by Johnson. In law, no less than in life, you cannot let a defendant use the ruse of his escape as a defence to truth.

4.15   Knowledge

The same issue was raised in the High Court in *RSPCA v. King* [2010] EWHC 637. This was an appeal from Portsmouth Magistrates' Court, which dismissed six summonses against Ian and Kathleen King alleging offences under the AWA. The DJ upheld a submission that there was 'no case to answer' because the information had been laid more than six months after the date of the alleged offences and so outside the limitation period. The prosecution sought to rely on the fact that a certificate is 'conclusive' evidence.

The certificate was signed by Jason Fletcher, the prosecution case manager, for the RSPCA. However, the copy attached to Fletcher's statement for the court was *unsigned*. The RSPCA claimed there was 'evidence' in Fletcher's statement of a certificate that complied with the AWA. The statement was evidence the proceedings had been commenced in time and was 'sufficient to justify the proceedings' that came to the prosecutor's 'knowledge' on 27 December 2007.

King claimed the prosecution was not entitled to rely upon that statement because:

(a)   Fletcher had not been called to give evidence and
(b)   the prosecution had not sought to introduce his statement before closing their case.

Therefore the court did not have any signed certificate that complied with the AWA. King made the point that this was no 'ambush' by the defence because it made clear there was a live issue as to the prosecution's date of 'knowledge'. It cross-examined a prosecution witness, Inspector Jan Edwards, who was referred to in Fletcher's statement, on that point.

The DJ concluded that the prosecution had failed to produce a signed certificate or other evidence to support its contention the information was laid within the six-month period. Therefore he could not 'rubber stamp' the signature of the head of legal services as the requirements of the AWA were not satisfied. He upheld the defence submission as the information was time-barred.

The RSPCA had to accept the exhibit did not comply with the section as it was unsigned. It argued that the court should look at the substance and not the form.

On appeal, Toulson LJ was dismissive of the submissions of the RSPCA from the outset: 'Given that a certificate in proper form is conclusive, subject to limited qualifications recognised in the case law, the court should not adopt a loose approach to the formal requirements of the subsection … A statutory certificate when in proper form forecloses the issue, subject to some limited exceptions. Therefore, there is good reason to require that the certificate should be in proper form.'

The reason Toulson LJ took that view was compelling as the dates were muddled and unclear. It was exacerbated by a fax from Fletcher that stated: 'Please note the date I signed the letter and the date on the letter are the same, being 29/10/08 and not 8/2/09 as in your draft statement. I am not sure where the date of 8/2 came from but you may wish to call me if there is confusion.' [Why did the prosecution not call this witness?]

Indeed, there was confusion because the letter of 9 February 2009 had been referred to in a schedule of 'unused material'– material known to but not relied upon by the prosecution which as a matter of fairness is disclosed to the defence lest it wish to use it – served by the prosecution, but there was no reference to a certificate dated 29 January 2008, nor had that ever been shown to the defence. The court concluded: 'These matters illustrate the point that a person who is signing a certificate intended to have effect under section 30 needs to have the relevant facts in mind at the time of making that certificate. They also illustrate the importance of requiring that a document should comply with the statutory requirements in form and in substance before being treated as a statutory certificate.' As the court remained unimpressed the appeal was dismissed.

That was the right decision because it put the RSPCA and all prosecutors on notice that it was essential they comply with the strict requirements of the AWA. Those conditions were strict for good reason. To gain the benefit of the requirements the prosecutor has the burden of fulfilling them. One depends upon the other because if a certificate was valid even if the prosecutor was unprofessional in relation to the correct procedure it would in time lead to a dilution of a provision that would be detrimental to a potential defendant. Worse than that, it would promote unfairness and injustice.

This provision is essential for a professional investigation as it allows prosecutors more time, but only if they can justify the delay and have not been dilatory in any way. Therefore this judgment should serve as a warning to all prosecutors that they fail those they are meant to protect if they fail to see this case as a signpost to the best practice. That reflects negatively on the pursuit of justice and the suffering of victims. Where law is concerned a loose use of language does not serve the community, the court or the animals. [See: **3.6**]

4.16   Date

The position of the prosecutor was spelled out in the clearest terms by the High Court in *Lamont-Perkins v. RSPCA* [2012] EWHC 1002. This was an appeal against two rulings made by HHJ Ambrose sitting at the Crown Court at Gloucester. [See: **4.12**]

Wyn Williams J made his view plain, namely that a certificate issued under the AWA is only susceptible to challenge on the grounds that an abuse of process has occurred in which some form of misconduct is involved.

When it was pressed on the point, the RSPCA was compelled to accept it had evidence sufficient to justify proceeding at an *earlier* date than it had claimed. There was evidence available to the court that 'strongly suggests' it considered it had sufficient evidence to justify a prosecution no later than 8 January 2008.

Wyn Williams J said: 'If the court remitted the case to the Crown Court they would probably conclude that the certificate … was plainly wrong.' However, even if the certificate is 'wrong' the court will still investigate whether the proceedings were brought within the time limit.

There was yet another surprising twist that had not been adumbrated. Wyn Williams J was not persuaded the evidence would demonstrate the proceedings were issued out of time. Then he went further in favour of the prosecution: 'A prosecutor must be afforded a reasonable period of time after obtaining the relevant evidence in order to form an opinion about whether the evidence obtained justified a prosecution. There is no evidence available which begins to suggest that the Respondent [RSPCA] considered it had sufficient evidence to justify a prosecution upon some dates between 4 September 2007 and 25 October 2007. These proceedings were commenced within six months of 25 October 2007.'

Wyn Williams J accepted that Lamont-Perkins had persuaded the court the procedure for determining the validity of a certificate was not that which was adopted in the Crown Court. The date was wrong. However, 'There is no material available to this court which persuades me that there is a possibility that the proceedings brought by the Respondent against the Appellant were issued outside the time limit.' Therefore the convictions were valid and the appeal was dismissed.

Wyn Williams J delivered a direct message to prosecutors for the future: 'This case has highlighted the need for *all* prosecutors to take great care when certifying a date under statutory provisions which have the effect of extending the time limit for bringing criminal proceedings. A prosecutor is exercising a crucial function when certifying such a date and it is incumbent upon the prosecutor to ensure the accuracy of the date.' [emphasis by judge]

When the prosecutor is less than professional, for him it is just another case that fails in embryo. However, for society that action might enable an animal abuser to avoid a valid charge. That is more than a slight blight on the community and the law as without this provision many cases of animal abuse would go undetected and the victims remain unprotected. Then any abuse could continue to affect the respective animals now and others in the future. As the power given to prosecutors is discretionary and wide, it has to be controlled by the court. The fine balance between the fairness to each party is the reason the court remains vigilant. The responsibility for adopting the right approach starts and ends with the prosecutors. Whether that is the CPS, the police, Defra or the

RSPCA is irrelevant. An unprofessional approach results in an injustice to the victim and society as well as bringing the law into disrepute.

The continuing importance of this issue is brought into focus by three recent decisions. In *Browning v. Lewes Crown Court* [2012] EWHC 1003, Browning applied for judicial review of the judge at the Crown Court as he stated her 'application is without merit'. She relied on several grounds that were related to the power to issue a certificate and the six-month time limit. Wyn Williams J dismissed each one in turn.

He said that the 'requisite knowledge' and the signature referred to the investigating officer not the 'prosecutor'. Neither was there any need to date the certificate nor serve it at the same time as the summons was served, as Browning claimed. That was the correct approach and consistent with the *Lamont Case*. This is an area fraught with problems that the court held the prosecutor must have in mind and here it did as the evidence proved.

In *Letherbarrow v. Warwickshire County Council* [2014] EWHC 4820, the High Court interpreted this area with a definite slant that assisted the prosecutor providing he acted strictly within the section. Bean LJ said, the section creates 'a long stop time limit of three years and a second alternative, six months beginning with the date on which evidence which the prosecutor thinks is sufficient to justify the proceedings comes to his knowledge. If the prosecution do nothing at all for more than two years, then stir themselves and issue summonses within five months of evidence coming to their knowledge, then they would be within the time limit …'

The interpretation by Bean LJ is instructive as it firmly sets out the favourable position of a prosecutor in investigating animal abuse. It confirms the decision to prosecute is a difficult one that must thereafter withstand analysis and being tested by cross-examination in court.

The problem reappeared in *RSPCA v. Webb* [2015] EWHC 3802, which involved an appeal by the RSPCA about a number of cats it had seized from Dean Webb. The sole issue for the court was whether it had filed the complaint within the time limit.

A vet visited the home of Webb on 9 February 2010. On 20 May 2010 she provided a witness statement confirming that the cats had a highly infectious feline corona virus. If the 'complaint' arose on 9 February it was 'out of time by one day'. It was in time if the complaint arose from the date of the vet's statement. A certificate was issued by the vet dated 9 February stating that three kittens were 'suffering' and a further 29 cats and kittens were 'likely to suffer'.

Beatson LJ in the High Court referred to the purpose of the section relating to 'animals in distress' and said: 'Although those provisions are concerned with what can be called urgent and possibly emergency situations, they show that what is relevant is the condition of the animal at the relevant time.' Consequently, the Crown Court was entitled to proceed on the basis that the crucial date was 9 February. As the RSPCA was outside the limit by a day, its appeal was dismissed.

A saving grace was tendered by Beatson LJ, who confirmed that it would be 'erroneous' to conclude that in all circumstances time would start running at the date of the seizure.' Nevertheless, the onus is on a prosecutor to act professionally throughout and calculate the date with the animals' fate in mind.

4.17   Post-Conviction Powers

All the sections from 32 to 45 provide the core punishment and powers following a conviction. They cover all aspects of the AWA from sentence to expenses. The powers govern the disqualification of the defendant from owning or keeping some or all animals. That is a significant part of the sentencing process, especially if the defendant has been convicted of an offence involving abuse of an animal and/or causing them unnecessary suffering. The purpose of any such sentence is to protect the respective animal and other animals from him in the future. [See: **6.1**]

Imprisonment or fine

4.18   Animal Welfare Act 2006 s.32

(1) A person guilty of an offence under any of sections 4, 5, 6(1) and (2), 7 and 8 shall be liable on summary conviction to

(a) imprisonment for a term of six months [51* weeks] or
(b) a fine not exceeding £20,000, or to both.

This section separates the varying degrees of the seriousness of the offence and provides a sentence that is supposedly commensurate with the gravity of the act for which a defendant was convicted. For an offence under sections 4 to 8 there is a present maximum of six months' imprisonment or a £20,000 fine, or both. [*The 51 weeks in the CJA 2003 has *not* been enacted.]

They all relate to the 'prevention of harm' category, which includes various forms of causing 'unnecessary suffering' and 'animal fighting' offences. Those carry the highest sentence available on a summary basis because they concern actual abuse of the animals.

The fine is proportionately high to reflect that fact, but as a penalty it is rarely a deterrent as the abuse is often linked to profit, be it by gambling or killing animals, or both. Further, it is pertinent to note that a fine is rarely paid. Usually they are ignored and forgotten as it is too costly to enforce the sum against a penurious criminal. So the fines tend to be 'written-off' by a concurrent sentence when a defendant reoffends.

A person guilty of a lesser offence under section 9, 13(6) or 34(9) is subject to the same sentence except it is limited to a fine up to level 5, which is presently £5,000. Those are concerned with failing in a 'duty of care' for the welfare of animals, being involved in an activity without a licence or registration and breaching an existing disqualification. It has the advantage of allowing the court to impose both imprisonment and a fine. A fine could be relevant, depending on its value, if the animal is sold or destroyed. [See: **3.9**]

A person guilty of an offence under regulation 12 or 13 relating to the 'promotion of welfare' is subject to the same sentence. The reason is that some breaches may be as serious as an offence under section 9 and so warrant the same sentence.

A person guilty of any other offence is subject to the same maximum sentence except it is limited to a fine up to level 4, which is presently £2,500. The lower offences attract the lowest sentences and include an obstruction of an inspector and failing to keep records. When that happens there are often more serious offences committed at the same time. Then a sentence for the more serious offence will be imposed to subsume the lesser one.

All the offences are summary only, which is a major problem within the AWA as the sentences are too low to prevent the prevalence and continuance of animal abuse. There is now no reason to retain that anachronistic tradition of markedly lenient sentences by the courts. There are offences that are so serious only a severe custodial sentence is sufficient to mark the gravity of them and to act as a deterrent to others. Only the Crown Court could impose an adequate sentence, but has no power to do so. The present limited sentences is a manifest inadequacy of the AWA. [See: **6.1**]

Deprive

4.19   Animal Welfare Act 2006 s.33

(1) If the person convicted of an offence under any of sections 4, 5, 6(1) and (2), 7, 8 and 9 is the owner of an animal in relation to which the offence was committed, the court by or before which he is convicted may, instead of or in addition to dealing with him in any other way, make an order depriving him of ownership of the animal and for its disposal.

When a person is convicted of one of the more serious offences the court can make an order depriving him of ownership of the animal. Deprivation of an animal can be an alternative or an additional sentence to imprisonment or a fine. Where the owner of an animal is convicted of an offence under this section the court has the same power of deprivation and disposal. So the court can order that the abused animal should be destroyed.

Destruction of an animal may be the only appropriate way of dealing with one that has been forced to engage in a 'fight'. The injuries suffered may be so severe that to allow the animal to live would only prolong the existing resultant pain. A sentence of death on the animal should then be treated as an *'aggravating'* factor, leading to a higher sentence for the defendant. The brief Guideline states 'serious injury or death' is one of the factors indicating a greater degree of harm, although the sentences are so lenient it is effectively meaningless. [See: **6.5**]

These powers within the AWA were introduced to counteract the weakness within the POA. The court can make 'directions' in relation to deprivation of the abused animal. The directions include a 'power of entry', which is essential in such a case as the animal may still be with the abuser. Where a court makes such an order it may appoint a person to carry out the directions to give effect to its order. The court can make the offender pay the expenses of the confiscation and of carrying out the order, plus any ancillary ones. We should adopt the American system as the abuser is the loser, paying for the cost of the injuries he has caused. [See: **3.8**]

As the order deprives an owner of an animal, it is limited to cases where there is an identifiable animal that has been abused. That proves the value of the power of an inspector to 'mark' an animal. The correct identification is crucial as otherwise the wrong animal could be subject to an order that affects its present and future. Where the animal has any dependent offspring, the power of 'deprivation' and 'disposal' extends to them too. Moreover, at worst the wrong animal could be killed while the right animal remains a victim. [See: **5.5**]

Although deprivation of ownership may be the sentence in its own right, that would not be the normal course. Usually the court would subject the defendant to an additional sentence. That goes to the root of the AWA as it is primarily to protect an animal and other animals in the future from the offender. The court has a duty to protect the abused animal now and those that may be abused by him in the future. Therefore there is an onus on the court to consider an order in every such case under this section. The duty is emphasised by the provision that if it fails to do so the court has to justify its decision. When a court fails to impose a deprivation order it '*shall*' give its reasons in open court. That mandatory duty applies to all courts dealing with such a sentence of animal abuse. If it is a Magistrates' Court it also has a duty to record its reasons in the register of its proceedings. That has a double benefit for the public as most such cases are dealt with in the Magistrates' Court. The court must consider that aspect of the sentence and any interested party can know its '*reasons*' lest there are grounds to appeal if it has made a wrong decision.

That position does not apply where a person is disqualified from owning or keeping animals. No reasons are necessary then as the disqualification order subsumes the deprivation. It is a more severe sentence that disqualifies the defendant from dealing with any particular animal or all animals. Disqualification is a more effective remedy and sentence.

When an animal is the victim of an 'animal fight', it does not normally constitute direct abuse by a human. Nevertheless, that could only happen if a human mind was the instigator of the criminal action. The kind of 'animal' is included in the generic reference rather than being specified. So besides the owner's own animal, the other victim could include a badger, fox or stag as the definition of an 'animal fight' is not limited to a 'protected' animal. The definition is exceptionally wide as it includes when a protected animal is 'placed … with a human'. That could catch a terrier man who deliberately traps a fox and prevents his escape by '*placing*' a dog in a face-to-face fight. [See: **2.13**]

'Disposal' applies to this section and throughout the AWA. All the courts dealing with animal abuse possess that power. While disposal can mean a transfer of ownership to a sanctuary or to another person, it includes every measure that can be ordered by the court. Hence it can mean the animal's death.

Disqualify

4.20   Animal Welfare Act 2006, s.34

(1) If a person is convicted of an offence to which this section applies, the court by or before which he is convicted may, instead of or in addition to dealing with him in any other way, make an order disqualifying him under any one or more of subsections (2) to (4) for such period as it thinks fit.

  Disqualification under this section disqualifies a person from:
  (a) owning animals,
  (b) keeping animals,
  (c) participating in the keeping of animals, and
  (d) being party to an arrangement under which he is entitled to control or influence the way in which animals are kept.

This section is positive when compared to the jejune provision that was in the POA. Disqualification is wide as a court can prohibit a defendant from having any involvement with animals at all. As the period that can be specified is a discretionary power according to the gravity of the offence, it can be any time up to a ban for life.

A defendant convicted of an offence under this section and any of the specified offences may be sentenced by the court to be disqualified for any period that it 'thinks fit'. The offences that can result in a disqualification are the main ones, including the various forms of causing 'unnecessary suffering' and 'animal fighting'. Those offences carry the highest sentences as they are concerned with the direct and deliberate abuse of an animal.

Disqualification alone can be a sentence in its own right. It can also be an alternative or an additional sentence to imprisonment and/or a fine. Disqualification alone as a sentence would be unusual given that it applies to the most serious offences. There is an additional power where a person breaches a disqualification that is of itself another offence. Such a breach is not uncommon as where people have an emotional attachment to animals or animals provide their living, they tend to adopt an ostrich-style approach and disregard the disqualification. When a person breaches the existing order the court can make a further disqualification that is more severe than the original sentence. Consequently, the original sentence could be doubled or extended into a life ban. The court could extend the terms and time of the disqualification, as well as imposing any other sentence.

The wide power to disqualify can extend to a person having any involvement with animals. That does not mean merely owning and keeping animals, but participating in the control of and having any 'dealing' in animals at all. Lest there is any doubt about the width of such a ban, it can include transporting and 'arranging' for the transport of them.

The defendant could be banned from even *'influencing'* the way animals are kept. However, in that event he has to be shown to actually do so by evidence, not mere suggestion, by proof rather than presumption. In *R (on the application of Patterson) v. RSPCA* [2013] EWHC 4531, Connor Patterson was convicted of 'animal cruelty' by participating in 'a blood sport'. He was disqualified for five years. When an RSPCA inspector visited Patterson's home he found a 'whole host of animals and birds along with Mr and

Mrs Patterson and their children'. The RSPCA claimed he was breaching the disqualification order. Patterson was convicted at the Magistrates' Court. He appealed on a point of law to the High Court. On appeal Patterson relied on the point he had 'passed title to all the animals to Mrs Patterson and she was now solely responsible for them'.

The evidence relied upon by the RSPCA was one of inference and assumption. Essentially it was submitting that whenever Mrs Patterson was absent or unavailable the appellant would be bound to be looking after the animals. He was the only available adult. Therefore Patterson was able to 'influence' the way the animals were kept.

In the High Court Blake J said: 'It is not sufficient that you are able to control or influence the way in which they are kept, you must be entitled to control or influence the way in which they are kept under an arrangement to which you are a party.' The prosecution relied on a presumption rather than proof. As the prosecution had failed to establish its claim by 'evidence', the conviction on that count was quashed.

A disqualification can be imposed in relation to animals generally or to animals of one or more 'kinds'. In *Ward v. RSPCA* [2010] EWHC 347, Openshaw J made a salient point about the character of Anthony Ward when the High Court dismissed his appeal. Ward was sentenced to a disqualification order on two previous occasions. The court included 'cattle' in the order, though the unnecessary suffering only related to two ponies.

Openshaw J upheld the disqualification in respect of both kinds of animals. He sagely concluded that the suffering caused by Ward, 'is just as likely to be directed towards his cattle as towards his ponies.'

The judge's percipient point confirms the guilt of an abuser is the crucial factor, not the kind of victim he abuses. A defendant who abuses an animal has the kind of 'bad character' that he would not distinguish one kind of animal from another.

When a defendant is disqualified he can apply for the ban to be lifted after one year from the date of the order. However, while that is the norm, when the order is imposed the court has power to specify a period during which the defendant may not make an application for a termination of the order. That enables the court to make an order that reflects the gravity of the crime. So the sentence could disqualify a person for, say, ten years and not allow him to apply for a termination for seven years. Part of the punishment is to protect all animals from the defendant now and in the future. [See: **4.29**]

Often because of the emotional attachment aspect of these cases the defendant lodges an appeal. In that event the court can suspend the order. The court can also allow the defendant time to make arrangements for any animal subject to the disqualification order. As the court's power is discretionary, it is significant that a disqualification is not automatically suspended pending an appeal. That is unlike all the other similar orders under the AWA.

In contrast, a disqualification can only be suspended pending an appeal by *'leave'* of the court. So the court can consider whether or not it would be prudent to allow the convicted defendant to remain in contact with and control of animals. The court would have to guard against giving him the opportunity for further abuse. The court would take account of his plea, the evidence, the gravity of the offence and his antecedents. If he has a violent character, given the 'link' between the victims being animals or people, leave should not be granted. [See: **17.14**]

A court is under a duty to consider disqualification in every case. Therefore, whenever the court decides not to make an order it *'shall'* give its reasons for the decision in 'open court'. Additionally, a Magistrates' Court must record the reasons and cause them to be entered in the register of its proceedings. That approach has several advantages in that it concentrates the mind of the particular court in respect of its duty to the community. The public knows the 'reasons' for its decision and the defendant is aware why he was or was not disqualified. That would be 'evidence' in any appeal or subsequent breach.

In *R (on the application of the RSPCA) v. Guildford Crown Court* [2012] EWHC 3392, a defendant was convicted of six charges under sections 4 and 9 in respect of three ponies. He was disqualified for three years. The court then amended the disqualification in relation to 'keeping of animals' by removing that limb as it was concerned he may breach it due to his lifestyle as a traveller and horse dealer. It was feared his mere presence in a horsebox driven by others might place him in breach of the disqualification. The RSPCA claimed the judge had no power to amend the disqualification. That was upheld by the High Court as a disqualification applied to *'all'* rather than some of the prohibitions. Given that the court has to give reasons for its decision to disqualify a defendant, it equally has to protect animals as against an abuser. Any human rights element apart, a disqualification protects animals in the future. As the defendant is the abuser his 'lifestyle' is secondary to the primary purpose of protecting his victim and others in the future.

The POA did not allow the court to make orders to protect animals owned or kept by the disqualified person. Indeed, it did not even allow the authorities to enter land to remove animals that were kept in breach of a disqualification order. In *Worcestershire County Council v. Tongue* [2004] EWCA 140, the Court of Appeal criticised this inherent weakness. This section and section 35 were introduced in an attempt to solve that problem.

Now the problem appears to be solved as the disqualification extends to all animals he has any 'dealings' with, in whatever capacity, be it ownership or otherwise. It would include every form of being involved with animals from 'custody' to 'care'. That is proof of the power of a disqualification if and when it is properly used by a court. The court can invoke the principle of the AWA to protect all protected animals from all abusers.

The principle in *Patterson* is right: the prosecution should have adduced admissible evidence, not a questionable inference.

Seizure of animals in connection with disqualification

4.21   Animal Welfare Act 2006 s.35

(1) Where
    (a)   court makes an order under section 34(1), and
    (b)   it appears to the court that the person to whom the order applies owns or keeps any animal contrary to the disqualification imposed by the order, it may order that all animals

he owns or keeps contrary to the disqualification be taken into possession.

Where a court makes a disqualification order, it is often the case that the owner still has custody or control of the animal in question and sometimes other animals too. When the disqualification is imposed the defendant's position immediately changes. Then the court has to take account of his position now and in the future. Thus all the animals he owns or keeps can be seized.

A court has a similar power where a person breaches an existing disqualification. It may be it only applies to certain animals. Then when he is convicted again the court may order that all the animals he owns or keeps contrary to the disqualification may be '*taken into possession*'.

All aspects of the animal's welfare have to be considered by the court. It has to consider those that have been seized by a court order, but do not belong to the defendant or to a person subject to the disqualification. Moreover, the offence could have been committed without the owner's consent or even knowledge. Then the court has power to deal with the animal in 'such manner' as the appropriate court may order. That takes account of the potential for an appeal by the owner or an interested party. The 'appropriate' court is the one that made the order or, if it was a Magistrates' Court, then it is one in the same local justice area.

As the court is dealing with the life and death of an animal that may be seen in emotional or financial terms, the court has to be aware of proprietary rights in the animal. A court cannot make a 'disposal' unless it has given the owner an opportunity to be heard, subject to discovering his whereabouts. In these days of technology that can track a person's movements this side of death, it would seem reasonably easy for the court to communicate with the owner. The court would have to discharge that duty before it acts without such consent or hearing his objection. However, the animal's welfare is the primary consideration. A court can act if it is satisfied it is not 'reasonably practicable' to communicate with the owner, although obviously the absent owner could be the abuser.

The person deprived of his animal by disposal has a right of appeal. If it was the Magistrates' Court it is to the Crown Court, and from the Crown Court to the Court of Appeal. When a person is dis-qualified his animals are taken into possession by a court order, which *'shall'* have effect as an order for disposal. Consequently, to continue consistency between deprivation and disqualification, the reference to 'disposal' of an animal includes destruction.

A court can combine a disqualification order with an order that any other animals he has may be seized too where continued owner-ship or possession would put him in breach of the order. Hence he may be convicted of animal abuse and disqualified for, say, ten years or life in respect of all or specified animals. Then others within that category or generally would be seized too as otherwise he would be in an immediate breach of the order. There is no point in protecting an animal while leaving others in danger with the same defendant.

To that extent this provision is wider than a deprivation order as that can only be made in relation to a convicted person. Under this section a seizure can be made against a person by virtue of the fact he is 'keeping' animals in breach of that order.

The owner is entitled to be given the 'disposal' proceeds less any expenses. It seems strange that the person who abused the animal may also profit from its death, especially as he could have been the one that caused the suffering or been instrumental in the resultant abuse. That power devalues the animal to an inanimate object by accounting for the value to the owner.

Section 35: supplementary

4.22   Animal Welfare Act 2006 s.35

(1) The court by which an order under section 35 is made may
    (a) appoint a person to carry out, or arrange for the carrying out of, the order;
    (b) require any person who has possession of an animal to which the order applies to deliver it up to enable the order to be carried out;
    (c) give directions with respect to the carrying out of the order;
    (d) confer additional powers (including power to enter prem-ises where an animal to which the order applies is being

kept) for the purpose of, or in connection with, the carrying out of the order;

(e) order the person subject to disqualification, or another person, to reimburse the expenses of carrying out the order.

An order has no effect until it is executed. These 'supplementary' provisions are in fact and effect similar to those relating to the deprivation order. The provisions allow the court to appoint a person to carry out the order and give directions to enable it to be done. This provides a power of 'entry', which is essential for the person appointed to fulfil his duty.

The monetary aspect is important as the court has to take into account the 'value' of an animal. As an animal is property like any other commercial item, the court has to exercise the power so 'any amount' the owner is entitled to as a result of the sale may be reduced by that sum if he is liable as a matter of law. That ensures whatever pain the animal has endured is balanced by the gain to the owner while endorsing the concept of animals as our 'property'.

The offender or 'another person' can be ordered to reimburse the costs incurred. That 'another' person, as he is not subject to a disqualification, must have some culpability or liability towards the animal. That would provide a reason for the court to make an order. Although that person may not have directly committed the offence he must have a 'responsibility' towards the animal which should reflect his contribution to the expenses. Without some connection by that 'another person' any order by the court would be open to challenge if it is irrational or unreasonable.

Destruction in the interests of the animal

4.23   Animal Welfare Act 2006 s.37

(1) The court by or before which a person is convicted of an offence under any of the sections 4, 5, 6(1) and (2), 7, 8(1) and (2) and 9 may order the destruction of an animal in relation to which the offence was committed if it is satisfied, on the basis of evidence given by a veterinary surgeon, that it is appropriate to do so in the interests of the animal.

The most serious offences under the AWA are those within sections 4 to 9. While a conviction within any of those offences has repercussions for a defendant, those are outweighed by the result for the abused animal. If there is such a conviction the court may order the destruction of the abused animal if it is satisfied 'on the basis of evidence given by a vet', that it is appropriate to do so in the '*interests of the animal*'. As it is evidence 'given' by a vet, it should be in open court. Then that allows the vet to be challenged by the owner, bearing in mind the court is under a duty to be 'satisfied' with the decision it should be exacting on behalf of the animal. It may be there is no cross-examination, no opposition and no one to counter the claim for destruction on behalf of the animal. The owner or abuser, if they are different people, may have absconded. [See: **2.7**]

Whatever is the procedure and decision, a statement from the vet that is 'read' out in court should not suffice for this section. That would detract from the severity of the sentence given there is no appeal from death.

As it is an order that once executed cannot be reversed, there are strict limits to that decision. A court may not make such an order unless it gives the owner an opportunity to be heard. That can be overcome if it is not 'practicable' to communicate with him. A court would find it hard to justify that position in these days of advanced technology making it relatively easy to communicate with someone, whether they are deliberately evading contact or not.

A fact to face is that often the abuser will have no interest in whether the animal lives or dies. Equally, he may have conveniently become incommunicado in order to escape prosecution or further costs. He may not even be the person who was convicted of the offence in question. Then there is a danger the court would only hear the vet's evidence as the prosecution expert. Such a procedure is contrary to the adversarial system as well as the 'interests' of the animal. Those interests could only fairly be considered by the court if the animal was represented by an independent body or an advocate as a 'friend' of the animal. That would assist the court in arriving at the right and reasoned decision. An 'intermediary' can be appointed on behalf of a vulnerable person to help the court. There is no reason why one should not equally apply to animals. Indeed there is a stronger reason for it to do so due to their lack of legal status.

Where the court makes an order for destruction it has the power to appoint a person to carry out the directions of the court. That also ensures the owner or person responsible would be liable to pay the expenses incurred in carrying out the order. Where the court makes an order for destruction the offender and the owner, if they are different, may appeal from the Magistrates' Court to the Crown Court, and from the Crown Court to the Court of Appeal.

This section applies to an animal that was in a 'fight'. An animal may be so badly injured by being the victim in a fight that it is in its interests to be relieved of the 'misery' by death. That applies to any animal, not only a protected one, by the definition of an 'animal fight'.

The question for the court is whether the injuries mean it is in that animal's 'interests' to die. That could be 'appropriate' because of the abuse by the perpetrator or the injuries sustained in fighting. An unusual aspect of this section states if the court directs death is in the interests of the animal that carrying out the order 'should not be delayed'. The court can only do so if it is satisfied on the '*evidence*' of a vet. That needs positive evidence to support a negative conclusion. After all, if the animal is going to be killed it is axiomatic it has to be as a result of conclusive evidence from an expert.

If the vet's expert evidence is challenged, a legal issue might arise. Then it would have to be conclusive so the court can rely upon it to exclude any potential appeal. There is no appeal within the AWA if the court directs that the order '*should not be delayed*'. Although that may exclude the ordinary avenue of appeal it would not exclude an application by case stated or judicial review. Each of those would apply if there was a point of law. Where it is a question of life and death, the High Court should intervene to become a voice for the legally voiceless. [See: **3.9**]

Destruction of animals involved in fighting offences

4.24   Animal Welfare Act 2006 s.38

(1) The court by or before which a person is convicted of an offence under section 8(1) or (2) may order the destruction of an animal

in relation to which the offence was committed on grounds other than the interests of the animal.

This is a somewhat startling section as it could exclude the main protection under the AWA. For if a person is convicted of a 'fighting' offence the court may order the death of the animal on 'grounds other than the interests of the animal'.

A court can override the 'interests' of the animal to live. As an animal would have been involved in 'fighting' at the instigation of humans it is unreasonable to kill an animal against their own interests. There is a restriction on the court making an order as it cannot do so unless the owner is given the opportunity to be heard. That can be displaced if the court is satisfied that it is not 'reasonably practicable' to communicate with the owner.

But what if the owner has deliberately absented himself in order to avoid detection? Or absconds during the trial with the inevitable verdict looming, so as to avoid a sentence? Where is the advocate for the animal to represent its 'interests' and ensure a 'fair trial'?

That restriction must be considered knowing the owner may be the perpetrator, but he has escaped conviction. The owner may have spent time and money training his animal to fight. Hence the last thing on his mind would be seeking an opportunity to be heard.

Where a court makes an order it may appoint a person to carry out the order and give directions for that purpose. It may make the offender pay the expenses of those carrying out the order, assuming he can be found. There is a restriction in that where the owner of the animal is not the offender he has a right of appeal. He can appeal from the Magistrates' Court to the Crown Court, and from the Crown Court to the Court of Appeal.

Animal welfare is the cornerstone of the AWA, reflected throughout in the offences and sentences. Yet here the animal's welfare could be overridden if it is considered to be aggressive and so could harm other humans, particularly children, if it is allowed to live. The animal's 'character' may have been formed and manipulated by the owner whose perverse interests are totally against the interests of the animal. An animal behaviourist should be engaged *by* the court given there is no appeal against death. [See: **4.23**]

The grounds that relate to other than the interests of the animal can apply to one that is a danger to public safety. The AWA deals with 'fighting offences' that are mainly aimed at the criminals and not directly concerned with the animal in terms of his welfare. Then if the animal is to be killed, the burden of death is for his own benefit. Conversely, this section gives a discretionary power to the court to destroy the animal even if it is against its 'interests'.

What evidence does the court rely on in respect of the animal? While there is a right of appeal to the Crown Court and the Court of Appeal, who would know or care enough to lodge an appeal for the animal ordered to die? That flaw in our law gainsays the ethos of the AWA.

Reimbursement of expenses relating to animals involved in fighting offences

4.25   Animal Welfare Act 2006 s.39

(1) The court by or before which a person offence is convicted of an offence under section 8(1) or (2) may order the offender or another person to reimburse any expenses incurred by the police in connection with the keeping of an animal in relation to which the offence was committed.

Expenses mount at every turn in the detailed investigation and prosecution of offences involving animals. They are the result of the many different services that might be employed by the police, including kennelling expenses and a vet. Preparing a case tends to be a time-consuming investigation. There is a constant problem in trying to obtain evidence that will be tested in court during a trial. The major obstacle stems from the fact the victim of any offence is vulnerable and voiceless, so can only suffer in silence. Moreover, the best evidence may be revealed by its death.

In *Gray v. RSPCA* [2010] the total cost in investigating the saga of suffering animals on the 'Hell Farm' run by the Gray family was approximately £1 million. As an investigation is usually prolonged, often made more difficult by unco-operative owners denying an obvious truth, the costs are generally disproportionately high in relation to a conviction. When a defendant is convicted he can also be ordered to make a payment of all or some of the costs and expenses relating to the animal. That includes the complete investigation namely pre-trial, during it and after the sentence. [See: **2.8**]

Above the general aspect of a claim for the expenses, this section adds a dimension in relation to 'fighting offences'. It is an acknowledgement that such cases are costly to prepare and present. In a case of animals involved in a fighting offence, the court may order the 'offender or another person' to reimburse the expenses incurred by 'the police' in connection with the keeping of an animal that is the victim of such an offence. Who is the 'another' person is not defined, but as he is not the offender, any expenses would have to be both balanced and fair. Any costs that are ordered cannot be disproportionate as that would be counter-productive in that it would lead to an appeal and escalate costs on each side.

Unlike the usual case of animal abuse where the prosecutor could make a claim for costs against a convicted defendant, this section applies specifically to the police. There are attendant expenses in fighting offences that can certainly escalate with the time a case takes to come to trial. The expenses borne by the police could be higher than usual for food and kennelling and veterinary treatment as it includes an animal that 'took part' in a fight in relation to the offence. It is not limited to the animals that were forced to fight. Depending on the circumstances, any offspring of the animals may also be 'taken into possession'. Any other animals owned or kept by the defendant may also have been seized if he was disqualified for the fighting offence. There are often numerous defendants implicated in 'fighting offences' as by its nature the violence instilled in the animals can only happen if there are many people willing to agree and participate in their conspiracy.

Those expenses continue to escalate as the police have a 'duty of care' for the welfare of any animals in their custody, regardless of whether they have been seized or rescued. We should make the perpetrator pay for his abuse as a positive move in the public interest. [See: **3.8**]

Forfeiture of equipment used in offences

4.26   Animal Welfare Act 2006 s.40

(1) Where a person is convicted of an offence under any of sections 4, 5, 6(1) and (2), 7 and 8, the court by or before which he is convicted may order any qualifying item which is shown to the satisfaction of the court to relate to the offence to be
   (a)   forfeited, and
   (b)   destroyed or dealt with in such manner as may be specified in the order.

It would be counter-productive to prosecute a person and then allow him to retain the apparatus he used to commit the crime. As criminals tend to be creatures of habit, the likelihood is he will commit similar offences in the future. An animal abuser will usually use equipment to train the animal to become aggressive or vicious, or may use equipment to abuse the animal. This section allows the court to order 'any qualifying item' relating to the offence to be forfeited and disposed of or destroyed.

A *'qualifying item'* includes anything that is designed or adapted for committing the offence. The items would include all the paraphernalia used by the amateur and professional animal abuser, whether they work in an abattoir or a science laboratory, or caused the suffering on an opportunistic basis. That could be a single occasion or many, as in the current case of the 'Croydon Cat Killer' who has habitually killed about 100 cats in the neighbourhood to date. When he is convicted, the equipment he used to kill the cats could be confiscated. The items would include any apparatus that is used for tail docking, mutilation, making poisons, fighting and causing suffering to an animal.

The items could have been part of the preparation rather than actual use. As the offences include an 'attempt', the items do not even have to have been used, but merely 'designed or adapted' for that illegal purpose. So a carborundum stone used to hone a machete to kill an animal would be liable to be forfeited. A kitten 'adapted' for training a pit bull terrier for fighting would be part of the apparatus. In that context the kitten would be an 'item' in law. [See: **1.2**]

The offence may have been committed by a person who is not the owner of the animal. The owner may not even be aware that his equipment was used. Therefore the court is restricted in making an order: a court *'shall not'* order anything to be forfeited if a person claiming to be the owner or 'otherwise interested in it' applies to be heard by the court, where he has shown 'cause' why the order should not be made. It would be plainly wrong to penalise the owner if he is not guilty. Others that may have an 'interest' in the potential order could include a bank, an employer, a finance company or a landlord. The defendant might have used a vehicle, hired equipment or leased a building to commit the offence. As the person claiming the interest has to show 'cause', he would have to adduce evidence to prove his claim and displace a potential forfeiture order.

The person claiming the 'interest' in the equipment would have to be free from blame. If he was culpable then any qualifying items could be forfeited as part of his criminal activity. In that case his culpability would destroy his ability to justify his claim.

Orders under section 33, 35, 37, 38 or 40: pending appeals

4.27   Animal Welfare Act 2006 s.41

(1) Nothing may be done under an order under sections 33, 35, 37 or 38 with respect to an animal or an order under section 40 unless
   (a) the period for giving notice of appeal against the order has expired,
   (b) the period for giving notice against the conviction on which the order was made has expired, and
   (c) if the order or conviction is the subject of an appeal, the appeal has been determined or withdrawn.

As a court may make an order that is against the interests of the animals, the defendant or the owner, it cannot be enforced if there is an appeal. An order cannot be enforced if there is time allowed for an appeal or one is pending. Then the order is suspended until either the period for an appeal has expired or the appeal has been determined or withdrawn.

That limit does not apply if the order is subject to a court direction that the animal is destroyed and it is in the 'interests of the animal' that their death should not be '*delayed*'. That would be extreme as in that case the injured animal is due to be killed. What if the vet is wrong? Noel Fitzpatrick has saved numerous animal's lives, notwithstanding neo-insuperable odds, as he uses a bold imaginative expertise and techniques using Meccano-type fixtures. Death for a human or an animal is usually a burden and rarely a benefit.

The court may make detailed directions in relation to the animal taken into possession, including appointing a person to carry out the order. As the appeal may be delayed and the main exhibit is an animal, the expenses continue to escalate for food and safety and shelter plus treatment. The court can order that all the attendant expenses relating to the 'removal' and 'care' of the animal are recovered.

Although the expenses relate to a criminal conviction, the sum a person is directed to pay is recoverable as a civil debt. That has the advantage it can be recovered by bailiffs seizing and selling his property and through the defendant's earnings.

When a deprivation order is made the defendant is sometimes inclined to sell the animal. Some abusers part with their animal to another member of the family, a man they met in the pub or a friend of a friend whose name they cannot now recall. Or sometimes the dog somehow mysteriously runs away and inexplicably is never seen again, as in *R. v. Richards* [2008] EWCA Crim 1427. If the order is suspended the person may not 'sell or part with' any animal to which the order applies. If he breaches that order, he commits another offence.

A disqualification order is the only one that is not suspended pending the appeal. An application has to be made by the appellant that the court can grant or refuse. That is a prudent course as it puts the onus on the defendant given that he is the abuser. If the court suspends the order until the result of the appeal, it can make directions in respect of the animal. That ensures the animal's welfare is taken into account regardless of how long it takes to list the appeal. The animal may need veterinary treatment; his condition may be critical and should not be delayed. Indeed, the court has a 'duty' to the animal so should not delay matters and keep him in custody as an exhibit. If its welfare is affected the animal should be granted 'bail' to a sanctuary rather than the owner.

A problematic area is that if a ban is not suspended the defendant could breach the existing order by continuing to 'deal' with animals while disqualified. Any other animals he owns or keeps contrary to the disqualification can be seized. A disqualified person, who would usually be a convicted abuser, may retain a right to the animals until his appeal is determined. That is contrary to the name and spirit of the AWA. It is one thing to suspend a disqualification of a driver pending an appeal, then if it succeeds he retains his licence. If it fails he loses his licence and the time that has passed prior to the appeal. Where an animal is concerned, the abuser should not retain his property as that is why he was disqualified. Thereafter all he has to do is pass the '*title*' in the animals to his spouse or partner or another person. The fact he lives with and perhaps works with a person on a daily basis is directly relevant to the relationship between him and the animals as the order was made to protect them. Therefore the terms of an order could be drafted to counteract any potential future breach as that would be consistent with the reason a disqualification was imposed. [See: **4.20**]

Orders with respect to licences

4.28   Animal Welfare Act 2006 s.42

(1) If a person is convicted of an offence under any of sections 4, 5, 6(1) and (2), 7 to 9, 11 and 13(6), the court by or before which he is convicted may, instead of or in addition to dealing with him in any other way
    (a) make an order cancelling any licence held by him;
    (b) make an order disqualifying him, for such period as it thinks fit, from holding a licence.

Allowing a convicted defendant to continue to trade under a licence is irreconcilable with protecting an animal. As he might be tempted to continue the abuse, it could be a licence to break the law. The court may instead of or in addition to any sentence it imposes, cancel 'any licence' held by him and disqualify him for a period from even holding a licence.

That disqualification may be for licences generally or relate to other kinds. As well as trading in animals, he may be a show judge of animals, may run a farm and may breed animals for sale. All of those activities could be curbed and controlled by the court.

The orders apply to the sections covering unnecessary suffering and abuse in various forms. They also relate to the 'welfare' of the animal and transferring an animal as 'a prize'. This section allows the court to control all such activities relating to the children and their parents.

The court may specify a period during which the offender cannot apply for termination of the order. If there is an appeal the court may 'suspend' the order pending the result. That would be unlikely if there was a blatant breach of the animal's welfare or if he has antecedents for animal abuse. Moreover, if an appeal is lodged it can be listed swiftly so a suspension would be unnecessary as well as undesirable. An 'expedited' appeal would be consistent with the protection of protected animals. The overarching factor to consider is that the animal may have already suffered and may continue to do so if an appeal is delayed. Then any delay is only favourable to the defendant who has caused the abuse.

Termination of disqualification under section 34 or 42

4.29 Animal Welfare Act 2006 s.43

(1) A person who is disqualified by virtue of an order under section 34 or 42 may apply to the appropriate court for the termination of the order.

Though the cases vary and are fact-specific, the sentences imposed are always unduly lenient. In *R. v. Wilson* the defendant, who beat and almost poisoned his pet dog to death with alcohol, was disqualified for a year. In *R. v. Bale* the woman who was captured on the internet catching a cat by the scruff of the neck and then abandoned her in a dustbin was disqualified for five years. In *Ward v. RSPCA* a farmer who had two previous convictions, on his third conviction for abusing animals was disqualified for ten years. Ward could not apply for a termination of the order for three years. [See: **4.20; 6.1**]

An application for termination of a disqualification can be made a year from the date of the order. That would not apply if the court directed a period longer than that before he could apply. When an application is made the court may terminate the disqualification. Alternatively, it may vary it by making it 'less onerous'. The court could refuse the application. In that event a person can reapply after a further year has passed.

When the court considers an application it 'shall have regard to the character of the applicant, his conduct since the disqualification and any other circumstances of the case'. Character is often significant in cases of animal abuse. There is a clear connection between animal cruelty and child cruelty: those children who are cruel to animals often become criminals who use violence on vulnerable people. Therefore this area should be more stringently assessed by the courts when sentencing an offender. The prosecution should inform the court of any relevant antecedent of the defendant exhibiting that connection of cruelty. [See: **10.9**]

The court could consider his 'character' in the criminal sense, particularly what constitutes a propensity for violence under the CJA. This potentially provides additional protection for animals. The result is a rapist, wife batterer or child abuser has a relevant *'bad character'*. He is the kind of character from whom people and animals need protection now and in the future.

A positive approach if a person breached the order would be to charge him with an offence. Then his 'character' and antecedents would be taken into account. That could justify a longer ban and prevent an application for a termination of it for a longer term. As a corollary, it would justify a longer sentence.

The court can specify a period during which a person may not make a 'further' application. If his character is in issue or his 'conduct' or 'any other circumstances', the court could prevent him from reapplying. Then he would serve the whole period of disqualification, which could be for life. The court could make it more onerous. A defendant may have been banned for ten years with a condition he could not apply for another two years. If after that time his application was rejected, the court could order that no application can be made for a further five years. So it becomes a minimum period of seven years.

A court can make the applicant pay all or part of the costs of the application. This does not depend on its success or failure, although failure may result in the court considering it was a frivolous application. Therefore he could be ordered to pay even if he was successful. The ban was only imposed because he was convicted. Bear in mind the application springs from his criminal conduct towards an animal he owned or abused, or both.

The 'appropriate' court at which the application should be made is to the court that made the order. If it was a Magistrates' Court it has to be one in the same local justice area. That has the advantage of local knowledge by the court. It would learn whether an animal abuser was a *'fit and proper person'* to own a dog. Although that applies to the DDA, the defendant's character is relevant for a court when considering the principles of the AWA too. [See: **17.12**]

Orders made on conviction for reimbursement of expenses

4.30 Animal Welfare Act 2006 s.44

Where an order is made under section 33(4)(e), 36(1)(e), 37(3) (e), 38(3)(e) or 39(1), the expenses that are required by the order to be reimbursed shall not be regarded for the purposes of the Magistrates' Court Act 1980 as a sum adjudged to be paid by a summary conviction, but shall be recoverable summarily as a civil debt.

The provisions throughout the AWA make people pay for the expenses incurred in looking after animals affected by the acts of owners or other offenders. Although the expenses incurred follow a summary criminal conviction, the sums specified 'shall' be recoverable as a civil debt. [See: **4.27**]

That has the distinct advantage of recovery by bailiffs or a court order against the goods and property of the convicted person. A fine is rarely paid and often is simply discharged by a short prison term. The civil debt is a more effective method of enforcement.

A person can be ordered to pay the 'expenses' of the orders in relation to all the offences. That includes deprivation and caring for the welfare of the abused animal. All those expenses can be recovered in the same way. It is yet another reason that the American approach to making animal abusers pay for the cost of their abuse should be adopted in the UK. Equally it should be part of the 'confiscation' regulations so a court could penalise abusers financially as even after the sentence is served the sums remain outstanding until they are paid. That enables a court to monitor a defendant lest he becomes financially viable later by the Lottery or an inheritance or otherwise. [See: **2.8**; **3.8**]

Orders for reimbursement of expenses: right of appeal for non-offenders

4.31   Animal Welfare Act 2006 s.45

(1) Where a court makes an order to which this section applies, the person against whom the order is made may
    (a) in the case of an order made by a Magistrates' Court, appeal against the order to the Crown Court;
    (b) in the case of an order made by the Crown Court, appeal against the order to the Court of Appeal.

The power to make an order for expenses to be paid can also relate to a non-offender. As the non-offender may be an innocent party he can appeal against any such order. He may have no knowledge of the acts of the offender or be responsible in any way for the abuse, yet be potentially liable for the expenses. In that event he may appeal from the Magistrates' Court to the Crown Court, and from the Crown Court to the Court of Appeal.

The attendant expenses in caring for the abused animal may be quite high as the care and treatment continues while he is recuperating. It may relate to food and shelter at a pound or sanctuary if the animal was seized by the police or, subject to the abuse, veterinary treatment. The animal, whether or not the owner is guilty, still needs care for its mental and physical welfare.

There would have to be some culpability or responsibility by the non-offender as otherwise he would be placed in jeopardy as a result of another person's vicarious abuse. If so, he could appeal by the standard process or if it was an 'unreasonable' decision by the court, that could be subject to judicial review.

5

ENTRY AND SEARCH

5.1 General

These sections cover and complete the circle of the AWA. They include the duties and the responsibilities of inspectors, powers of entry and search as well as the general interpretation of the terms used throughout the AWA.

5.2 Animal Welfare Act 2006 s.51

(1) In this Act, 'inspector', in the context of any provision, means a person appointed to be an inspector for the purposes of that provision by
   (a) the appropriate national authority, or
   (b) a local authority.

Although many animal welfare organisations have an interest in the mechanism of the AWA, the inspector is the aorta of the Act. The inspector's powers are wide even as investigative powers go. All the power that governs the search and seizure of animals rests with the inspector. An Inspector is defined as 'a person appointed to be an inspector for the purposes of that provision by the appropriate national authority, or a local authority'. His role applies to '*any*' provision of the AWA. Inspectors are the artisans that monitor and operate the provisions of the Act.

Guidance may be issued by the national authority that the local authority 'shall have regard' to in appointing the inspectors. It may compile a list of persons whom it considers suitable for appointment by the local authority. The list may indicate some are considered 'suitable' for all purposes or only a particular purpose. That would depend upon their experience and qualifications. A person appointed as an inspector is likely to be qualified in animal welfare, an RSPCA officer or an animal behaviourist.

Any expert may make a bad decision, but usually he has a responsibility for his actions. However, an inspector 'shall not' be liable in any '*civil or criminal proceedings*' for anything done in the 'purported' performance of his functions under the AWA if the court is satisfied that the act was done in 'good faith' and that there were 'reasonable grounds' for the act. That is unusual as an inspector could act in good faith, but have questionable judgement. Equally, a court would be challenged to find the grounds were unreasonable if he 'acted in good faith'.

There are different burdens of proof in civil and criminal proceedings. The civil court could find his act, even in good faith, to be unreasonable, while a criminal court could find it was reasonable. In the event of a trial the first one heard would be likely to be the criminal matter. Though not decisive, any judgment in one action would have evidential weight in the other.

The protection is limited to the inspector. Any 'relief' from civil and criminal liability does not extend to 'any other person' in respect of the inspector's act. If the inspector's act passes the test of 'reasonable grounds', that would be persuasive in respect of any person who is charged with him or instead of him. That point could be used to support a defence or an application of an abuse of process. It must be noted it is in the 'purported' performance of the inspector's 'function'. The subjective element protects the inspector on the touchstone of competency and honesty.

A problem would arise if an inspector recklessly or intentionally acted outside his powers while 'purporting' to be acting within those powers. Then this protection of his inspection role would probably not apply as it is beyond his specified function.

5.3   Animal Welfare Act 2006 s.52

A warrant is the lifeblood of the AWA. As it is so wide and effective against a citizen, one of four conditions must be met before a warrant can be granted. Significantly those conditions apply to private dwellings and other premises. A warrant is essential to deal with urgent situations and to act in an emergency on behalf of a suffering animal. The conditions attached to a warrant serves to protect an occupier in normal circumstances as he must be informed of their pending visit. In extreme cases he is not informed where there is a degree of urgency. That approach echoes the ethos of the AWA in protecting animals from present and future suffering. The conditions have been analysed in an earlier chapter as it is relevant to several sections throughout the AWA. [See: **4.3**]

5.4   Animal Welfare Act 2006 s.53

Schedule 2 (which makes supplementary provision in relation to powers of entry, inspection and search) has effect.

This section protects two parties, namely those seeking evidence and those subject to the searches. The entry may be under a warrant or otherwise.

Schedule 2 grants extra power to the police and inspectors in relation to their investigation. The powers are supplementary to those in the body of the AWA. They give extra protection to an inspector and the police, as well as those who are assisting them.

An unusual but positive aspect of the AWA is it places a burden on the defendant himself. A 'qualifying person' includes the occupier and any person who appears to be responsible for animals there. Those persons must assist the inspector if he requires their help.

More than them, it includes persons who appear to be 'under his control' too. That clause gives claws to the inspector to grasp the essence of his power by putting an onus on the abuser or one associated with him.

The 'qualifying person' can include the licensee where the condition specifies that an authorised activity can be carried out on his premises. That could result in a potential defendant helping the person with the power of entry to gather evidence, which is then used to prosecute him. It is in fact even stronger than that position where a potential defendant can become an actual one as to refuse such assistance is itself an offence. Hence any co-operation or lack of co-operation could count against him. In a sense it is a form of self-incrimination. Then again, the victim has suffered at his hands and remains helpless without human aid.

5.5   Schedule 2

Functions in connection with inspection and search

This is a power that puts into practice the investigation of the potential offence. In that respect it allows a person exercising the power to:

(a) inspect an animal found on the premises;

(b) inspect any other thing found on the premises including a document or record;

(c) carry out a measurement or test of an animal found on the premises;

(d) take a sample from an animal found on the premises or any substance on the premises which appears to be intended for use as food for such an animal;

(e) mark an animal found on the premises for identification purposes;

(f) remove a carcass found on the premises for the purpose of carrying out a post mortem;

(g) take copies of a document or record found on the premises in whatever form it is found;

(h) require information stored in an electronic form and accessible from the premises to be produced in a form in which it can be taken away and in which it is visible and legible or from which it can readily be produced in a visible and legible form;

(i)   take a photograph of anything on the premises;

(j)   seize and detain or remove anything which the person exercising the power reasonably believes to be evidence of any non-compliance, or of the commission of any offence, relevant to the purpose for which the inspection or search is made.

If an inspector is gathering evidence by searching the premises, the persons there have a duty to assist him. Those persons must co-operate with the inspection and allow the inspector or officer to seize anything he reasonably believes to be evidence of non-compliance or the commission of an offence. Their duty to co-operate applies to anything found during the inspection or search that is classed as 'evidence'.

While it states 'anything', that does not include any item that is subject to 'legal privilege'. As a matter of principle, such an item would be excluded from that power.

This section allows discretion to the investigator to gain the evidence that can be used as it is or seized for a later analysis. Items taken can be retained as exhibits for a pending trial or for forensic examination. Whatever is taken must relate to a 'relevant offence', defined as 'any offence under any of the sections 4 to 9, 13(6) and 34(9)'. Those relate to the most serious offences of causing 'unnecessary suffering' and the 'duty of care' plus offences such as breaches of the licensing and registration conditions and a disqualification order. [See: **4.4**]

The power of Schedule 2 lies in the sanction. A failure to comply with a relevant request of the investigator is an offence. Although such co-operation may be against his own interests, it is not his choice to refuse. Once the request is made, he must comply or he will fail in his duty to co-operate. It is an all-embracing duty as an 'intentional obstruction' of any power is an offence. The investigation is intended to take the occupant off-guard. If notice is given to a potential offender he would have the opportunity and temptation to destroy available evidence. That could include the abused animal, often the best evidence in any proceedings. If he succumbed to the temptation, any destruction of the evidence would be an offence. The evidence can only be gained by the hand of a human in his inspection or by a post-mortem examination. This power recognises the unique position of animals as victims within our legal system.

Power to stop and detain vehicles

5.6   Animal Welfare Act 2006 s.54

(1) A constable in uniform or, if accompanied by such a constable, an inspector may stop and detain a vehicle for the purpose of entering and searching it in the exercise of a power conferred
    (a) by section 19(1), or
    (b) by a warrant under section 19(4) or 23(1).

When committing illegal activities involving animals, especially badger baiting, dog fighting, fox hunting and hare coursing, and transporting them in breach of a court order, the transgressors usually use vehicles. So the AWA provides the power to the police and inspectors to stop and detain vehicles.

A constable in uniform has extensive powers of search and inspection under this section. An inspector's power is limited as he has to be 'accompanied' by a constable. They can detain the vehicle as long as reasonably required to carry out a search or their investigation. The search may be connected to any 'related' power under the Act. Therefore it would allow the police to undertake forensic tests, which could relate to the vehicle and any blood, carcasses, weapons or other evidence found within it. The investigator could then widen the initial reason for the detention of the vehicle as it could lead to the detection of other offences, discovered at that time or later.

More than common criminal acts such as animal fighting and illegal hunting, it applies to activities committed illegally such as transporting emaciated cattle and horses to and from the abattoir. As the definition of 'premises' includes 'any vehicle … or movable structure', this is a wider power of 'entry' than at first appears as PACE applies to the AWA. [See: **4.5**]

A constable can stop and seize a vehicle to seize an animal used in fighting. That power can emanate from a 'reasonable belief' or a reasonable suspicion or a warrant. The effect can span activities from rescuing animals in distress to inspecting farms. [See: **3.5**]

5.7   Animal Welfare Act 2006 s.55

(1) Where an inspector appointed by the appropriate national authority certifies in writing that he is satisfied that an offence under or by virtue of this Act is being or has been committed on board a vessel in port, the vessel may be detained.

Animals are protected under the AWA when in the air, on land or on the high seas. The appetite for animals for food, pets or fashion ornaments continues to expand exponentially and internationally. That upward curve leads to worldwide trade, which puts animals at risk of abuse. People with money and myopia tend to use elephant tusk ivory as an aphrodisiac, which is palpably false as well as a criminal offence.

An inspector's power extends to most forms of travel. The inspector can certify in *'writing'* that he is 'satisfied' an offence within the AWA is being or has been committed on board a vessel in port. Following the issue of his certificate, the vessel may be detained. As it is an important document for the person on whom it is served, there are precise points relating to the contents. The certificate *'shall'* specify each offence. So the inspector's reason for his decision identifies the unlawful acts. Then the defendant knows what he has done or is doing wrong. As the penalty can be to detain the vessel, the inspector has to be on sure ground as his 'reasons' forms the evidence validating that detention.

The Merchant Shipping Act 1995 allows specified officers to detain a ship. They may detain a ship if it leaves a port without having permission to do so. Significantly, that section *'shall apply'* as if the power of detention was conferred by the AWA. Hence it extends the inspector's investigative power to include the sea.

A certificate 'shall', as soon as reasonably practicable, be served on the master of the vessel. Then the master knows the reason for the detention and can take legal action to protect the vessel, crew and himself. Once a vessel is detained it may be kept until the national authority 'otherwise directs'. The ship and crew may be foreign and need interpreters to understand the charge and during an interview under caution.

Regulations within the AWA allow for changing conditions to cover new forms of transport. The definition of premises 'includes any vehicle, vessel, aircraft or hovercraft; any tent or movable structure'. That would include provision for the detention of any aircraft or hovercraft in relation to offences contrary to the AWA. All the other powers of entry and search would also apply. A 'protected' animal may be a cat that is a mascot on board a Greek ship or a straggly dog companion with a travelling crusty master. The investigation would include searching a yacht in the Isle of Wight, a hovercraft and a tent found with a traveller on the way to an annual music festival.

Obtaining of documents in connection with carrying out orders

5.8　Animal Welfare Act 2006 s.56

(1) Where
　　(a) an order under section 20(1), 33(1) or (2), 35(1) or (2) or 37(1) has effect, and
　　(b) the owner of an animal to which the order relates has in his possession, or under his control, documents which are relevant to the carrying out of the order or any directions given in connection with it, the owner shall, if so required by a person authorised to carry out the order, deliver the documents to that person as soon as practicable and in any event before the end of the period of ten days beginning with the date on which he is notified of the requirement.

Wide powers of investigation into animal abuse would be valueless without a power to obtain the evidence that underpins the abuse. That evidence is essential for those persons charged with carrying out the 'directions' of the court. A person authorised to carry out the order can request relevant documents from the owner, who has a 'duty' to supply the documents within ten days.

As this power follows a conviction, the power must enable the authorised person to have the documents relating to the animal even if there is a pending appeal. Where the court makes a direction that deals with how an animal is to be treated during any suspension of the order, the investigation can continue pending the result. Whilst the order may be suspended pending an appeal, the owner remains under a duty to supply the documents. That is a reasonable request as the abused animal may literally and legally be on the verge of death.

A person who fails 'without reasonable excuse' to comply with a request commits an offence. Significantly that places a burden on the owner for he is the one who would probably possess the documents. Even if he does not he would have the legal power to obtain them. Therefore any excuse tendered would have to be legitimate and bear scrutiny. An 'excuse' that is unreasonable will not excuse criminal culpability. [See: **3.8**]

Offences by bodies corporate

5.9   Animal Welfare Act 2006 s.57

(1) Where an offence under this Act is committed by a body corporate and is proved to have been committed with the consent or connivance of or to be attributable to any neglect on the part of
   (a) any director, manager, secretary or other similar officer of the body corporate, or
   (b) any person who was purporting to act in such capacity he (as well as the body corporate) commits the offence and shall be liable to be proceeded against and punished accordingly.

The AWA makes people who are in a position of authority vicariously liable for those whom they supervise or may have control of and over as employees or contractors. It would not be limited to a vicarious liability, but could relate to a joint and individual liability too. Therefore it would apply to all persons in a company who act in their own right and those whom they directly and indirectly control.

The liability extends to those in charge of the activity leading to the abuse. In effect it covers any activity within a company that affects animals where the corporation is involved. That includes its officers and extends to any person 'purporting' to be acting in such a capacity. That targets all those who are directly and indirectly in control of animals.

A company can allow all the members to be in control of its affairs. That status will not stymie the aim and effect of the AWA to protect animals. Where the affairs of a body corporate are managed by its members, the liability applies in relation to the *'acts and defaults'* of a member as if he were a director of the corporation.

This section catches all those involved as may have done so by actual 'consent' or even 'connivance', while for others it may be the result of 'neglect' by them. This catch-all section relates to a person who is in an official capacity as well as those 'purporting' to act in any such capacity. That would include ostensible authority. This section shows the strength of the AWA: it captures those responsible for causing the abuse of animals under their control by widening the net of their accountability and guilt.

Scientific research

5.10   Animal Welfare Act 2006 s.58

(1) Nothing in this Act applies to anything lawfully done under the Animals (Scientific Procedures) Act 1986.

The use of animals for experiments and vivisection is and always has been a controversial area of the law. While scientists have a vested interest in carrying out such procedures for reasons of their livelihood and research, equally many animal welfare bodies have criticised those acts as being immoral and wrong. The present Act controlling such procedures is called the Animals (Scientific Procedures) Act 1986 [ASPA]. The first Act to control those carrying out experiments was aptly titled the Cruelty to Animals Act 1876.

It is beyond doubt that the 'procedures' allowed under the ASPA are against the welfare of the animals. Most are to test various products or research by experiments on animals and finally, when they have been so used, killing them. To protect those engaged in such activities there is a complete exemption from prosecution if they are acting within the conditions of their licence. The premises where they carry out their experiments are similarly protected. An inspector cannot enter or inspect or search those premises for the purpose of investigating or ensuring compliance with the conditions of the AWA.

Significantly, the AWA does not apply to any act 'lawfully done' within the ASPA. Even the core 'duty' of a person for an animal's welfare does not apply to an animal kept at a 'scientific procedure establishment' for use in 'regulated procedures', breeding or bred there, or being supplied for use elsewhere in regulated procedures. Hence, the ASPA is so wide it allows 'procedures' bound to affect the animal's welfare to be performed that would otherwise be an offence. So the scientific gain cancels the calculated animals' pain to make their suffering legal.

As the exemption applies to *'anything lawfully done'*, if the scientist carried out an experiment that is not allowed under his or her licence granted by the Home Office, it would still be an offence. There would have to be reliable evidence from a 'whistle-blower' as evidence gained under the Freedom of Information Act 2000 would be rarer than truth as the area is deliberately completely cloaked in secrecy. If it was gained then a warrant could be issued that would allow the inspector to enter the premises without informing the experimenter. Conversely, it is an offence under the ASPA to disclose confidential information gained by an experimenter in discharging his function.

Some places under the ASPA have a dual purpose of being a farm and an experimental place. If the 'farm' is not a designated 'scientific procedure establishment', an inspector could visit the premises to check whether an offence has been or is being committed under the AWA. That power will only apply to animals that he reasonably believes are bred or kept for 'farming purposes'. Thus the power will not extend to animals bred or kept for an *'experimental or scientific'* purpose.

How wide the ASPA is in practice can be seen from section 2: A regulated procedure is any experimental or other scientific procedure applied to a protected animal that may have the effect of causing it pain, suffering, distress or lasting harm.

For the avoidance of doubt it confirms that the death of the animal subjected to an experiment is not an 'adverse effect'. Consequently, the animal's death is not classed as 'lasting harm'.

Meanwhile, a significant increase in animal experiments is contrary to the promise of the Coalition government in 2011 that it would, 'work to reduce the use of animals in scientific research'. In 2012 there were 3.7 million procedures, a total that is 40% higher than in 2002. In 2015 the figure increased to 4.14 million.

In 2016 Cruelty Free International [CFI] applied for judicial review against the government approval for a firm to breed dogs for medical experiments. The application was dismissed. The CFI said: 'The European Directive requirement [2010/63] for giving dogs used in highly unpleasant tests just a little protection has, with this judgment, been swept away.'

Sir Roger Bannister, the legendary athlete and doctor, while in his medical practice some years ago wanted to test pyrogens. With the same spirit that made him the first 'four minute miler' in the world he explained: 'To test my hypothesis I needed someone to experiment on, so I experimented on myself. It was dangerous, but it gave me the chance to verify my theory, and save lives.'

Fishing

5.11   Animal Welfare Act 2006 s.59

Nothing in this Act applies in relation to anything that occurs in the normal course of fishing.

Given the continuing controversy over hunting that sprang from the Burns Report in 2000 and resulted in the Hunting Act 2004, this section seeks to avoid any such doubt about the legality of fishing. What is or is not the 'normal course' of fishing is not clear. Certainly it is often claimed by anglers that fish are 'cold-blooded' and so do not feel pain. That is used by them to distinguish fishing from 'blood-sports' such as hunting that involves killing 'hot-blooded' animals. Anglers then claim it is not cruel or concerned with the animal's welfare. Yet the *Report of the Panel of Inquiry into Shooting and Angling* by Lord Medway [1980] confirmed that the evidence for fish feeling pain is similar to that of other vertebrate animals.

This section limits the activity to what is the *'normal'* intrinsic part of the fishing process. Consequently, if a person uses some form of fishing before or during or after the catch which is not part of the 'normal' course of fishing, he could be caught by the net of the AWA.

Legal fishing is limited to the ordinary activity of anglers. If an unusual-shaped hook used was a particularly barbaric method that caused severe pain or a fish was battered by a weapon while it was still breathing, that could be abnormal and therefore unlawful. This section accepts the 'normal' activity is impliedly cruel. That is the reason it is legally exempt. Angling is analogous to experiments legalising what would otherwise be illegal. It is a question of degree. An abnormal activity is prohibited and so potentially illegal.

A fish may be a 'protected animal' if it is under the control of a person, whether it is gained by a competition or by leisure. A gold-fish at a fair is no different than one at a trout farm or in a pet shop.

The permitted course would include the use of live bait. However, the common practice of 'catching and releasing' fish has not been tested in court. Professor Victoria Braithwaite assessed the position with the gimlet eye of an expert: 'In Germany for example, laws forbidding the intentional release of fish over a certain size have now been passed ... a similar ruling was also recently introduced in Switzerland ... Catch and release is an ethical issue; knowing that fish feel pain and can suffer raises questions about whether it is appropriate to allow fish to be caught multiple times ...'

Answering the question posed in her book, *Do Fish Feel Pain?* [2010], Braithwaite puts the position beyond doubt: 'Yes, they do. As demands for good animal welfare increase, this answer will change the way we think and act. Some will struggle with this change. Fish are still perceived as "different", but the deeper we delve, the more we recognise and appreciate many similarities with birds and mammals. The fish pain debate is gaining momentum.'

Meanwhile, researchers at Edinburgh University have also con-firmed that fish do feel pain. Dr L. Sneddon said: 'There were "pro-found behavioural and physiological changes" shown by the trout after exposure to noxious substances [that] are comparable to those seen in higher mammals.' Janicke Nordgreen of the Norwegian School of Veterinary Science came to the same conclusion. [See: *Science Daily*: 12/1/10]

Many anglers' practices are suspect and unlikely to be consistent with the welfare of fish. Katherine van Ekert, president of the Australian organisation Sentient, has criticised the killing of tuna in the old La Mattanza ceremony saying: 'The fish were shown to be lifted by hooks after attachment. The suspension of the tuna's body weight is expected to cause pain and stress to the animals, as too would the tearing of their tissues as a result of gravity working against the hook.'

The *Pour l'Egalitie Animale* [PEA] Marchers Against Racism and Sexism and Speciesism in Geneva in 2016 stated: 'Fish cannot cry out to express their suffering, but this does not make their suffering and death any less terrible when they die by suffocation in fishing nets.' Jonathan Balcombe has explored the secret world of fish for over three decades. His analysis in *'What A Fish Knows'* [2016] covers every aspect of their lives from birth to death including their risk from predators of the piscine and human kind. Balcombe proves they are emotional and intelligent and sensitive. They suffer pain and loss no less than the men who kill them by hook or line or net. His treatise examines the anglers' notion that fish feel no pain when dragged from the lake or ocean and nails that falsity with undiluted truth.

Perhaps Byron said it all with insight in his message to angler Izaak Walton: 'The quaint, old, cruel coxcomb, in his gullet should have a hook, and a small trout to pull it.' [See: *Don Juan*; **2.3**]

Crown application

5.12   Animal Welfare Act 2006 s.60

(1) Subject to the provisions of this section, this Act and regulations and orders made under it shall bind the Crown.

The AWA binds all government departments and other public bodies that are part of the Crown. Nevertheless, the normal practice is the Crown is not subject to criminal liability. Yet as the Crown is heavily involved in many areas of animal welfare, it is essential that it is bound by the AWA. To some limited extent it is, as the High Court can *'declare'* the questionable conduct is unlawful, be it an act or omission. That would unquestionably cause the conduct to be changed and controlled in the future.

The exemption from criminal liability applies to the Crown as an entity. Any person would be liable if he or she does not share that exemption as this section states it *'shall'* apply to such persons. So the employees and staff are liable just as any other person would be. If they were not, the exemption would be a shield from the sword of prosecution, providing a privilege to cause unnecessary suffering to animals.

The exemption applying to the Queen may extend to her land. The Secretary of State may certify that entry to Crown premises should not be exercisable if it is not in the 'interests of national security'. An inspector or a constable does not have the power of entry granted under the AWA to enter the private estates of the Queen. However, obviously offences may well be committed there no less than anywhere else. If an offence has been committed, they could enter but will require permission to enter her land. Many members of the royal family and their visitors use guns for shooting birds. As a consequence the Queen and her estate should not be exempt from the provisions of the AWA as otherwise it could prevent the detection of serious offences against people and animals.

Sometimes you can be serendipitously in an area whoever you are. Prince Harry was seen wandering near the woods where a hen harrier was shot. However, he did not hear or see any activity relating to the illegal shooting. [See: *Inglorious*: Mark Avery: (2015)]

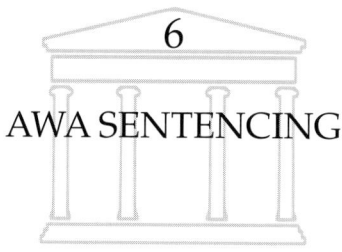

6

AWA SENTENCING

6.1 Powers

The powers under the AWA are:

(a) Imprisonment for six months and a fine or both;
(b) A Deprivation Order;
(c) A Disqualification Order.

The Sentencing Guidelines range from 26 weeks' imprisonment to a small fine.

6.2 Summary

Throughout the last two centuries the courts have consistently imposed lenient sentences on defendants convicted of animal abuse. That judicial approach remains the same under the AWA. Prison is rarely imposed even in the most flagrant cases. The maximum sentence is inadequate though it is due to be increased to 51 weeks' imprisonment. If that was doubled it would still be woefully low.

6.3 AWA

How effective the AWA is in practice can be gauged by the acid test of sentencing that rests with an astute judiciary. In case after case it has failed victims, animals and society. This small sample typifies where the problem lies:

1. In 2015 a gang of four 16-year-old youths stole a tiny puppy, a Chihuahua–Yorkshire terrier-cross called Chunky, from his owner's garden. The gang then tortured Chunky for hours. They punched and kicked him, fed him drugs and broke his neck. They lit an aerosol deodorant can and set fire to Chunky's eyes and face. They fractured his leg and caused bruising to his groin and finally dumped him, leaving him for dead. The following day Chunky was found by a member of the public. When Chunky was examined 'the injuries were so severe that despite the fantastic veterinary care, medication was unable to numb the pain'. Chunky was so injured and in such pain 'initially they thought he'd been in a road traffic collision'. The youths were unmoved about Chunky's injuries during the interview. The grandfather of one of them 'cried when he heard the evidence read out of Chunky's ordeal and torture'. Each defendant received a one-year referral order, so they meet a panel to 'discuss' their offending behaviour.

2. Kerstin Vockert had been advised and warned about the neglect of her dogs in 2012 by the RSPCA. She ignored the warning. In 2015 she had two dogs, a shih-tzu called Happy and a cocker spaniel called Millie. The fur of both dogs was badly matted. Happy was found wandering loose on the road. He was found to have a prolapsed eyeball, which was concealed because of his matted fur. His eye could not be saved. When she was traced the woman lied and denied owning Millie. Later she admitted she had taken her to be euthanised that morning. She claimed Millie was suffering from cancer. There was no evidence to support her claim. The inspector believed she killed Millie to prevent him discovering the truth about her condition as Millie's matted state was worse than Happy. The inspector and a vet, who were particularly familiar with matted dogs, said: 'Millie's condition was the worst they had ever seen.' Millie was encrusted with faeces. The vet opined it would have taken 'many months to get in that condition and the elderly dog would have been in constant discomfort'. The euthanasia was by intercardiac injection, which was 'a painful process and an unacceptable method to perform on a conscious dog'. Millie's matted condition was so bad a post-mortem

examination revealed that 'it would have restricted her ability to walk'. Vockert was convicted and fined £620. Vockert was a veterinary surgeon with her own practice.

3.   In 2014 a defendant teenager was arrested for unrelated matters. His mobile phone was examined. It showed him holding down 'a terrified' white Staffordshire bull terrier, called Tyler, and 'punching him 36 times in the chest and abdomen, then kicking him in the face'. Tyler can be heard 'yelping and crying'. There was further footage of his abuse to a tortoiseshell cat. The thug can be seen kicking the cat 'forcefully in the pelvis'. The cat is 'heard to scream' and is 'thrown in the air by the force of the blow'. The attacks on the dog and cat seemed to be for his 'entertainment' as the name of the film of the cat was LOL, as in 'laugh out loud'. During the interview the video of the animals was shown to the defendant, who 'showed no emotion'. An RSPCA inspector said the attacks were 'utterly abhorrent'. He said: 'I have seen a lot of terrible things in my job, but I felt physically ill watching this footage. What makes it worse is that he seems to have seen it as some form of entertainment.' The defendant received a rehabilitation order.

4.   In 2015 the Lancashire Police acted with the RSPCA's Special Operations Unit as there was intelligence about two men involved in an organised dog fighting ring. During their investigation they found a pit bull terrier, Dingo, who was 'scarred around his face and legs' as well as a 'healing injury to his foreleg' and a 'large portion of one ear was missing'. Two other dogs were found without food and water and were in an 'unsuitable environment'. Two more dogs were found at another address and were peppered with 'old scars'. Numerous items that are the paraphernalia of the professional dog fighter were found including a fan, a ceiling hook, a flirt pole, a working treadmill and blood-spattered carpet. A vet confirmed that the 'scar patterns' on four of the dogs were 'caused by fights of significant duration, on multiple occasions'. Three defendants were convicted of dog fighting offences under the AWA. The DJ said they were 'knowingly and willingly involved themselves in an industry that perpetuated injuries to animals … and been involved at an organisational level … over a period of time.' Each defendant received a suspended sentence.

5. In 2016 Darren Millington 'admitted killing and mutilating a total of nine birds after a drunken row with his girlfriend'. Jo Bannerman, his girlfriend, was 'terrified' when she called the police because Millington 'threatened to kill her dog'. The prosecutor said: 'When she looked outside she saw that the coop has been destroyed and nine chickens had been killed by having their heads removed'. The magistrate at Exeter Magistrates' Court said: 'The attack was vengeful and extremely distressing for the victim.' Millington was sentenced to a 12-week 'overnight curfew' and compensation for the chickens and a tablet.

6.4   Prison

1. In 2014 a defendant from Suffolk was convicted of three offences in relation to Whiskey, his piebald pony. Whiskey had been left lying in an open field and then dragged behind a tractor to an open shelter, where he was 'propped up on a cold concrete floor without adequate bedding.' When Whiskey was found by the RSPCA inspector he made no attempt to stand up. The vet confirmed he was 'suffering from severe worm infestation' and was in 'an advanced state of emaciation'. His quarters were soaked in urine. Whiskey was euthanised to end his 'acute suffering'. On passing sentence the DJ said the defendant 'shows absolutely no remorse or willingness to accept responsibility for his actions now or in the past'. He was sentenced to 23 weeks' imprisonment. His appeal against sentence was dismissed. The reference by the DJ to his 'past' was the fact that this was the *fifth* time the defendant had been convicted of abusing animals.

2. In 2014 Katy Gammon abandoned her boxer dog, Roxy, leaving her without food and water with the result she starved to death. Roxy was so 'desperate' she chewed at the kitchen door, which had been tied shut with a rope by Gammon. The boxer had emptied mop buckets in her 'desperate search for water'. Meanwhile, Gammon had piled tins of dog food and dog 'treats' outside the kitchen 'just feet away from where Roxy' was trapped inside. The 'remains' of Roxy were not discovered for ten weeks. The RSPCA inspectors had to remove Roxy's remains with a snow shovel as they were 'maggot-covered' and

'so badly decomposed'. A post-mortem examination revealed that Roxy had suffered 'starvation and dehydration' leading to a 'prolonged and painful' death that may have lasted as long as six days. Roxy would have become blind and fallen into a coma before dying of organ failure. Gammon was sentenced to 18 weeks' imprisonment. Gammon was a practising solicitor.

3. In 2015 a woman arrived home and found her puppy, Babs, in a 'restless' state. Unknown to her partner, a personal trainer, the next day she took Babs to a vet. Babs showed signs of 'extreme pain'. She was found to have a compound break to her jaw, a fractured neck and possibly a fractured skull. The vet considered they were 'non-accidental injuries'. The woman's partner had admitted to her that he 'swiped' Babs off the bed. The woman then recalled 'the deaths and disappearances of a number of other animals he had owned' and 'a disturbing history of animal abuse came to light'. That 'history' involved a cat, other puppies and seven rabbits. They had all been subject to the 'care' of the man and all ended up missing or dead. Finally, the man admitted causing the injuries to Babs. The RSPCA inspector called the cruelty 'stomach-churning'. The DJ said: 'In the context of this case, you are one of the most danger-ous men in relation to animals that I have come across.' He was sentenced to 18 weeks' imprisonment.

Due to the severe overcrowding in our prisons it is now unusual for most prisoners serving a short sentence to serve the full sentence. They are usually released after a much earlier time on licence or an electronic tag under the 'Home Detention Curfew Scheme' [HDC]. Most prisoners in that category would be released after serving a quarter of their term.

A sense of perspective can be gleaned from this general example: if you imagine the worst form of animal abuse a person could commit, the maximum sentence that could be imposed would be six months' imprisonment. If the defendant pleaded guilty he or she would be entitled to a discount of up to one third. Therefore the maximum sentence would immediately become 18 weeks. Prisoners serving a sentence of less than 12 months only serve one-half of the term. With the HDC he or she would be sent home after about a month.

6.5 Guideline

Such suffering by animals at our hands happens every day in every county throughout the UK. Such sentences show how the courts and so the community view animal abuse. Rarely, even in cases of extreme abuse, does a court impose a custodial sentence. Even when one is imposed it is either suspended or for such a short term as to be futile as a punishment, deterrent, rehabilitation or retribution. Those sentences send out a beacon sign to the perpetrators and the public: animal abuse is undesirable but unimportant.

These cases prove the AWA has an inadequate sentencing regime for cases of animal abuse. As there is a defined 'link' between animal abuse and human abuse, the type of crime a defendant commits where the victim is an animal has a resonance beyond the offence. An abuser of animals has a defined propensity to be violent towards vulnerable people. [See: **4.29**]

Our courts follow the guidance of the SC which supplies them periodically with Guidelines for particular crimes. In relation to the AWA, the Sentencing Guideline recommends a 'starting point' of:

(a) A High Level Community Order for:
Several incidents of deliberate ill-treatment/frightening animal(s); medium term neglect.

(b) 18 weeks custody for:
Attempt to kill/torture; animal baiting/conducting or permitting cock-fighting etc.; prolonged neglect.

The 'Range' for those offences at (a) and (b) are:

(i) Medium Level Community Order to 12 weeks custody.

(ii) 12 to 26 weeks custody.

A brief analysis of that Guideline will illuminate the problem within our legal system. For *'Several incidents of deliberate ill-treatment'* the likely sentence is a Community Order. That is 'recommended' by the Sentencing Council (SC), which would be referred to by the judge when sentencing. Even within the suggested 'Range' the maximum is 12 weeks' imprisonment.

For an *'Attempt to kill/torture; animal baiting'* the likely sentence is a short custodial sentence. Even within the suggested 'Range' the maximum is 26 weeks' imprisonment.

Significantly, these sentences are based on a defendant pleading 'not guilty'. If he pleads 'guilty', he would be entitled to a discount, which could be as high as 33%. Therefore for *'Several incidents of deliberate ill-treatment'* the term in the Range would be reduced to eight weeks. If that term was imposed – which would be rare anyway – the defendant would serve half and probably be released after a fortnight.

Therefore for *'attempting to kill/torture; animal baiting'* the 'Starting point' could be 12 weeks and the 'Range' would be reduced to 18 weeks. If that term was imposed the defendant would serve half and probably be released after about a month.

Whatever the gravity of the abuse, the maximum sentence is six months' imprisonment. Animal abusers are treated leniently by the courts because the AWA and the Guideline is manifestly weak in practice and principle with regard to the sentences.

6.6   Maximum

In 2016 the RSPCA protested against the leniency of the sentences for causing animals 'unnecessary suffering'. During 2016 the UK government has sought consultation from interested parties as to the sentence for domestic animals. Both are right to do so.

The sentences for animal abuse have always been far too low. A maximum of six months' imprisonment is the sort of sentence reserved for average traffic offences. The DDA suffered from the same approach from 1991 until 2014. Then the sentence was increased from two years' to 14 years' imprisonment. That should be a datum for the AWA to follow in its legal footsteps.

The present sentences imposed are futile as a punishment and too lenient to be a deterrent.

6.7 Culpability

The SC has introduced a new Guideline relating to sections 4 and 8 and 9 of the AWA. It is to be effective from 24 April 2017. In general the approach and steps to be taken are similar to the present position.

All the categories are relating to 'Culpability' that is either high or medium or low, namely:

Factors indicating high culpability:
Deliberate or gratuitous attempt to cause suffering/prolonged or deliberate ill-treatment or neglect/ ill treatment in a commercial context/a leading role in illegal activity.

Factors indicating medium culpability:
All cases not falling into high or low culpability.

Factors indicating high culpability:
Well intentioned but incompetent care/mental disorder or learning disability, where linked to commission of offence.

However, on the crucial question of sentencing the policy remains as weak as ever as they recommend these terms:
'Starting point' of 18 weeks custody for 'high culpability' in causing 'greater harm' which is death or serious injury/harm to animal; high level of suffering caused.

For 'medium culpability' causing 'greater harm' the 'starting point' is a 'medium level community order'.

For 'low culpability' causing 'greater harm' the 'starting point' is a 'Band C fine'.

Three points have to be remembered in considering this new Guideline:
All of those sentences relate to death of or serious injury to the animal.

Anything less than a 'high culpability' leads to a non-custodial sentence.

As a Band C fine has a 'starting point' of '150% of relevant weekly income' an unemployed defendant would be treated with even more leniency.

Moreover for all animal abuse falling outside of the category of 'greater harm' the recommended sentence is a community order or a Band B fine that is '100% of relevant weekly income'.

Given that the maximum sentence remains at six months, this Guideline is as anodyne as the previous one. On every level it uses leniency as a cornerstone for animal abuse sentencing.

6.8   Increase

While the problem of undue lenient sentencing for animal abuse has rumbled on for some time, recently it has attracted the interest of various animal welfare bodies including the Battersea Dogs and Cats Home, the League Against Cruel Sport and the RSPCA. That problem has also been adopted and addressed by various Members of Parliament. All these organisations and people were calling for an increase in the maximum sentence to 5 years' imprisonment. As a result the subject was debated in Parliament on 24 February 2017. The decision was postponed as the Second Reading of the Animal Cruelty (Sentencing) Bill was adjourned until 24 March 2017.

Finally in April 2017 the Committee delivered their Report. Their conclusions on the multiple 'recommendations' for their consideration are borne of a general failure to understand animal welfare and particularly the sentencing of animal abusers. The 'recommendation' was for the maximum sentence to be increased to 5 years' imprisonment. Although that is still too low the Committee concluded that 'Current sentencing practice for offences of animal cruelty in the Animal welfare Act 2006 does not suggest that the courts are finding current sentencing powers inadequate.' What that bland view proves is that their grasp of the issue is inadequate. That self-serving statement underlines how they have failed to understand the impure truth about animal abuse and undermines the value of their views. Their superficial Report only serves to show that the Committee never understood the problem and certainly do not attempt to offer a solution.

To have a sense of perspective on our present failure it has to be borne in mind that we introduced the first major animal welfare legislation in the world. Now our sentencing for animal abuse is more lenient than numerous countries, at least 30 in Europe alone, including Austria and Bulgaria and Czech Republic.

Nevertheless even the proposed 5 year sentence is still unduly lenient as the animal abuser would end up spending a much lesser term in prison as a result of these factors: (a) a one-third discount of the term is allowed for a plea of guilty and (b) prisoners usually only serve half of the sentence imposed and (c) the early-release on licence system after a quarter of the term and (d) the ever-present and increasing level of prison overcrowding. All these factors mean a defendant who is sentenced to say three years' imprisonment would usually end up serving less than a year. [See: *Do we need an Animal Abuser Register?* BBC Wildlife Magazine: January 2017: N. Sweeney]

6.9   Arrow

The AWA has sound principles that protect animals and ensure that we care for their welfare. By controlling the owner's conduct towards their animals, we can shape those principles. Law as an instrument of social change strives slowly towards a sound sense of natural justice. A valid law aspires towards justice for all that inspires a community to follow as well as lead. We should shoot an irretractable arrow towards the target of justice for animals that our present system serves the least yet deserve it most.

Dangerous Dogs Act 1991

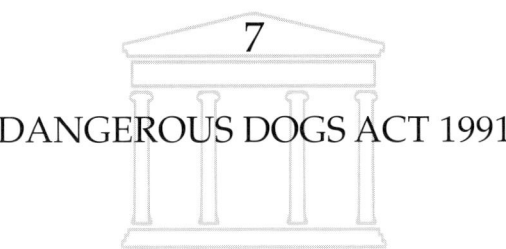

7

DANGEROUS DOGS ACT 1991

7.1 Bias

The DDA was introduced for a positive reason. After a spate of dogs running riot and biting members of the public who were friends and strangers, the government was forced to act. The result was negative. The DDA was a badly drafted Act that induced confusion in judges and dog owners. In 25 years nothing has changed.

The DDA was draconian in the literal and legal sense. It contained two provisions that were contrary to the normal principles of criminal law: (a) if a dog was a particular 'type' it was deemed to be dangerous and doomed to die as (b) the burden of proof is on the defendant to prove it is not of that type.

This Act did and does trouble judges. Their unleashed comments underlined their frustration given its provisions produced a legalistic dog's dinner:

Rougier J said in *R. v. Ealing Magistrates' Court ex parte Fanneran* [1995] 160 JP 409: 'Whilst acknowledging the obvious need to prevent the dogs which are, or have become, savage from injuring people, yet it seems to me that the Dangerous Dogs Act 1991 bears all the hallmarks of an ill-thought-out piece of legislation, no doubt in hasty response to yet another strident pressure group. Add to that the foolish nephew, an observant and zealous policeman and the result is that a perfectly inoffensive animal has to be sent to the gas chamber, or whatever method of execution is favoured, its only crime being to have a cough. It would take the pen of Voltaire to do justice to such a ludicrous situation.'

Even after it was in force for many years, Underhill J said in *Bogdal v. Regina* [2008] EWCA Crim 1: 'It may be anomalous that one particular kind of private space – namely the common parts of a building shared by more than one dwelling – should have been specially brought within the statutory definition when others are not; but this is a notoriously ill-conceived statute, and it is not for us to seek to re-draft it.'

7.2   Onus

The effect of the DDA was not limited to legal confusion. The website endangereddogs.com highlights the case of Ebony, a 'rescued' dog who had been abused by a former owner, was alone and frightened in a car. The police arranged for a vet to anaesthetise her. Ebony was then killed. Despite their belief and acting purely on appearance, after her death they discovered she was not a pit bull terrier but a friendly Staffordshire bull terrier too frightened of them to move. The site also cites the case of Mark Amston, who was so worried that he did not have insurance for his pit bull terrier, Sandy, he had her put down. The following day he hanged himself. His suicide note said: 'Me and Sandy will never be parted again.' Dewi Pritchard Jones, the coroner, said: 'In this case it was a family pet that had to be put down, not a fierce animal. There was no evidence that this dog was fierce. I think the lesson from this death is that legislation should be based on reason and not on panic … [his death] was a consequence of legislation rushed out and not properly thought out.'

A well-drafted Act is even more necessary now than before as in the summer of 2016 through to the present autumn there was another spate of dogs biting people, particularly children. There were 1,160 hospital admissions for dog bites to children under nine years old in England in 2013. In 2014–5 that figure continued to escalate. There were also many unprovoked attacks by dogs on Guide Dogs for the Blind, which has increased from a rate of eight to ten a month. There are a total of 200,000 people being bitten by various dogs every year. It is a problem that will not disappear. We have to concentrate on the irresponsible owner.

In May 2016 a man and two women were arrested following an incident where a dog, not a banned breed, went wild and bit 11 children in a park. In the same week a pet dog, which again was not a banned breed, attacked and killed his owner. In September 2016 Chewy, a pet Pomeranian, 'walked through a hole' in the fence of a neighbour's property and was allegedly attacked by the neighbour's Alsatian. Chewy had a wound and despite a blood transfusion, bled to death. Whatever the merits of each case, they all prove branding a breed and killing a 'type' of dog is misconceived.

Postmen are more prone than the average person to be attacked by dogs when delivering letters. In 2015 there were 2,660 attacks on postal workers. The attacks increased by 10% during the summer holidays. It is such a normal part and parcel of the problems faced by postal workers doing their daily duties that the Royal Mail now releases the statistics during its 'Annual Dog Awareness Week'. [See: **17.3**]

The statistics tell their own worrying story. While thirty-one people have been killed by a dog since the DDA was introduced, twenty-six people have been killed by dogs in Britain in the past decade. The admissions to hospital as result of dog bites have risen by 76%. In relation specifically to 'postal workers' the figure subject to attacks by dogs is assessed to be 5,000.

An irresponsible owner will allow and sometimes even encourage his dog to be aggressive. Ultimately, it is usually the owner that causes the problem. That is why the DDA places the onus on the owner. That is where it properly belongs because the control is in his or her hands.

7.3   Future

Now we have the opportunity to balance discrimination of dogs within a system that would reflect the view of the judges in *Knightsbridge Crown Court v. The Commissioner of Police for Metropolitan Police v. Wells Street Magistrates' courtex parte Crabbe* [1996] EWHC 380.

McCowan LJ delivered a masterly description of what the trial process should achieve: 'I would not criticise the Commissioner for making the application, it is important, in my judgment, that if the application were to be made, no steps should be taken which would prevent the dog having a fair trial. The relevant facts were that the applicant had no legal aid, no right of appeal to the Crown Court and no means to pay the £300. As I say, £300 is an inordinately high sum. A much fairer sum could surely have been achieved by having the dog examined at another police station or, perhaps better still, at the police dog kennel. As it was, by insisting on a figure of £300 contribution to be made by the Applicant, the Commissioner made it well near impossible for the Applicant to get a fair trial for his dog.'

McCowan LJ concluded: 'There was not, in the result, a fair trial.' The court quashed the destruction order on Elsa. A rehearing was ordered before a different Stipendiary Magistrate.

Collins J added: 'It seems to me that it is all the more important that the magistrate, before whom the matter comes, ensures that there is a fair trial; in particular, that the owner of the dog, who is disputing the application that it will be destroyed, be able to produce all the evidence that he wishes, providing of course that evidence is relevant.' [See: **13.4**]

Their brother judges have similarly shown a prescience that augurs well, assuming others follow their guidance. Irwin J in the High Court in *Housego v. Canterbury Crown Court and the Crown Prosecution Service* [2012] EWHC 255 concluded with a succinct comment observing what is so often overlooked by the court to the detriment of the owner as well as his dog: 'After this dog has been kept on death row, so to speak, for more than two-and-half years, it is time she was reprieved.'

Moses LJ added: 'I agree. I only wish to express the gratitude of the court, both to solicitors acting in effect for the dog and to counsel and, of course, to Mrs Todd of the Lord Whisky Animal Sanctuary, all of whom are to be congratulated for their persistence in this appeal, faced with the erroneous approach of Mr Recorder Byrne.' [See: **11.2**]

Yet caution is necessary as a report from the RSPCA, *Breed Specific Legislation – A Dog's Dinner*, [2016] delivered a stinging critique of the DDA. The report confirms the welfare of many people and their dogs have been subject to the inherent prejudice in the DDA.

Taking all those views as an accurate and reliable guide gives some hope for the DDA to be interpreted in a manner that promotes the ever-fleeting forms of fairness and justice. In *R. v Hastie* [2016] as an echo of the 'death row' reprieve, a pit bull terrier, Stella, was rescued by HHJ Cottle at Exeter Crown Court. Even then there has to be vigilance for the voiceless as Stella was condemned to a destruction order by the Magistrates' Court and her release was initially opposed by the prosecution and the police. Finally they only changed their mind at the Crown Court. [See: **17.10**]

In that vein it is valuable to consider the tale of Tyson, who was killed because of the various organisations' failure to make a legal application to save his life. They should have known better. In that respect Tyson was not alone. His plight was repeated and endorsed by the Magistrates' Court in Dorset, where Hopper had spent two years in isolation in a cage whose dimensions were the size of a small table top used to play solitaire. Following that court order against him, after two years in total isolation he was only released by death. [See: **17.9**]

It seems inexplicable there was no appeal from that decision as the dog's character can be changed by the character of the owner. Punish the owner by all means, but destroying the dog is neither the best nor the only solution. The severity of the law should be reserved for those cases where the reckless owner fails to control his dog. Equally it should balance the fate of the dog with the inherent fairness of the law itself. That depends on the sapience of our judges, whose function must be to ensure the dog as well as the owner has a 'fair trial'. For in matters of life and death nothing less than that process will do.

8

DDA IN ACTION

8.1   Dangerous Dogs Act 1991 s.1

(1) This section applies to
    (a) any dog of the type known as a pit bull terrier;
    (b) any dog of the type known as the Japanese tosa; and
    (c) any dog of the type designated for the purposes of this section by an order of the Secretary of State, being a type appearing to him to be bred for fighting or to have the characteristics of a type bred for that purpose.

Initially the Act was limited to the pit bull terrier and the Japanese tosa. The Secretary of State introduced the Dangerous Dogs (Designated Types) Order 1991 which amended the DDA to include:

    (a) any dog of the type known as the Dogo Argentino; and
    (b) any dog of the type known as the Fila Braziliero.

At first it appears strange to have the *'type'* of dog specified rather than a *'breed'*. However, on analysis the reason becomes clear: specifying breed would limit the definition to a kind of dog with a background and character within a certain category. By using 'of the type' a much wider variety of dogs can be caught within that term.

A new type of dog bred by badger baiters is a cross between a bull terrier and a lurcher. The result is a cross upon a cross dog. The temperament of such a dog could well be cross too, though that may be the intention of the breeder. The Secretary of State could amend the DDA by including such a 'type', if it was not already banned.

8.2   Type

Shortly after the DDA was introduced, the leading case of *R. v. Crown Court at Knightsbridge ex parte Dunne; Brock v. Director of Public Prosecutions* [1993] 4 All ER 491 was decided by the High Court. Each was an appeal, *Dunne* by judicial review and *Brock* by case stated. The cases were heard together because the point at issue in each one was the same, namely the meaning of 'any dog of the type known as the pit bull terrier'.

Gary Dunne was charged with having a pit bull terrier in a public place without it being muzzled. He was convicted at Wells Street Magistrates' Court and appealed to the Knightsbridge Crown Court. The court decided that (a) Dunne had failed to prove his dog was not of the type known as a pit bull terrier, but (b) the prosecution failed to prove that the dog was unmuzzled. Therefore the court allowed Dunne's appeal.

Dunne was advised he could not appeal against the Crown Court's conclusion that his dog was of that type. Therefore he applied and was given leave for judicial review seeking: A declaration that the Crown Court erred in its interpretation of the phrase 'any dog of the type known as the pit bull terrier', and that on a proper construction of the statute the word 'type' should be defined in its technical sense – here equivalent to 'breed' – rather than given a broad, popular meaning.

Karen Brock was convicted of having a dog in her possession or custody that was a pit bull terrier. She admitted that she had such a dog and that it had not been neutered, tattooed, implanted, insured or registered. Therefore she was subject to the prohibition against Buster.

The Crown Court accepted the evidence of the prosecution's witnesses and rejected the evidence on behalf of Brock. It found the characteristics of Buster 'substantially conformed to the American Dog Breeders Association [ADBA] standard and was of the type known as the pit bull terrier'. Therefore Brock had failed to adduce sufficient evidence to rebut the *'presumption'* that her dog was of that type, so the court dismissed Brock's appeal.

In the High Court Glidewell LJ said the phrase 'of the type known as the pit bull terrier' meant the word 'type' has a meaning different from and wider than the word 'breed'. The Crown Court was therefore entitled to use the ADBA standard as a guide. However, both courts were also entitled to find on the evidence that the fact that a dog does not meet that standard in every respect is not conclusive. Thus both courts could properly conclude that a dog was of the type known as pit bull terrier if its 'characteristics substantially conformed to the ADBA's standard' or if the dog 'approximately amounted to, was near to, or had a substantial number of the characteristics of the pit bull terrier as set out in the ADBA's standard'.

In *Brock's Case* the Crown Court stated 'that in determining whether a dog was "of the type known as a pit bull terrier" the behaviour of the dog, whether or not it had shown dangerous proclivities, was irrelevant'. The High Court rejected that decision. The ADBA's standard stated the dog should have various characteristics including 'gameness' and 'aggressiveness'.

Glidewell LJ said those two are aspects of 'behavioural characteristics'. By the ADBA's standard it is relevant to consider whether or not a dog exhibits the behavioural characteristics of a pit bull terrier. Consequently, evidence of the dog's behaviour cannot be irrelevant.

Thus the declaration sought by Dunne was refused. The appeal of Brock was allowed as it raised evidence of Buster's 'behaviour', which was wrongly considered to be inadmissible.

Nothing much has changed since *Dunne* as while a pit bull terrier has a total of 54 characteristics, a lot fewer than that number plus a dog's appearance are enough to ensure he is seized and killed. The documentary *The Dogs on Death Row* on BBC1 on 24 January 2012 proved looks can still kill.

Professor John Bradshaw in *In Defence of Dogs* [2012] states legislating against a breed can only be justified if there are biological reasons making the breed aggressive. If the main cause is irresponsible ownership using the dog for fighting 'then outlawing one breed is unlikely to solve anything'.

Bradshaw's point is unassailable, yet that is the reasoning relied upon by court after court to condemn a dog as being of a certain type with the consequence of ordering their destruction.

Even with 57 characteristics, the tale of Tyson tells its own truth about the prejudice that proves if looks could kill in respect of a dog they probably will. *Tyson's Case* is instructive as the authorities apparently misunderstood the position with the result that the dog was duly killed because of his appearance. No one considered the elementary legal point of seeking assistance from a court by applying for Tyson to be registered.

This problem was accentuated by the seizure of 22 dogs in 2014 by the Merseyside Police. They were all family pets. The pets were all perfunctorily euthanised by the police within hours of being seized. All the dogs were *'exempt'* under the DDA, but the respective owners had not allegedly complied with the particular rules pertaining to the Index of Exemption. Several owners took action against the police. While the police stood firmly by their action the High Court found their practice and procedure was unlawful. Why the police believed they could just destroy people's pets without a court order remains a mystery. [See: **12.3**]

The essential point that cannot be ignored is that only the court, rather than the CPS, police, Defra or any other body, can decide whether a dog should live or die. An incisive observation was made by McCowan LJ in *Knightsbridge Crown Court v. The Commissioner of Police for Metropolitan Police*: 'After all it is for the court to decide whether the dog should be destroyed and not the Crown Prosecution Service.' Then the procedure and the decision is known to the owners and openly seen to be fair and judicious. Even a dog is entitled to 'a fair trial'. More importantly, then the owner can be heard and has a right of appeal. Unlike those people in Liverpool, to have value for an owner the appeal has to be while his or her dog is still alive.

The proper approach for the welfare of dogs and letter of the law is to apply to the court for a declaration and, if necessary, a change of the keeper as in *R. v. Hastie*. The position and the decision was clarified by Collins J in *R (Sandhu) v. Isleworth Crown Court* [2012] EWHC 1658. He said: 'All that the court can do, and should do, if satisfied that the dog in question would not constitute a danger to public safety, because it does not have the inherently dangerous characteristics that pit bull-type dogs are believed to have, is make a contingent destruction order if asked to do so, so that attempts can be made to obtain a certificate of exemption. After all, that would not be altogether surprising because if a dog is not to be regarded as a danger to the public, then it is *prima facie* wrong that the dog's life should be brought to an end.' [See: **17.10**]

8.3   Drunk

The prohibition on such dogs extends to allowing them to be a danger to the public at large. So the owner or person in charge cannot allow the dog to be in 'any place' unless they are muzzled and kept on a lead.

The state of the owner affects the fate of the dog. In *DPP v. Kellett* [1994] Crim LR 916 the prosecution appealed against a decision of the Crown Court to allow Kellett's appeal against conviction. Kellett was charged with being the owner of a pit bull terrier, which she had 'allowed' to be in a public place without being muzzled or kept on a lead. The animal was registered as a pit bull terrier and otherwise complied with the Act. It escaped from her flat as the front door had been left ajar by Kellett because she was drunk. The issue was whether Kellett had 'allowed' her dog to be in a public place.

The prosecutor argued that although 'allow' imported an element of *mens rea* [guilty mind] into the offence, her drunkenness was irrelevant. As the offence was a crime of '*basic*' intent – rather than a '*specific*' intent offence such as with intent to endanger life or murder – Kellett's state could not be a defence. So the prosecution appeal was allowed.

'Allow' implies knowledge and consent on the part of the person concerned. That remains the same whether Kellett was as drunk as david's sow or as sober as a judge.

8.4 Blameless

The DDA is strictly interpreted in respect of any available defence. In *Cichon v. DPP* [1994] Crim LR 918 the defendant was convicted of allowing a pit bull terrier to be in a public place without being muzzled. He appealed against the sentence to the Crown Court. Cichon claimed his mitigation revealed a defence, so his guilty plea at the Magistrates' Court had been equivocal. The Crown Court refused to remit the case for trial, but stated a case.

The mitigation was that Cichon removed the muzzle because his dog had kennel cough. Therefore it was cruel to keep the muzzle on whilst he was coughing. Cichon claimed that was a defence of 'necessity'. The questions for the divisional court were (a) whether the plea was equivocal and (b) whether the refusal to remit the case was right.

Schiemann J said: 'The Act does not in terms (and nor in my judgment does the common law) allow the person in control of the dog to make a value judgment as between what is good for the dog and what is good for the rest of mankind ... We have here an absolute prohibition and a breach of that prohibition is to be followed by an order for the dog's destruction however blameless the dog and its owner.' Necessity as a defence did not apply.

Kennel cough [acute tracheobronchitis] is a problem for a dog such that *Vetstream* advises that: 'It is very contagious and will spread rapidly around the dog population ... it causes coughing that can go on for a month in some cases ... If your dog normally wears a collar, take this off, to stop it irritating his throat, and exercise him outside with a harness or halter and lead.'

If a person had an allergic reaction to an electronic tag he had to wear as a condition of bail he would have a defence of necessity if he had to remove it. A prisoner charged with an offence of escape could rely on necessity if he had fled from a burning cell. It would not matter whether the fire was started by an accident or arsonist. What is the difference when compared to a kennel cough, a drink of water or an involuntary vomit? Why should necessity be available for a man, but denied to the owner of a dog?

Dickson J in the Supreme Court of Canada dealt with the point in *Perka v. The Queen* [1984] 13 D.L.R. (4th) 1. A cargo of cannabis due for Colombia was offloaded into Canada. The captain took that action to save the ship from sinking. The court confirmed the defence of necessity as: 'The objectivity of the criminal law is preserved; such acts are still wrongful, but in the circumstances they are excusable. Praise is indeed not bestowed but pardon is …'

If the kennel cough was such a condition that as a result of the muzzle not being removed the dog choked and suffered or died, the defendant could be charged with failing in his duty of care under the AWA. As it is 'very contagious' perhaps the only lawful course was for Cichon to keep his dog indoors. Though necessity knows no law, the idea is trumped by the irrevocable injustice suffered by Cichon's dog.

8.5   Abandon

Abandonment is a constant problem in our society as people routinely abandon their pets. Often they will simply move away and leave their animals to fend for themselves. The worst way they act is to simply leave a house full of dogs to starve to death. The animals then try to survive as best they can, sometimes by eating their former companions. There are more than 100,000 dogs abandoned every year, that is more than 250 a day. Usually the owners escape prosecution while the animals lose their lives.

It seems it can be difficult for some people to determine whether a dog has been abandoned. Although a dog may appear to have been abandoned the owner may have merely 'forgotten' he or she had left her ageing, ailing pet dog alone in a tent when she left the Glastonbury Festival. Lynn Southway, the manager at *Happy Landings*, where Dolly was recovering, said: 'She was found in a very bad state. There was a cardboard box with some food in it and a bowl, which I'm hoping had water in it at one point but she was visibly distressed. She has terrible pain in her ears from all the mud, she keeps shaking her head. Her claws have grown and now wrap around her paws. At night I have to sit with her like a child to get her to sleep because she's so shaken. She obviously hasn't been taken care of well at all.' Dolly, the elderly white lurcher, was later reunited with her owner. The *Happy Landings* staff said: 'Although we have concerns and unanswered questions legally, we have to hand her back.' Why the staff had that view is unclear as 'legally' the 'unanswered questions' remain as to why the owner was not prosecuted for an offence under the AWA. [See: **2.14**]

When a dog is separated from his owner it can be a cause of stress for the dog. It can create 'separation anxiety', which leads to a dog becoming angry or frightened, or both. In relation to the DDA, it should not be overlooked that Dolly was cold, lost and alone when she was first encountered by the staff gathering the abandoned property left by people at the festival. When the person entered the tent he might well have been attacked and bitten by Dolly. For it would have been an instinctive reaction to defend herself against him given he was a complete stranger in her territory. In that event her owner, if she could be found, could have been guilty of the *aggravated* offence and Dolly could have been destroyed. Even if her owner was not discovered, Dolly would have been liable to be killed by law.

Following a popular fantasy series, *Game of Thrones* and the *Twilight* films, which feature wolf-like breeds, the Siberian husky became a fashionable breed. As they grow and demand a lot of exercise and no longer 'look like cuddly toys' they are abandoned on the streets. According to the UK animal charity Blue Cross: 'Record numbers of Siberian huskies and other wolf-like breeds are being abandoned each year, with the past five years seeing a 700% rise ...'

Abandoned dogs are a problem that demonstrates a licence for *all* dogs is essential. Our politicians' continued failure to protect the public is mirrored by their failure to protect dogs from irresponsible owners. A licence is the legal answer and social solution. [See: **17.11**]

8.6   Process

While the prosecution has the advantage of the 'presumption' that has to be proved by the defence, it still has to follow the proper process.

In *R. v. Liverpool Magistrates' Court ex parte Slade* [1997] EWHC 529 there was an application to quash the decision of the Stipendiary Magistrate, who refused to 'stay' an information against dog owner Noel Slade. At a hearing on 4 May 1995 it was made clear the sole issue was whether the dog involved was a pit bull terrier and the defence indicated it intended to call an expert witness. The trial was fixed for 16 June but the defence was granted an adjournment because its expert was unable to attend court that day. The prosecution also intended to call an expert witness. The trial was fixed for 7 September. On that date, due to an administrative error, the expert witness for the prosecution could not attend because of a commitment at Doncaster Crown Court. The magistrate refused to adjourn the case.

The prosecution, in the absence of that witness, decided to call no evidence. The information was dismissed. The next day, the dog, which was in police possession, was returned to Slade. In February 1996 a new piece of information was laid against Slade with respect to the dog alleging he was in charge of the dog in a public place after he collected it on 8 September. The defence sought a 'stay' as it was an abuse of process. The magistrate refused that application.

In the High Court defence counsel submitted there was an abuse of process because by returning the dog on the following day the court played a crucial role in allowing him to commit the offence with which he was now charged.

Maurice Kay J said: 'It was wholly inappropriate and wrong for the Commissioner to take the second proceedings against this applicant … It matters not precisely what label is put on that analysis but in my judgment it is an abuse of process and ought to have been held to have been such.'

Pill LJ said: ' … the applicant was allowed to take the dog out of police custody and into a public place unmuzzled. He had expert evidence in his favour and he had been acquitted of the charge against him. On the evidence, there is no reason to doubt that, the prosecution not having proceeded against him on the previous day, and the charge having been dismissed, he reasonably believed he was entitled to act as he did. Unknown to him, the prosecution had already decided to base a further charge against him on observing him leave the police station in such circumstances.'

Pill LJ analysed how the prosecution and the police had acted and induced a belief in Slade that he would not be prosecuted. He said:

'The statutory provisions were such that the trial court, by way of mitigation of sentence upon conviction, was not in a position to protect him (or his dog) from the unfairness of the procedure followed. Given the consequences of a conviction, it was unfair to try the accused for the offence and offensive to the court's sense of justice and propriety, so as to be an abuse of process.'

If the prosecution was able to take advantage of its own error or bad practice to condemn a dog to death it would destroy more than the dog: it would reflect badly on the integrity of the court and the raw essence of the law. This decision is one of the growing few in this area that takes account of the fact that the *'thing'* being affected is a living creature whose life is balanced in the scales of the court's judgment. *Slade's Case* is a positive example of the judicial process in practice being applied to protect the system and the victim.

Other especially dangerous dogs

8.7 Dangerous Dogs Act 1991 s.2

(1) If it appears to the Secretary of State that dogs of any type to which section 1 above does not apply present a serious danger to the public he may by order impose in relation to dogs of that type restrictions corresponding with such modifications, if any, as he thinks appropriate, to all or any of those in subsection (2) (d) and (e) of that section.

The Secretary of State can impose an order in relation to dogs of any type that are not 'prohibited' within section 1. He has to consider that those other types of dogs *'present a serious danger to the public'*. In that event he can impose restrictions with such 'modifications', if any, as he thinks fit to all or any of those contained in section 1. That would apply to any dog that is not one of the four prohibited ones and any new designated dogs. So there would have to be something about them that makes them *'specially'* dangerous over and above the natural disposition of any dog to defend his territory and himself.

That would allow for changing conditions, including where a type of dog was suddenly stricken with some behavioural problem and had to be curbed while in public, though he was not a 'fighting' dog *per se*.

Before making any order, the Secretary of State *'shall'* consult with persons having *'relevant knowledge and experience'* in order to determine whether he should make any order at all. If it is necessary then the content is equally relevant to the submissions of the third party. The persons to be consulted include (a) a body concerned with animal welfare and (b) one concerned with veterinary science and practice and (c) one concerned with breeds of dogs. That ensures a balanced and fair approach covering most appropriate areas, though it is not limited to those bodies. That approach is adopted when considering whether such restrictions are necessary when they are not dealing with designated dogs. It is necessary as it is easy for a government to introduce legislation in this area that continues the tradition of Draco.

The third parties ensure there is a legal brake on a potential arbitrary power. An excellent example of the effect of the consultations can be seen in relation to the AWA in *R. (on the application of Petsafe Ltd and another) v. Welsh Ministers* where they included the Kennel Club, the PDSA and the RSPCA. [See: **2.18**]

While this provision states he shall consult such bodies as 'appear to him' to have the relevant knowledge or experience, if he fails to do so it could give rise to an application of judicial review. The consultation is intended to be even-handed and fair-minded. If he consulted bodies that did not possess that 'relevant knowledge or experience' it would reflect upon his judgement and equally be open to challenge by judicial review. The criterion is a balance of views *before* a decision is made. That is positive as it seeks to negate any creeping crony bias, profit-motivated nepotism or political chicanery. [See: **2.10**]

8.8   Wry

The value of an expert's view is it can place a dog's behaviour in its proper perspective. The opinion of Tina Delaney, an animal welfare manager in Newham Council in East London, is instructive: 'I do not believe any breed of dog is a bad dog. It is the result of bad training or the wrong training.'

The value of a dog can be assessed by another expert's view, PC Martin Parker of the Metropolitan Dog Service, who said: 'It would be impossible to police the streets of the capital and our streets without our canine partners.'

It has to be remembered that, although it is regrettable, accidents can happen whereby even a trained dog can become out of control. That can be seen by the tragic case of Irene Collins, a 73-year-old woman who gave the police permission to 'search her home and garden' to chase 'a drugs suspect' in Middlesbrough. In the event the police German shepherd went into the kitchen and attacked Mrs Collins. A week later, Mrs Collins died in hospital from her injuries.

Certainly it would be a harsh law that would result in the death of the dog in such circumstances. That is the reason for the exemption in respect of the dog that extends to his handler by section 10 of the DDA: ' … but references to a dog injuring a person or there being grounds for reasonable apprehension that it will do so do not include references to any case in which the dog is being used for a lawful purpose by a constable or a person in the service of the Crown.' That 'purpose' protects the police. Harsh maybe, nevertheless it is pertinent to note the protection was limited as the dog was destroyed.

With a wry irony it is relevant to consider the case of Eddie, an Akita, who won a Crufts rosette 'for obedience', receiving a Good Citizen Award at the Birmingham dog show in 2013. A few hours later, as Eddie and his owner, Lorain Ronis, posed for a photograph he suddenly attacked Louise Nelson and bit her knee and hand. As they posed Eddie tried to attack another Akita, Banks. Nelson was standing nearby when she was attacked: 'I tried to get out of the way but it grabbed hold of my knee and was shaking my kneecap.' Ronis claimed Eddie was not aggressive and that Banks attacked him first. She claimed Nelson 'told me "dogs will be dogs, don't worry about it".' Ronis was prosecuted for allowing Eddie to be dangerously out of control in a public place. Although she denied the offence, Ronis was convicted and in 2014 was sentenced to a one year community order.

Neither the police dog nor the Crufts dog in those cases was a banned breed. Neither of the dogs involved in the death of Clifford Clarke nor Eliza-Mae Mullane were a banned breed. The position remains the same for the four dogs that killed Jade Lomas-Anderson at her friend's home. [See: **19.1**]

It proves the problem is not the breed but the one who holds the lead – or fails to do so.

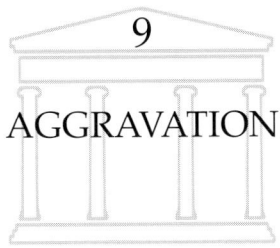

9
AGGRAVATION

9.1 Dangerous Dogs Act 1991 s.3

(1) If a dog is dangerously out of control in any place
   (a) the owner; and
   (b) if different, the person for the time being in charge of the dog, is guilty of an offence, or, if the dog whilst so out of control injures any person, an aggravated offence, under this subsection.

As the DDA is aimed at protecting the public from dangerous dogs, section 3 is its heartbeat. This deals with dogs that are dangerously out of control in *'any place'*. Its purpose is to ensure persons who own or are in charge of a dog are in control of its behaviour. Otherwise they will be controlled; their dogs will be too. If they fail to do so the consequences are that it could lead to a charge of manslaughter, though it is conceivable in certain circumstances it could even lead to one of murder.

Many criminal gangs now adopt 'status' dogs as a weapon of choice to protect them and impress their friends while frightening their enemies. As a result, the Metropolitan Status Dog Unit was set up in South London specifically to seize such dogs.

Given the proclivity of criminals, especially drug dealers, to possess dangerous dogs as an ersatz weapon that are sometimes encouraged or even trained to attack the police, there is no reason why the owner could not be charged with murder. An interesting historical case is outlined in E. P. Evans idiosyncratic book, *The Criminal Prosecution and Capital Punishment of Animals* [1906], where he documents one of the last animal trials in Switzerland in 1906. Scherrer, his son and their dog attacked a man called Marger, intending to rob him. During the attack the man was killed and all three were charged with murder. All three were convicted and the two men were sentenced to life imprisonment. Their deemed legal 'accomplice' was executed.

In *R. v. Singh* [2011] EWCA Crim 1756, although there was a complete conflict of evidence, the prosecution alleged the two defendant brothers intended to rob their victim using two pit bulls as a joint weapon. Circumstances may change, but the passing of a century has not inhibited the legal position.

John Barrington tells an oxymoronic tale in *Of Men and Dogs* [2013] of a dog and his owner on the Scottish Borders. The dog was so gifted he went out alone and stole an 'entire heft of sheep'. The rustled sheep were hidden and disguised by the farmer, then sold through the markets. Eventually their ruse was discovered and both the farmer and his accomplice dog were tried for sheep rustling. They were both convicted and, as was normal at the time, each was sentenced to death. The farmer was hanged. The dog was 'to meet the same fate, but somehow eluded the hangman's rope. It is whispered that it was quietly relocated'.

Now the Anti-social Behaviour, Crime and Policing Act 2014 [ABCPA] has extended the definition from 'public' to '*any*' place the potential liability of every dog owner has increased. Depending on what happens it would at least lead to the simple offence and potentially the aggravated one. The combination of place and the lack of control can lead to the twin risks of an irresponsible owner and a dog devoid of a master. Moreover, a dog can now be destroyed by law even if no offence has been committed. [See: **17.1**]

9.2 Expertise

Fortunately the courts can often be persuaded by expert evidence relating to the dog in question. It can result in either a severe or a lesser sentence for the defendant and his dog. Just how important an expert can be is exemplified by the Scottish case of *Swankie v. Procurator Fiscal* [1998] Scot HC 3. Terrence Swankie pleaded guilty as the owner of a collie-type dog that was dangerously out of control.

Swankie was not present when the case was listed, but had submitted a letter of explanation. The procurator fiscal informed the sheriff that Alastair Gardiner had walked with his granddaughter past the gate of Swankie's home, when the dog ran towards them, jumped over the wall and approached them barking and growling. He successfully fended off the dog. About 15 minutes later a neighbour heard the sound of breaking glass and, on looking out, saw the dog running along the top of the wall. The dog jumped off the wall, ran towards a postman, barking and growling, and backed him up against a wall. The postman used his bicycle to ward off the dog. Gardiner came out of his house and together they chased the dog away, which then went back to its own garden. The police were called and when they interviewed Swankie the dog was on a lead and was excitable, but not aggressive.

The sheriff invited Swankie to attend court and give evidence to show that the dog was not dangerous as his letter was inconsistent with the prosecution case. Swankie could only explain the *second* incident when the dog broke the window and escaped. However, as that did not explain the *first* occasion the sheriff concluded there were *two* incidents of aggressive behaviour by the dog. Lord Kirkwood, in the High Court, said: 'The sheriff then invited the appellant [Swankie] to provide him with evidence, perhaps from a veterinary surgeon, but the appellant declined to provide any evidence. So he concluded that the dog was a danger to the public ... and he reluctantly made an order that the dog was to be destroyed.'

Swankie had misunderstood the situation. He did not realise he was being invited to lead evidence to show his dog was not dangerous and did not appreciate he was to be destroyed.

The Appeal Court then made a crucial point in relation to the circumstances. It was thought 'there had been two separate incidents, the first of which was unexplained, had weighed heavily with the sheriff'. However, on analysis that was wrong: it was one *continuous* incident in that the dog had somehow broken the glass, was frightened, escaped and then attacked two people. Lord Kirkwood said: 'On the basis of Mr Gardiner's statement, there had not been two separate acts but one continuous incident after the dog had fallen out of the window. In these circumstances it was understandable why the appellant could not give an explanation for two separate incidents 15 minutes apart, as the account the procurator fiscal had given the sheriff was factually inaccurate.'

Once Swankie realised the seriousness of the situation, Lord Kirkwood said 'he had obtained evidence which clearly showed that the dog was not dangerous'. The court had a report from 'Dr Roger Mugford, Head of the Animal Behaviour Centre, Chertsey in Surrey ... Dr Mugford stated that the dog was a good-natured and much loved family pet who had never previously been the subject of a complaint or caused danger to the public ... We were also told that numerous references had been obtained from neighbours and friends to the effect that the dog was a good-natured family dog.'

The 'new' information enabled the court to allow the appeal and quash the destruction order.

The absence or presence of an expert is of such importance that without it the fate of a dog can be sealed in law. In *R. v. Harry* [2010] 2 Cr. App. R. (S) 395 it made the difference between life and death. The Crown Court judge refused an adjournment for an expert report and ordered that Millie, a female crossbred bull terrier, and Snoop, a male English bull terrier, should both be destroyed. Unusually, the Court of Appeal considered a provision in the Criminal Appeal Act 1968 that allows the court to receive evidence that was not adduced earlier in the proceedings if it is '*in the interests of justice*' to do so. As a result the court considered the report and quashed the order for destruction in respect of each dog. [See: **10.3**]

In *Swankie* Lord Kirkwood referred to the fact the court was 'told that numerous references' had been obtained to the effect that the dog was 'a good-natured family dog'. When the author represented the owner of a 'rescued' dog who bit a postman, a petition from the neighbours was adduced as evidence of his 'character'. The dog, a friendly Jack Russell terrier, was abused by his former owner, a cruel, violent man. As a result he was traumatised and feared all men until he got to know them well. His treatment by the abuser had marked him forever. He saw the postman as the ghost image of his former abuser revisited.

Given the ABCPA, now expert evidence is not merely admissible but relevant as the court 'must' consider both the 'temperament' and 'past behaviour' of the dog.

How a dog's life is determined by the defence can be gleaned from *R (on the application of Kenton Hooker) v. Ipswich Crown Court* [2013] EWHC 2899. Kenton Hooker was the owner of a three-year old German shepherd dog. He pleaded guilty at the Magistrates' Court, which ordered the dog to be destroyed. The defence did not bother to obtain an expert's report. Hooker appealed to the Crown Court, which upheld the order. The defence had not bothered to obtain an expert's report. Hooker appealed to the High Court. Lord Justice Treacy said: 'The judge [at the Crown Court] commented that no animal behaviour consultant had provided any material to the court and that indeed was the case.' Finally, the defence obtained two reports from an expert. Treacy LJ said: 'We are not minded to consider the contents of those reports.' As a result the 'rescued' dog was ordered to be destroyed.

What could be less in the 'interests of justice' than to order the death of a dog because of the failure of the defence to obtain an expert report?

That was misplaced and should not be repeated as it is contrary to principle in that the court punished the dog for the defendant's failure. The fair and just course is that laid down by the Court of Appeal in *R. v. Harry*. Then if necessary the court can criticise the defence and order costs against it. The court was wrong to ignore a report so as to condemn the dog to death. As the failure was addressed, albeit late, the defence should have appealed. [See: **10.4**]

The ABCPA also serves to show that the Crown Court in the *Hooker Case* was wrong to dismiss the appeal and kill the dog. At the least it could and should have adjourned the case in order to allow – or indeed 'order' – the defendant to obtain the relevant evidence of the dog's character. Now under the ABCPA the court is under a positive duty to adjourn the case for that purpose so it can perform its duty.

Therefore, whether the defendant has failed or succeeded to obtain evidence of the dog's character is not the crucial point as the onus is on the court itself to do so. If the *Hooker Case* was before the court now it should not be decided in the same way. The failure by the court to do so would provide grounds for an appeal. There is no reason why the court should not, and indeed every reason why it should, expect the prosecution to provide that 'evidence' as part of its case. That is consistent with the ABCPA and its duty to the court as a 'minister of justice'.

An expert is now essential in most cases in order to properly prepare and present the defence. With the amendment by the ABCPA and the revised sentencing, within that Act and by the SC, it is advisable to obtain a report in every case. Failing to do so would be a failure of the defence duty. That duty extends to the court and the prosecution. [See: **17.2**]

The Court of Appeal analysed the competence of expert witnesses in cases concerning dangerousness and destruction orders relating to dogs. The action taken by the court proves the importance of such evidence.

In *R. v. Rogers* [2016] EWCA Crim 801, on 30 June 2014 at about 8 a.m. Georgina Rogers was walking with her two Staffordshire bull terriers, Bailey and Socks, in Watling Park, Burnt Oak in London. Bailey was a bitch whom Rogers had owned since she was a puppy. Bailey was about seven years old. Socks was a male dog who was about ten years old. Both of the dogs were on leads. Bailey's lead was a retractable one that extended beyond Rogers' control. It was inappropriate for her dog as it should have been a short lead.

Jon Gadigbe was walking his dog, a Rhodesian Ridgeback, named Zeus. He was not wearing a muzzle. The dogs belonging to both Rogers and Gadigbe became involved in a fight. The judge, Mr Recorder Etherington QC, described it as a 'frightening incident'. He found that Rogers had no 'idea how to bring either of her dogs under control'. Further, she lacked 'the strength or training to manage them'.

Richard Bingley was walking his own three dogs, which, on witnessing the 'dog fight', he tethered to a tree. Bingley intended to assist in controlling the dogs involved in that fight. During the 'disturbance' Bailey slipped her lead, ran off and attacked one of Bingley's dogs, an Irish terrier. Bailey bit the terrier on his hind leg.

Bingley tried to protect his dog. In the event Bingley was bitten on his ankle, hand and knees. He needed medical treatment and had to stay in hospital. He missed five day's work. The judge found that Bingley was not to blame for his own injuries.

Two of the dogs, including the Ridgeback, were injured in the initial fight. The judge found it was 'unnecessary' to decide which of the dogs began the fight.

Rogers pleaded guilty at Wood Green Crown Court to being the owner of a dog that had caused injury while dangerously out of control in public and the owner of a dog dangerously out of control. The judge made a contingent destruction order for Socks and a destruction order for Bailey.

Dr Davidson, a vet and the principal of a small animal veterinary clinic in the Home Counties, gave evidence for the defence in a written report that was adduced at the Crown Court. The judge took that into account in making his decision of destruction.

Rogers appealed in relation to Bailey. The appellant counsel claimed that the judge was wrong to order the death of Bailey. He should have ordered a contingent destruction order as he did for Socks.

Dr Shepherd was described by the Court of Appeal as an 'eminent dog psychiatrist'. Dr Shepherd, who did not appear at the Crown Court, prepared a report and gave evidence at the Court of Appeal. There appeared to be a disagreement between both of the experts as to the proper approach to be taken in considering how a court should resolve a dispute as to the disposition of a dog deemed to be 'dangerous'. In turn that was the underlying reason for the approach of the Court of Appeal.

Lord Chief Justice Lord Thomas [LCJ] said: 'There was a significant dispute between the experts as to issues relating to qualifications, expertise and to the video recording of examinations. Dr Shepherd appeared to insist, for example, that only those certified as Clinical Animal Behaviourists are sufficiently qualified to give evidence in this kind of case. We would invite the Royal College of Veterinary Medicine (to whom a copy of this judgment will be sent) to consider whether it should give guidance on these and other matters which would prevent similar disputes arising in the courts in the future. Very important issues relating to the safety of the public and very strong feelings on the part of owners and those injured by dogs can arise in cases under the Dangerous Dogs Act [1991]. For this reason it is a matter of some importance that the court should be able to have confidence that a person put forward as having the requisite expertise to give an opinion about matters, such as temperament, going to the heart of the issue whether a dog poses a danger to public safety, is appropriately qualified to express that opinion, and has sufficient data to support it.'

Within that judgment the court considered the subject of when they would receive *'fresh'* evidence that was not adduced in the lower court. The court held the decision was whether to admit fresh evidence is 'case and fact specific'. So each case will be decided on its own facts. Lord Thomas LCJ said that evidence that could and should have been raised at the original trial will only in *'exceptional circumstances'* be admitted on appeal. In the absence of some reasonable and cogent explanation for the original omission, it is highly unlikely that the 'interests of justice' test could be satisfied. In sentencing appeals, the court will scrutinise intensely any application to give a factual explanation that was not put before the sentencing court.

If the evidence was available it seems a strange decision not to present it at the original court. While who to call as a witness is a judgment call for every advocate, the problem remains that unless there are 'exceptional circumstances' the evidence will not be admitted in the Court of Appeal. In that event the likely result is the appeal will fail and the dog will die.

An aspect of the case that troubled the Crown Court judge and was endorsed by Lord Thomas LCJ was that the owner 'had not the first idea what to do to control Bailey when it broke away from her to attack the other dog'. Yet that 'important issue, which in many cases will be determinative, is the capability of the owner of the dog to control it' was not addressed during the appeal.

Defence counsel accepted that 'the way in which the expert evidence was presented to this court and to the judge was, as is evident from what we have set out, wholly unsatisfactory'. Lord Thomas LCJ concluded that: 'This is an extraordinary case in that what has been put before us by the appellant has undermined the evidence of an expert on whom the appellant sought to rely at Crown Court.' Given those obstacles relating to the owner and the manner the expert evidence was presented, the judgment of the Court of Appeal is not surprising. So the appeal failed and the dog would be destroyed.

An expert's role is so important in law that his or her analysis can determine the guilt of a defendant. In 2015 a tomography test carried out at a veterinary hospital on behalf of Nottingham University proved that a badger had been unlawfully killed by a gang of men using six dogs and shovels. The forensic tests confirmed that the DNA match on the shovel and a bloodstained vest worn by a defendant belonged to the same badger. Two of their dogs tested positive for the DNA of a badger. All four defendants were convicted.

An expert has the advantage for a court of providing evidence that is balanced and independent. His or her evidence tends to serve the interests of justice. The defence must be aware of that fundamental position.

9.3 Lead

The propensity of criminals is to possess dangerous status dogs that are sometimes used as a weapon no less than a gun or a knife. Then such a dog may be factually and legally equally 'dangerous'. If the dog injures any person, those liable are guilty of an *aggravated* offence. That liability would extend to both parties, namely (a) the owner and (b) if different, a person for the time being in charge of the dog.

The spread of liability was considered in *L v. Crown Prosecution Service* [2010] EWHC 341. The High Court clarified the meaning of being 'in charge' and confirmed that control is not relinquished by a temporary transfer of the leash. DJ Gott, at Newham Local Justice Area, found the defendant guilty of being in charge of a dog, a Staffordshire Terrier, which was dangerously out of control and caused injury to Toby Rajit. The co-defendant, Louie Green, was charged with the same offence. Green claimed duress, saying he was 'scared' of the co-defendant, L. Given the circumstances of the incident plus the relationship between the defendants, both were convicted.

The DJ made these findings of fact:

(a) L handed the lead to Louie while he tied his shoes;
(b) Louie ran at Toby shouting, 'get him, get him' and released the dog off the lead;
(c) The dog bit Toby, causing an injury that became infected and required an operation;
(d) Louie was in physical control of the dog when the dog attacked Toby.

The question was whether L was still in charge of the dog. L claimed he was not in charge at the crucial time because at that moment Louie had the lead and was in control. As the section states '*the person*', it was wrong to treat two persons as being in charge of the dog.

The DJ rejected L's submission and found him guilty because:

1. Louie and L knew the dog was dangerous as they were present when he bit a person on a recent previous occasion.
2. L was in effective control of the dog and in charge of him at all times.
3. Although Louie was in physical control, L was still in charge of the dog.

In the High Court Elias LJ said: 'In short, the view of the judge was that both were in charge, Louie had physical control, but the appellant retained effective control. The judge posed the following question for the court: "Was I wrong in law to find that the appellant could remain in charge of the dog despite the transfer of physical control to Louie and to find that both defendants could be in charge of the dog at the relevant time?"'

Elias LJ concluded the DJ did not make an error of law. The dog responded to the commands of L both before and after Louie took physical control. L would remain in charge of the dog if he was let off his lead in the park. Therefore he remained in charge even if there was a temporary period when he put the dog in physical control of Louie. As L had the legal authority to retrieve the dog at any time he was in a position to control the dog.

That was the right conclusion as the transfer was only temporary, while crucially the dog responded to the 'commands' of L. Given the relationship between a dog and his owner, with a word he could have ended the attack before it began, or at least while he was attacking the victim. Though L could have used his voice to make a difference, his culpable choice was silence. Therefore their joint knowledge led to their joint liability.

9.4   Charge

The length of time in *L v. CPS* was the focal point. In *R. v. Rawlings* [1994] Crim. L. R. 433 the Court of Appeal considered the transfer that involved keeping a dog for a longer period. Rawlings was charged with being a person for the time being in charge of a dog dangerously out of control that injured a person. Rawlings was looking after an Alsatian dog for a man who was in prison. She fed and exercised him. One afternoon the dog left the house and injured a nine year old boy. Rawlings had been out at work during the morning, returned home and then went out shopping; while she was shopping the dog got out, although she had locked the house. Rawlings' defence was that the woman with whom she lived had returned and was in the house when the dog escaped. So she denied being the person in charge 'at that time' within the meaning of the DDA. The judge directed the jury that she remained responsible even though she was out shopping. She appealed against conviction on the ground the judge had misdirected the jury and effectively withdrew her defence from them.

The court allowed the appeal as 'being in charge' was a question of fact and degree. There was an issue as to whether at the time the dog left the house Rawlings was still 'in charge' of him. Although the court considered that there was 'powerful evidence that she was', the judge should have left the issue to the jury. The decision was for them alone. Their decision is more significant given the increase in sentences by the ABCPA. [See: **S1**]

Rawlings, position was different from *L v. CPS* as there Louie and L were together in close proximity at all times throughout the incident. Although Louie had the lead, L had the authority and a voice the dog recognised. As L was present before and during the attack he could have stopped the dog in his tracks. The dog's recognition of his master's voice imbued L with the ability to control his dog's response. His choice was to allow the attack to happen and continue. In contrast, Rawlings had left the house. At that time the dog was in the company and control of the other woman, who had the choice and voice to exercise her authority over him. Rawlings was not capable of controlling the dog while she was absent from the house. So it was arguable as a matter of fact and degree that Rawlings was not in charge at the relevant time. Indeed, that is the reason the defence exists. [See: **9.8**]

9.5   Strict

When a dog injures a person while the owner is in charge, the fact that behaviour is unknown or unusual will not provide a defence. Then, if the dog bites the DDA does too. It will only be in extreme circumstances that the owner is not liable in law.

In *Regina v. Bezzina* [1994] 99 Cr. App. R. 356 the Court of Appeal held that although there was a *'presumption'* of law that *mens rea* was required before a person could be held guilty of a criminal offence, that presumption could be replaced where a statute was concerned with an issue of social concern and public safety. Hence, where a dog acts in a way that gave grounds for a 'reasonable apprehension' he would injure someone, an absolute liability is imposed upon the owner of that dog.

In 1993 Bezzina was convicted at Southwark Crown Court of an aggravated offence. An order was made that his dog is destroyed. He appealed on the grounds the judge had erred in ruling the offence was one of 'strict' liability.

Kennedy LJ said the words 'dangerously out of control' imposed a 'strict' liability on the owners of dogs of all sorts that are in public places. It was an objective standard of 'reasonable apprehension' that was not related to the state of mind of the dog owner. He explained that 'dangerously out of control' means if the dog is shown to be acting in a way that gives grounds for a reasonable apprehension he would injure anyone, liability follows. Then if a person is injured 'there must have been, immediately before the injury resulted, grounds for reasonable apprehension that injury would occur.'

A point made on behalf of the owner was that he or she may have no realisation that the dog is liable to behave in a way that will cause injury to anyone until, for example, a child pokes the dog with a stick and the dog reacts. The court was dismissive of the idea saying: 'That, indeed, may be the case. But it seems to us that Parliament was entitled to do what in this piece of legislation we find that it has done, namely to put the onus on the owner to ensure, if that is likely to happen, he takes steps which are effective to ensure that it does not, either by keeping the dog on a lead or keeping the child away from the dog or whatever may be appropriate in the circumstances.' The court dismissed the appeal.

Several areas of concern arise from this case. A perfectly well-behaved dog might be killed as a matter of law because he reacts to being poked with a stick by a child. That is unjust. What if the child pokes it into the dog's eye? Why should such provocative behaviour result in a criminal liability? That is using the law as a stick to beat the owner and the dog. A *'reasonable apprehension'* of injury cannot exist if up until the exact moment the dog reacts he had been pacific and the reaction was purely an instinctive reaction because he was suddenly poked in the eye by a child waving a sharp stick. Then it is not the dog that is not being controlled by its owner, but the child who was not being controlled by his parents.

Like humans, animals can suffer from P-TSD. Like the soldiers they serve beside, the dogs of war are subject to the psychological stress that affects the soldiers. Stanley Coren, a professor of psychology, said: 'In the past, the clinical world would have said you were crazy and anthropomorphising but the condition is now widely accepted.' When a dog affected by stress is hit or kicked without reason and bites his attacker, is his owner assumed to have a reasonable apprehension of that reaction? Are all dog owners deemed by law to be psychic?

If a dog unexpectedly bites a person and is immediately restrained thereafter, that cannot amount to a reasonable apprehension that it *'will'* do so. As 'apprehension' is 'anticipation especially with fear or dread' something that is unknown cannot induce that knowledge. *Bezzina* is a bad decision that has been followed in subsequent cases where the reasoning is similarly flawed. The necessary apprehension is neither reasonable nor real. The judicial attempt to try and justify the position in subsequent cases has resulted in confusion rather than clarity. [See: **16.6**]

A dog that suffers from P-TSD or is recovering from an operation may not be dangerous at all, but if he is kicked may defend himself or his owner. Indeed, expert evidence would be admissible if it would tend to prove that the dog reacted as he did because his master or he was attacked. That would be relevant to and assist any decision of a magistrate or a jury as to conviction and sentence. Provocation should be a defence at best and at least provide mitigation that could avoid a destruction order. After all, for humans provocation is a defence to murder.

Pitchford J in the Court of Appeal made a notable point in *R. v. Holland* [2003] 1 Cr. App. R. (S) 60 when he said: 'The recorder expressly excluded the idea that the dog was being teased or tormented.' The Crown Court and Court of Appeal concentrated on that point. Thus if the dog had been *'teased or tormented'* and then reacted, such evidence was relevant and admissible. [See: **10.7**]

Now 'expert' evidence is not only admissible, it is a prerequisite of the conditions the court has to address in considering the dog's fate and future. It is time for *Bezzina* to be revisited and revised to avoid injustice to an owner and his dog. [See: **16.3**]

9.6   Notice

Even with such severe measures the concept of natural justice cannot be ignored. In *R. v. Trafford Magistrates' Court ex parte Riley* [1995] 160 JP 418, Riley, the owner of a dog, had an argument with her friend. Following the dispute and without Riley's knowledge, her friend took the dog to a nearby car park. Although the dog was on a leash, as her friend was unable to control him he bit a police officer. A summons was issued against her friend. She pleaded guilty and the magistrates ordered the destruction of the dog. Riley applied for judicial review of that decision, claiming that she ought to have been given notice of the hearing.

The High Court held that although the magistrates had no discretion in whether to order the destruction of the dog, if Riley had been notified she could have attended the hearing and argued that in the circumstances the prosecution was an abuse of the process. Riley may have argued that the car park was not a public place – [an important legal point at the time] – or that the friend had entered her guilty plea maliciously. In any case concerning the destruction of property, the rules of natural justice required a known owner of property to be given the opportunity to be heard. The conviction and order for destruction were quashed. The matter was remitted to the Magistrates' Court.

That decision was not because the dog was a living creature, but purely that he was a person's *property*. Though the 'place' has changed, the legal principle remains the same. [See: **10.5**]

9.7   Fitness

The owner may have a defence if he was not in charge of the dog at the material time and he proves the person who was, was someone whom he 'reasonably believed to be a fit and proper person to be in charge of it'. That has the advantage for the owner as a defence, especially as he would have been absent or not in charge of the dog at the 'material time'. It could be temporary possession by the other person while the owner used a public toilet, or longer if he went to the dentist. Equally it applies if the owner allows the person to take his dog to the park, where he then bites someone. As it is for the defendant to 'prove' the person was a 'fit and proper person' to be in charge, the burden is on him to establish the defence.

The transfer could be for a longer period, such as when the owner is on holiday, or in hospital or prison. Then the character of the one he chose could provide a defence.

The defence was considered by the Court of Appeal in *R. v. Harter* [1998] Crim. L. R. 336. Harter was convicted of being the owner of a dog dangerously out of control. At a time when Harter was absent, a tethered dog bit a visitor to his scrap yard. His daughter, who also worked at the scrap yard, was present. When he was interviewed, Harter said: 'The Harter family own the dogs.' The co-defendant, his daughter, gave evidence that she was the owner of the dog in question. She produced evidence he had been sold to her *alone*. Harter's defence was that he was not the owner.

The court held the judge should have directed the jury that if they found Harter was the owner, then they should consider the statutory defence. His failure to direct the jury was a material non-direction. As that went to a substantial defence, the conviction was quashed.

The Crown Court judge overlooked the important point that if the defendant believed his daughter owned the dog the jury might have concluded he was the family pet, so Harter was a co-owner. Harter should have been able to 'prove' the dog was in the charge of a person whom he reasonably believed to be a fit and proper person.

Now it is a stronger position as the court is under a mandatory duty by the ABCPA to assess whether the one in charge of the dog is '*a fit and proper person*'. The importance of that duty is that the answer affects the fortune of the dog as well as his owner. A fitness for purpose places a duty on the owner to choose a person who is capable of controlling his dog. Choosing the right person is crucial. The wrong choice would mean for one it could be prison and for the other it could be death. [See: **17.12**]

9.8   Transfer

The Court of Appeal considered that defence again in *R. v. Huddart* [1999] Crim. L.R. 568. Huddart was the owner of a Rottweiler dog. A Rottweiler was roaming on its own and bit a man exercising his dog in a field. The issue for the jury was whether the Rottweiler that bit the man was the same dog owned by Huddart. His defence was his dog had not left his garden at the material time, so it was another Rottweiler that bit the man. Although there was no formal transfer of the dog to her, Huddart claimed his wife opened the door of their house to let the dog into the garden. At the trial the judge directed the jury to disregard that defence. Huddart appealed, contending the judge's direction was wrong.

The court held that the defence was not intended, where a dog was kept at home, to analyse which member of the family was in charge at any one moment. The fact the door the dog escaped through was opened by a member of the family rather than by the owner was not evidence the charge of the dog had been transferred. The defence operated only if there was *'evidence'* the dog had been transferred to someone other than the owner. There had to be evidence that supported the inference that the owner had for the time being divested himself of responsibility in favour of an identifiable person. Here there was no evidence to support the inference the dog was transferred from the owner to his wife. To adopt such an approach would be artificial and contrary to the purpose of that defence. As the judge was right, the appeal was dismissed.

The court was concerned the 'statutory defence' would be diluted and become ineffectual. There was no evidence Huddart had transferred the charge to his wife. A point Huddart had perhaps overlooked was if there had been a transfer his wife could have been liable. [See: **9.3**]

The court restricted the defence to cases where the owner has taken action to transfer the charge of the dog to another. That would apply to someone such as a vet, a kennel, a neighbour, or a cohabitant as in *R. v. Rawlings*. [See: **9.4**]

In the Scottish Case of *Swinlay v. Crowe* [1995] SLT 34 the High Court confirmed that when an owner transfers the charge of his dog to another person his responsibility for the dog then ends. His responsibility is regained if and when he retakes charge of the dog. That is part of the reason the court is strict in its interpretation of the section for otherwise there would be a legal limbo where no one is liable. That would not assist the owner, the dog, any victim, the public or the law.

Given the choice between a dangerous dog without an owner or a doubt as to who is in charge, the court places the burden where it properly belongs: it remains on the defendant to establish his defence. Then at least the owner could be liable. It also allows the court to protect the dog from an irresponsible owner and probable death. [See: **Chapter 17**]

9.9   DA

The Dogs Act 1871 [DA] is an additional power for the prosecution under the DDA. Using the DA has a distinct advantage for the prosecution. The jurisdiction of the English courts applies even if an offence is committed outside England. Neil Shufflebottom went to Scotland on holiday and stayed in a caravan where his dog bit Charlotte Gabbittas and caused her 'serious injuries'.

When he was charged before Stockport Magistrates' Court he claimed it had no jurisdiction to hear the case. In *The Queen on the application of Neil Shufflebottom v. Chief Constable of Greater Manchester Police* [2003] EWHC 246 the High Court rejected his claim.

Mackay J said: 'Dog owners within the jurisdiction who own dogs wherever they may be, or wherever they may have been, whose conduct, wherever it took place, evidenced the proposition that they were dangerous dogs, thus giving rise to a consideration of the appropriateness of one or other of the remedies available … that was so notwithstanding the fact that the supporting evidence justifying the complaint arose from an incident outside their jurisdiction and indeed, outside the jurisdiction of any English court.'

Even with the ABCPA, that advantage for the prosecution within the DA remains.

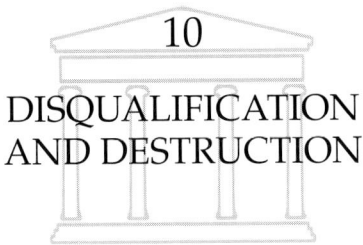

10

DISQUALIFICATION AND DESTRUCTION

10.1 Dangerous Dogs Act 1991 s.4

(1) Where a person is convicted of an offence under section 1 or 3(1) or (3) above or of an offence under an order made under section 2 above the court

   (a) may order the destruction of any dog in respect of which the offence was committed and, subject to subsection (1A) below, shall do so in the case of an offence under section 1 or an aggravated offence under section 3(1) or (3) above; and

   (b) may order the offender to be disqualified, for such period as the court thinks fit, for having custody of a dog.

(1A) Nothing in subsection 1(a) shall require the court to order the destruction of a dog if the court is satisfied

   (a) that the dog would not constitute a danger to public safety

   …

When the DDA was introduced numerous dogs were rounded up and destroyed, often without cause or reason. The comment in *Cichon v. DPP* by Schiemann J was typical of the court's concern: 'We have here an absolute prohibition and a breach of that prohibition is to be followed by an order for the dog's destruction, however blameless the dog and its owner.' [See: **8.4**]

This amendment under section (1A) governs the court's discretion. The court does not have to order its death if it is satisfied the dog would not constitute *'a danger to public safety'*. [See: **11.4**]

10.2   Principles

The Court of Appeal set out the guiding principles for the court to apply in the leading authority of *R. v. Flack* [2008] 2 Cr. App. R. (S) 70. Flack pleaded guilty to being the owner of a dog, Star, which caused injury while dangerously out of control. He also pleaded guilty to being in charge of a dog, Snoop, while dangerously out of control in a public place.

A couple walking through Ridgway Park in Lymm, Cheshire, with their three grandchildren noticed two dogs running towards them. One of the dogs attacked the female member of the couple, causing a severe wound to her leg. Flack pleaded guilty on a specified 'basis'. The Crown Court made a contingent destruction order in respect of Snoop and a destruction order in respect of Star. The appeal was limited to Star.

Silber J said: 'The basis upon which the appellant pleaded guilty was that an unknown third party had opened the gate behind which the dogs were secured, thereby allowing them to escape.'

Dr Candy d'Sa, an animal behaviour consultant, explained that she carried out an assessment of the dogs Star and Snoop over a period of two hours. She concluded that they were both sociable to people, very friendly and very playful with each other. In her report Dr d'Sa said that Star was a neutered bitch Rottweiler crossed with a German Shepherd dog. She was used as a therapy dog to visit the elderly in care homes. This had required rigorous training so far as her temperament was concerned. Dr d'Sa considered that Star and Snoop were friendly and interactive and they responded to commands. The dogs displayed no signs of aggression. She considered that the cause of the attack might possibly have been that the dogs had been anxious on escaping from their garden and that they had reacted with fear to unfamiliar stimuli. Her conclusion was that there was no evidence that Star or Snoop were inherently aggressive or dangerous dogs and that Flack showed he was a capable and an experienced dog owner.

There were eight references before the recorder in respect of Star. The grounds of appeal were that Star did not constitute a danger to the public and therefore should be exempted from destruction. It was contended there should have been stringent conditions upon Flack in relation to the future behaviour of Star with the sanction of the dog being destroyed if he failed to comply.

Silber J set out the 'relevant principles' in respect of a dog whose owner has been convicted under section 3. Those are:

1. The court is empowered to order the destruction of the dog.
2. Nothing shall require the court to order the destruction if the court is satisfied that the dog would not constitute a danger to public safety.
3. The court should ordinarily consider, before ordering immediate destruction, whether to exercise the power … to order that, unless the owner keeps it under proper control, the dog shall be destroyed ('a suspended order of destruction').
4. A suspended order of destruction may specify the measures to be taken by the owner for keeping the dog under control whether by muzzling, keeping the dog on a lead, or excluding the dog from a specified place or otherwise.
5. A court should not order destruction if satisfied that the imposition of such a condition would mean the dog would not constitute a danger to public safety.
6. In deciding what order to make, the court must consider all the relevant circumstances, which include the dog's history of aggressive behaviour and the owner's history of controlling the dog in order to determine what order should be made.

The recorder did not consider a suspended ['*contingent*'] destruction order. Star had not previously been aggressive. There was evidence from an animal behaviour consultant. It was a relevant factor that Flack was a man of good character. Silber J said the recorder made: 'No order disqualifying him from owning or being in control of dogs. We are not surprised by that conclusion. It is clear from the evidence before us that the appellant is a competent and conscientious dog owner.'

As a result, the court quashed the order for destruction. Silber J said: 'Instead we make an order that, unless the appellant keeps Star under proper control, she will be destroyed. We also impose the same conditions that were imposed in relation to Snoop: (1) Star shall be muzzled in public places at all times; (2) she must wear a special collar to keep her under control; and (3) she must be kept on a lead at all times in public.'

The principles specified in *Flack* have become the benchmark for the courts in subsequent cases. They are fair in aim and approach by taking into account the factors that affect the public, the owner and the dog. In making their assessment the court took into account the expert evidence and the 'character' of the appellant and his dog. That approach is even more relevant as a result of the ABCPA and the Sentencing Guidelines. [See: **19.4**]

The principles in *Flack* are the bellwether for other courts to follow in the future. A sound decision which has heard that clang is *R. v. Devon* [2011] EWCA Crim 1073 where the Court of Appeal quashed the destruction order and substituted a contingent one. The Court made it conditional on the dog being rehomed with a suitable owner. [See: **17.10**]

10.3   Neutered

The principles framed in *Flack* were followed in *R. v. Harry* [2010] EWCA Crim 673. Jamie Harry appeared at Mold Crown Court and pleaded guilty to two counts of being in charge of a dog that caused injury while dangerously out of control in a public place. Count 1 related to an English bull terrier known as Snoop. Count 2 related to a Staffordshire bull terrier called Millie. Harry was sentenced to a 12 months' conditional discharge. A destruction order was made for both dogs. Harry appealed against that order.

Harry arrived at his parents' home at Chestnut Avenue. His parents were absent. At that time the dogs were living inside as his parents were having building work done to the rear of the property. Harry released the two dogs into the garden. The builders had been told to ensure that the side gate, which gave access to the front of the house and the road, 'remained closed at all times'. Naturally, one of the workmen left the side gate open. As a result both dogs escaped into the street.

The victim walked towards his car parked outside his girlfriend's house. The dogs ran towards him. At first they appeared friendly. Then Snoop jumped up and bit the victim on his legs and stomach and back. He ran to his girlfriend's house, which was locked. He then ran to a neighbour's home. The dogs followed, both biting him on his back. He stumbled, threw his jacket at the dogs but they continued chasing him. He arrived at another house on Chestnut Avenue and a resident let him in. He trapped one of the dogs' heads in the door. The victim was taken to hospital and made a good recovery.

In the Court of Appeal Davies J said, Harry 'accepted that the gate had been left open. A letter was before the court from D & K Home Improvements Limited confirming that at some time during 13 August 2008 the gate was left open by mistake by one of the building team. In that letter Mr Small, a director of the company, stated that at all times when the work was being carried out the dogs had been in their cage and even when they were let loose in the back garden they caused no harm to any member of staff and were playful'.

Davies J said Harry was a man of good character and pleaded guilty on the 'basis' the workmen had left the side gate open and he had let the dogs out without first checking that the gate was secure. It was accepted by the recorder that Harry and his parents were conscientious dog owners, who cared for their animals and who had an excellent record of animal ownership. Neither dog had ever done anything of this nature before and neither dog had shown any propensity to act in the way that each did on this single occasion. The court was shown photographs of the accommodation that had been built for the dogs at the rear of the property since completion of the building works. It was an enclosed and roofed kennel that would significantly reduce the chance of the dogs being able to escape.

The court cited and relied upon the principles Silber J specified in *R. v. Flack*.

Davies J added: 'It is the appellant's case that if the recorder was considering a destruction order, he should have allowed the application made on behalf of the appellant to adjourn that part of the hearing, to allow for the preparation of a report on the dogs by an animal behavioural consultant.'

The court relied on the Criminal Appeal Act 1968 [CAA], which allows the court to receive any evidence relating to the appeal if it is in the 'interests of justice' to do so. [See: **9.2**]

That evidence was a report prepared by Madeleine Forsyth, a veterinary surgeon, who examined both dogs in the absence of their owner, but in the presence of a police officer and a representative from the kennels where they had been placed after the attack. She found Millie to be in good physical condition, extremely friendly and placid in manner, displaying no aggression, either to herself or her main handler from the kennels. She was in no doubt that Millie was a friendly domestic pet.

Forsyth described Snoop as a good example of his breed and in good bodily condition. She found him to be friendly and amenable to verbal command. He allowed examination without objection. He showed no signs of aggression, but was boisterous and powerful. Neither dog displayed any aggressive attributes as a normal behavioural characteristic. The manner and demeanour of each dog was entirely consistent with the status of a friendly family pet.

The court made a contingent destruction order for both dogs with a condition (a) they were kept under proper control and restraint and (b) Snoop had to be neutered within 56 days.

The gate was opened by a third party who had disobeyed a direct instruction. Nevertheless, Harry was at fault to a degree in failing to check that the gate was secure before he let the dogs out. The onus was on him to do so.

The ABCPA endorses those sound principles in relation to the owner and his dog. [See: **17.12**]

10.4   Identity

The practical importance of *R. v. Flack* can be seen from the Court of Appeal decision in *R. v. Davies* [2010] EWCA Crim 1923. Davies was convicted at Harrow Crown Court. The particulars of the offence were important as they alleged that he 'on the 5th of September 2008 was in charge of a *dog* which was dangerously out of control in a public place, namely Larkspur Close, Kingsbury, and whilst so out of control injured Caroline Foley'. [Emphasis added by the judge]

Mrs Recorder Bickford-Smith sentenced Davies to a community order and made a destruction order for his Alsatian dog. The appeal was limited to that order.

Caroline Foley, a neighbour of Davies, was walking her dog on a lead towards a green space at the bottom of her road. At the same time Davies was walking his two dogs, an Alsatian and a Labrador. They were not on leads or otherwise controlled in any way. They ran towards Foley and attacked her dog. She tried to pull her dog away and in doing so placed her hand over its chest. One of Davies' dogs bit her finger, inflicting a large open wound. She could not tell which of the two dogs had bitten her.

The two limbs of the appeal were that (a) the recorder was wrong to find that the Alsatian bit Mrs Foley and (b), if the first limb fails, the recorder was wrong to make a destruction order rather than, at most, a contingent destruction order.

In considering whether the sentence was right Mackay J said: 'It is the appellant who is seeking to displace a mandatory consequence and it is the appellant who will normally be the owner of the dog or a person entrusted with its care and who will be best placed to know about and adduce evidence of its characteristics. Such evidence may be of an expert nature (as was led in *Flack*) or it may be lay evidence relating to such matters as the dog's character, demeanour and general past behaviour. But the matter does not end there, because section 4A allows for a contingent destruction order even if a destruction order, mandatory or discretionary, is otherwise appropriate. That section was construed by this court in *Flack* by Silber J … in an analysis with which we agree.'

The problem was the recorder was not referred to any of those provisions. Initially 'she was under the impression that as she had identified the Alsatian as the biting dog a destruction order was mandatory … Defence counsel accepted that and said no more. He made no application to lead any evidence on this topic. He did not refer to the case of *Flack* or to the further obligation to consider a contingent destruction order.

So both the recorder and the defence were at fault. The court concluded that the order for destruction must be quashed. It was replaced by a contingent destruction order that the Alsatian must be muzzled and kept on a lead.

It is significant that the court not only followed *Flack* in aim and effect, but that Mackay J stated that defence counsel did not refer to it 'or to the further obligation to consider a contingent destruction order ...' That placed a duty on the defence as well as the court. After all, the court can only act on the evidence it is presented with rather than indulge in speculation. That duty is on the defence by the ABCPA as the court has a mandatory duty to '*consider*' the character of the dog and his owner. The court can only fulfil its own duty if the defence fulfils its too. So the court can expect each party to produce the evidence that enables it to comply with its statutory duty. Moreover, given its duty to the court as a 'minister of justice', it places a positive duty on the prosecution too. If either or both fail to do so the onus is on the court to adjourn the matter for the representatives to obtain the relevant evidence. The failure by the court to fulfil its own duty would provide a ground for an appeal. [See: **4.2**]

That avoids an unjust decision such as in *Hooker* where the High Court upheld the Crown Court order for destruction rather than a contingency destruction order. The High Court noted that the defendant did not produce any evidence in the Crown Court from an animal behaviour consultant, though he could have done so. Consequently, as his dog had bitten a person and caused injury the court had no 'reassurance' that he would not do so again.

Yet the defendant was a dog owner for 30 years and of good character. Further, he had retired due to ill-health and needed the help of his dog to climb stairs. Finally, the defence obtained two reports from an expert. Treacy LJ said: 'We are not minded to consider the contents of those reports.' As a result the 'rescued' dog was ordered to be destroyed.

Their peremptory approach, even if the owner and the defence were in the wrong, was unfair. The court could and should if it felt it was warranted 'punish' the defence by a costs order against it, not a destruction order killing the dog. That would have been a fair trial, now it would be contrary to the court's statutory duty under the ABCPA. If this unjust decision was followed, an appeal should be lodged.

A critical distinction that highlights the poor judgment in *Hooker* is that in *Rogers* the defence had the evidence at the Crown Court, but chose not to use it. In *Hooker* it only obtained the reports *after* the trial at the Crown Court for the appeal. [See: **9.2**]

10.5 Natural

The principle of natural justice demands that a person is informed if he is to be deprived of his property. It does not even matter whether the order is right or wrong as a matter of law. The important principle remains that a person's property cannot be destroyed without his knowledge and the opportunity to raise an objection to that result. In *R. v. Ealing Magistrates' Court ex parte Fanneran* it was Fanneran's nephew who pleaded guilty to being in charge of a pit bull terrier in a public place without it being muzzled, contrary to the DDA. He had removed the muzzle in order to allow it to be sick. When the defendant appeared before Ealing Magistrates' Court he was fined and the dog was ordered to be destroyed. Fanneran, who was the owner of the dog, obtained an injunction restraining the police from destroying the dog and applied for judicial review of the magistrates' decision. She submitted that as she was not notified of the hearing the magistrates' order should be quashed. The High Court held that, although in all probability the presence of the applicant at the hearing would not have made any difference, the fact remained that she should have been told of the hearing. Her application for judicial review was allowed as the magistrates failed to follow the tenets of natural justice. The destruction order was quashed and the case remitted to the Magistrates' Court.

Staughton LJ said: 'The notion that when the rules of natural justice have not been observed, one can still uphold the result because it would not have made any difference, is to be treated with great caution. Down that slippery slope lies the way to dictatorship.'

Rougier J said: 'No one can ever say for certain what must have happened in the circumstances which have not, in fact arisen. The robing rooms up and down this land are full of strange tales of seemingly impregnable cases foundering on some unforeseen forensic reef. It is not, in my opinion, for this court to employ its imagination to postulate facts which might or might not have succeeded had the rules of natural justice been followed.'

A rubber duck hooked by a child at a fairground and a real one hooked by an angler are just *'things'* as a matter of law. Legally the duck is classified no differently than the angler's hook. Nevertheless, one reason that is stronger than most leans inexorably towards natural justice in this kind of case: unlike the normal case of destroying a person's personal property that can easily be replaced even at a price, a dog that becomes a corpse cannot be revived. [See: **9.6**]

10.6   Appeal

As the person convicted may not be the owner of the dog, there is a right of appeal by the owner to the Crown Court. This allows the owner the opportunity to avoid the order for destruction, as in *Fanneran*. Then the dog cannot be destroyed pending the appeal.

The court order cannot be effective:

(a)   until the end of the period for giving notice of appeal against the conviction or the order; and

(b)   if notice is given, until the appeal is determined or withdrawn.

When a person is convicted of these offences he is often reluctant to hand over the dog in question, which is often his pet. Sometimes he transfers the dog to another person so he cannot be traced. Therefore the court has power when it makes such an order to appoint a person to arrange the destruction and require any person having custody of the dog to 'deliver it up' for that purpose.

The court may order the defendant to pay all the attendant expenses of destroying his dog. It may make him pay for the dog's keep prior to and pending the destruction. If the offender is ordered to pay those expenses it can be enforced as if it were a fine imposed on conviction. Therefore, as with any actual fine, it could lead to imprisonment if it is unpaid. Unpaid fines are often 'written off' by a court with a concurrent sentence when the offender reoffends.

10.7   Disqualify

A person may be disqualified for any period up to and including a life ban. Whatever the period, a person may apply for a termination of the disqualification a year after the date of the order.

The Court of Appeal considered the position in *R. v. Holland* [2003] 1 Cr. App. R. (S) 60 and gave useful guidance to any subsequent court that had to deal with an application by a disqualified person. Elizabeth Holland pleaded guilty at Liverpool Crown Court to allowing a dog she was in charge of to enter a property in Strawberry Road and injure an eight year old child, Kathryn. Her son left his Staffordshire bull terrier, Rickson, with her. On Sunday afternoon her neighbours were entertaining their family, including their grandchildren. Two of the grandchildren were in the garden playing with a ball when the dog forced its way through wire fencing and ran towards the children. Rickson attacked one of the children, Kathryn, gripping her ankle, then her leg and finally her clothing in the vicinity of her chest.

Pitchford J said: 'The ferocity of the dog's attack and its determination to remain locked on the child was such that it was able to resist punches and blows with a mop handle. It desisted only when the appellant called the dog away.' Kathryn was taken to hospital where it was found that she had an injury just above the right knee that would leave a permanent scar. Holland was fined, ordered to pay compensation and disqualified from having custody of a dog for ten years. Rickson was ordered to be destroyed. She appealed against the length of the disqualification and the destruction order for her dog.

From the start the court was unsympathetic generally and dismissive of the evidence presented in support of the appeal. Pitchford J said: 'There was before the recorder and before us no evidence that the dog was other than a danger in circumstances such as we have just described. The recorder expressly excluded the idea that the dog was being teased or tormented.' Hence it would have relevance if that were the position. [See: **9.5**]

A petition signed by number of people who lived in the area of Liverpool before it moved to be with Holland at Strawberry Road, confirmed Rickson was not a dangerous dog. Pitchford J pointedly said: 'No doubt those persons who felt able to make that assertion would have made it on the day before this incident occurred. We are bound to say that it provides no evidence of the type which the court would require to avoid an order for destruction.'

The court was provided with a letter from Kenneth Fogg, headed, 'Sublyme Bull Terriers' of Stockport in Cheshire. Pitchford J said: 'Mr Fogg makes it clear that he does not have a veterinary qualification and that the purpose of his visit to see the bull terrier named Rickson at the council kennels in Birkenhead was to assess the well-being of the dog. He specifically did not express any opinion about the circumstances in which the dog came to be housed in council kennels. Again, we find ourselves quite unable to attach to this letter any weight for the purpose of reaching a conclusion whether this was a dangerous dog in circumstances such as we have described.' Given those circumstances the court's view remained hostile. [Why did the defence not obtain an expert's report?]

The court was equally unsympathetic to Holland. Pitchford J said: 'The purpose of the disqualification is both punitive and preventative. As to the punitive element as it concerns this particular case, we have been provided with a number of testimonials from persons who know both the appellant and the fact she has possessed dogs over many years.' The court remained unimpressed so the disqualification remained.

Pitchford J went further: 'It is asserted before us today, without evidence in support, that the grandparents have in fact moved. There is no confirmation of that bare assertion. In any event, it seems to us that fact alone would not meet the recorder's concerns as to the nature of the animal which the appellant might keep at this property in future.' [Why did the defence not present evidence rather than a 'bare assertion'?]

In contrast to the defence, the court had 'sympathy with the recorder's purpose … A balance should, however, be struck between the sensitivities of the victim on the one hand and the restriction on the freedom of the custodian on the other. Disqualification prohibits the appellant from keeping not merely an aggressive or dangerous dog, but any dog at all.'

The court went much further by placing the case in context for the future lest Holland make another application. Pitchford J said: 'We consider that the recorder was right to conclude that the risk of emotional, if not physical harm, to the child was a continuing one and that the onus of demonstrating that she was a fit and proper person to have custody of a dog should remain with the appellant … We would not intend to bind the court which hears such an application, but it is likely to be measured against the proposals of the appellant, first, as to the breed of dog she proposes to keep; second, as to the existence of secure fencing around her property; and, thirdly, who are her neighbours at the time when the application is made.'

The result was a foregone conclusion: they dismissed the appeal and confirmed the dog's death.

While the decision was no surprise, the absence of evidence of an expert who could have examined Rickson after the event is surprising. That is usual and one that often finds favour with the court. Notwithstanding there appears to be a paucity of evidence available on Rickson, nevertheless the court was wrong to be so dismissive of the evidence provided by the petition and Fogg and the references on Holland. All of that is admissible and relevant to the decision of the court. Indeed, it is specifically referred to in the leading authority of *R. v. Flack*. Such evidence may be of an expert nature or lay evidence relating to such matters as the dogs character, demeanour and general past behaviour. [See: **9.2**]

The elementary practical solution to the problem would be for the defence to seek the permission of the court to adduce further evidence and agree to an undertaking as to the owner's future conduct. Being unimpressed with the quality of the defence evidence imbues the feeble reasoning and error of judgment by the court in failing to order an adjournment. Why did the court not simply adjourn the hearing, of its own motion or a defence application, to obtain the evidence that could have saved the dog's life? [See: **10.8; 11.2**]

The Court of Appeal has confirmed the position in *R. v. Baballa* [2011] 1 Cr. App. R. (S) 50 where Swift J put the duty of the judge beyond doubt: 'It seems that … the case of *Flack* was not brought to the judge's attention. We consider that, if it had been, and if he had followed the approach set out in that case, he could and should have been satisfied that a contingent order of destruction would suffice.'

A solicitous lesson that the court in *Holland* should have followed in fairness to both the defendant and her dog was delivered by Davies J in *R. v. Harry* [2010] EWCA Crim 673: 'It is the appellant's case that if the recorder was considering a destruction order, he should have allowed the application made on behalf of the appellant to adjourn that part of the hearing, to allow for the preparation of a report on the dogs by an animal behavioural consultant.' [See: **10.3**]

As a matter of practice the defence should unquestionably provide an expert report for the court as to the character and disposition of the dog on the *first* appearance, namely in the Magistrates' Court. If it is favourable it should save the dog. If though it is favourable a destruction order is still imposed, it would provide a ground of appeal. If a report is not available an adjournment should be sought to obtain one. If it is refused it would be a ground of appeal that would be persuasive in any appeal court.

Following the introduction of the ABCPA, the need for an expert report is now *essential*. The prosecution and defence could and indeed would be failing in their duty to fail to obtain one. As a corollary the onus is also on the court to adjourn the case if one is not available. So *Holland* should not be followed in future as more than merely a bad decision, it is irreconcilable with the principles promoted by the ABCPA. Being unimpressed by the defendant and the defence may lead to a costs order. It is not a legal reason to kill his dog. [See: **9.2**]

10.8   Undertake

The Court of Appeal solved a potentially problematic legal point in *R. v. Haynes* [2004] 2 Cr. App. R. (S) 9 using first principles to find a fair resolution. Rodney Haynes was convicted at Woolwich Crown Court of three counts of being the owner of a dog that was danger-ously out of control and injured a person. The three counts related to the same incident. Haynes owned three dogs. He lived in a block of flats that adjoined two play areas, one for children and one for dogs. Haynes took his dogs to exercise in the dog play area. There was a hedge with a gate at each end. Haynes left the dogs there while he had a conversation with a neighbour on the balcony. The dogs escaped from their play area and attacked a seven year old girl who was riding a bicycle. They ran towards her, knocked her off her bike and surrounded her. The girl was taken to hospital and found to have grazes on her abdomen, superficial wounds to the front of her thigh and a graze below her eye. She was allowed to go home after about an hour.

Haynes pleaded not guilty. He did not dispute that the child had been attacked by his dogs, but suggested that the dogs had escaped from the dog area as a result of some other person opening one of the gates. He was convicted by the jury and sentenced to an order of forfeiture of the dogs and disqualified from keeping a dog for three years.

In the Court of Appeal HHJ Roberts said Haynes had suggested that someone, possibly the little girl, must have opened one of the gates of the dog area and thus allowed them to escape. So the incident was unforeseeable and there was no actual fault on his part. He added, 'however, the offence is … of strict liability and the jury had little alternative but to convict him.'

The court was sympathetic from the start to the position of Haynes as the appeal raised an unusual point of law and practice. The specialist in animal behaviour found that the dogs were in excellent condition and that they did not show any signs of aggression. He recommended that Haynes should be permitted to retain one dog, which should be surgically castrated. The other two dogs should be allocated to other owners. However, the power available to the sentencing judge did not permit him to make such an order. As the judge was satisfied the dogs did not constitute a danger to public safety, a destruction order was inappropriate. There was no statutory power to disqualify a person from having custody of more than one dog and to specify conditions under which an offender might be permitted to retain one dog. Reluctantly the judge made an order of disqualification on Haynes and as a consequence ordered forfeiture of the dogs.

The court's view was instructive as it shows how a professional defence team should act. HHJ Roberts said: 'Before the trial the appellant's solicitors had very sensibly instructed the well-known specialist in animal behaviour, Dr Roger Mugford, to examine all three dogs in police custody. Dr Mugford is the head of a referral practice which specialises in the treatment of aggressive dogs. He conducted his examination with a visiting Canadian animal behaviourist. He examined each dog on their own. He found that they were all in excellent condition … None of them showed any signs of aggression. They played happily and appropriately and related well to another dog to which Dr Mugford introduced them. He described them all as friendly and attractive dogs, individually a delight, and he did not think any of them on their own presented a danger to the public. He attributed the incident to "pack behaviour" when left without human supervision and he thought their motives were more likely to have been playful than aggressive. However, as he rightly stated, whatever their motives were, the outcome for the little girl must have been extremely frightening and her physical injuries could well have been more serious.'

Dr Mugford recommended that none of the three dogs should be destroyed. He considered only one dog, Bow, should be returned to Haynes and that a condition of the return should be that it is surgically castrated. The remaining two dogs should be transferred to the Metropolitan Police, which would arrange to rehome them.

The court resolved it by a judicial percipience that satisfied Haynes and saved the dogs. HHJ Roberts said he did not criticise the recorder. However, there was another course open to him that if he knew of he would 'almost certainly have followed. In deciding whether to make a disqualification order and whether to order the forfeiture of any or all of the dogs, he was entitled to have regard to any voluntary undertaking offered by the appellant as to the appellant's future conduct. Such an undertaking would not form part of any court order, but it could be reduced into writing and a copy provided to the police …'

An undertaking without a sanction would be valueless. So the court spelled out the consequences to Haynes: 'It would follow that in the event of any further offence being committed by the appellant and it being found that he was in breach of his undertaking, that breach would be treated as a serious aggravating factor and would almost certainly lead to the loss of the dog or dogs in question.'

Haynes impressed the court as, regardless of the recommendation of Dr Mugford, it concluded: 'We have not insisted that the appellant should include in the undertaking an agreement to have Bow castrated. That is a matter about which the appellant has very strong feelings, which we understand, and we do not feel that it is necessary to include that in the undertaking, so it is not included in it.'

After Haynes gave a *signed* undertaking, the court quashed the disqualification order and the forfeiture order relating to Bow. The defence approach was a prime example of good practice in gaining the expert evidence *before* the trial, which found favour with the court. [See: **10.7**]

10.9   Character

When the court considers an application for removal of a disqualification it may have regard to the applicant's 'character', his conduct since the disqualification was imposed and any 'other circumstances' of the case. It may then grant or refuse the application. Whatever its decision, the court may order the applicant to pay all or any part of the costs of it. If the application is refused, then no further application can be made until a year after the date of that refusal.

The concept of 'character' is very wide following the changes by the CJA. Any violent offences the applicant has been convicted of meanwhile could reflect on his character. There is a well-proven connection between violence to animals and people as a person with a propensity for violence can affect his conduct with dogs. A violent owner can change the character of his dog, making him violent too.

Moreover, unlike the AWA, there is no provision for preventing a person from making an application after the one-year period. By the AWA the court can specify a period in which the defendant cannot apply or reapply. That is just another deficiency of the DDA. [See: **4.29**]

The orders are enforced by the court in relation to any person who has custody of a dog in contravention of an order or fails to comply with a requirement imposed under this section. He is thereby guilty of an offence. He would be liable on conviction to a fine. Such a sentence seems and is unduly lenient as by then he has already been convicted of a serious offence. That reflects the inherent weakness of the DDA.

How a person acts and reacts to any disqualification can be decisive in such an application. If he applies for termination of the order: 'The court may have regard to the applicant's character, his conduct since the disqualification was imposed and any other circumstances of the case.' That spells out the importance of character, which is often significant in cases of animal abuse.

The connection between animal cruelty and child cruelty is accentuated by the fact those who are cruel to animals as children often graduate to use violence on people. In 2012 a boy put a neighbour's cat in a microwave oven. As the boy was eight years old he was below the age of criminal responsibility. He is a potentially dangerous child who with time might turn to violent crime. How will he behave in 2020?

The ABCPA has underlined the relevance of the 'character' of the owner and has even balanced it against the character of the dog. Therefore, the court should hold the 'good' character of the owner in favour of his dog. Conversely, the court should not hold his 'bad' character against his dog. It is a stronger reason not to kill his dog if the defendant has used his violent nature to change the creature's character. Otherwise that would mean the dog is a victim twice over, once by his owner and then by the law. [See: **11.2**]

A chilling confession by Anthony Stravato is a warning to the authorities and the community. He served eight months in prison for offences including torturing, mutilating and killing his mother's cat. Stravato boasted on Facebook that: 'as n ill be tha next serial killer since i have a serial killer trait. im sure i knew it already. i used to watch my cats die all tha time when i was young so i began to be fasinated with death when i was 6.' *(sic)*

When he was asked why he 'keeps killing animals' he said: 'yes i do like it i enjoyed it.' *(sic)*

Stravato is a registered Level 3 sex offender, which means he is highly likely to reoffend. [See: National Link Coalition: Link Letter: September 2016]

10.10   Nerves

How a court interprets an Act is a measurement of the twin limbs of its aim and policy, as a court can stifle a particular practice or promote another procedure. Tina Delaney, Newham Council's animal welfare manager, is charged with monitoring the behaviour of dogs and owners. You could find no better example of a bad practice than an irresponsible owner who did not properly care for her dog, Bruiser, by ignoring the requirements of the law as to castration, registration and vaccination. Additionally, she failed to use a muzzle whenever she took her dog out in public, which was rare anyway. As a result, Bruiser was anti-social and ill at ease on the streets. He became a 'problem' dog, and was branded as a pit bull-type as well as being 'aggressive as a result of being nervous'. Delaney confirmed that consequently the problem was solved by the court ordering Bruiser to be killed. [See: *Animal Saints and Sinners*: BBC1: 25/8/14]

By using the revised SC Guidelines and the ABCPA provisions, the courts can control irresponsible owners. To that end the courts must move away from their present approach of judicial pussyfooting in protecting the owner while punishing his or her dog by destruction. A defendant who is at fault because of the inadequacy of the defence evidence should be penalised by ordering costs against him. Killing his dog is neither judicious nor just.

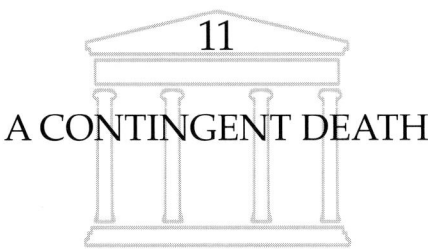

11

A CONTINGENT DEATH

11.1 Dangerous Dogs Act 1991 s.4A

(1) Where
  (a) a person is convicted of an offence under section 1 above or an aggravated offence under 3(1) above;
  (b) the court does not order the destruction of the dog under section 4(1)(a) above; and
  (c) in the case of an offence under section 1 above, the dog is subject to the prohibition in section 1(3) above, the court shall order that, unless the dog is exempted from that prohibition within the requisite period, the dog shall be destroyed.

A 'contingent destruction order' is now a major part of the DDA. The court can impose conditions relating to the owner and the dog that 'suspend' a destruction order. That has been endorsed by the Court of Appeal as the *initial* step to be considered and taken rather than the immediate destruction of a dog. [See: **10.2**]

It applies where a person is convicted of having a prohibited dog or an aggravated offence of causing injury. Then if the court does not (a) order destruction of the dog and (b) where the dog is the prohibited type, his future depends on whether there is an Exemption Certificate. Then unless the dog is exempt from prohibition, within the requisite period, the dog *'shall'* be destroyed.

A court could order the owner to contact the authorities within two months, the 'requisite' period, to seek 'exemption'. Then he must contact the appointed Agency, Defra, which controls the Index of Exempted Dogs. The court may extend the period. No details are given as to the criteria, but as in the circumstances his dog's life is at stake, the owner would need a sound reason for seeking an extension, especially as it follows from a conviction. If it was withheld on 'unreasonable' grounds it could be subject to a judicial review. [See: **11.4**]

The test for when a mandatory and discretionary destruction order applies has been clarified by the High Court in *Kelleher v. DPP* [2012] EWHC 2978. Victoria Kelleher was the owner of two dogs, Amber and Shadow. Both dogs were subject to control orders following previous incidents in public places. Neither of those incidents resulted in any injury to a member of the public. The present incident arose in 2009 when Shadow escaped from Kelleher and attacked another dog, Wooky. Shadow was muzzled at the time. While Kelleher tried to regain control of Shadow, she lost control of Amber, who attacked Wooky too. Amber bit Wooky. Although Wooky's owner was 'exceedingly upset and distressed' he did not 'suffer any direct injury' from Amber or Shadow.

After Kelleher pleaded guilty to two offences, the Magistrates' Court ordered destruction of her two dogs. The recorder at Bristol Crown Court upheld that order.

On appeal Collins J said the recorder '… did get it wrong … section 4A applies to both aggravated and non-aggravated offences. The power to make a destruction order applies in both cases. The distinction … is that in the case of an aggravated offence there must be a destruction order unless the dog would not constitute a danger to public safety, and in the case of a discretionary order the court has to decide whether it is appropriate in all the circumstances, having regard to the facts, to make a destruction order … the test, which, as it seems to me, should be applied in either case, essentially relates to whether the dog is a danger to the public.'

As more than two years had elapsed and both dogs remained well-behaved in public, the court quashed the orders and remitted the case to a differently constituted Crown Court.

Kelleher was a far-sighted decision as though it was in 2012, and pre-dates the ABCPA, it reflects the principles in the Act that places a mandatory duty upon the court to *'consider'* the character of the dog. The fact the dogs were 'well-behaved' for more than two years reflects positively on them and their owner. That goes to the core terms of 'temperament' and 'past behaviour', which are the determining conditions for the court under the ABCPA, though that Act did not come into force until 2014. Crucially, if it was a choice between the bad character of the owner and the 'well-behaved' dog it would place an onus on the court to choose a course to protect the dog, not the owner. [See: **10.4**]

The misinterpretation by the police of the power they possessed was considered when they seized and killed the 22 pet dogs in Liverpool in 2014. Chief Inspector Chris Gibson, of the Matrix Serious Organised Crime Uniformed Services Wing, said the reason was: 'The action taken across Merseyside … today is solely in relation to banned breeds, which have been given exemption by the courts.' All the 22 dogs were killed by the police without a court order. The legality of the action of the police was subject to judicial review by ten of the owners whose dogs were destroyed. [See: **12.3**]

11.2   Otherwise

The power was considered by the High Court in *Housego v. Canterbury Crown Court and the Crown Prosecution Service*. Timothy Housego pleaded guilty to three charges of being the owner of a dangerous dog out of control in a public place. The magistrates made an order for the destruction of his dog, Kelly. Housego appealed against the destruction order to Canterbury Crown Court. Before the appeal was heard, the police seized Kelly and placed her into the care of Margaret Todd at the Lord Whisky Animal Sanctuary. Housego renounced ownership and applied for Kelly to be permitted to stay at the sanctuary.

The Crown Court heard evidence from the owner of the home, Todd, as well as an expert report from Dr d'Sa. They considered that would be a satisfactory arrangement. Todd and the sanctuary staff were able to keep Kelly safe. Despite those manifest favourable features, Mr Recorder Byrne decided to dismiss the appeal.

Irwin J then set out the progress of the appeal: 'On 8 April a pre-action letter was sent to the Recorder, making the point that the dog was not going to be returned to the owner, that a suspended destruction order could properly be made and asking for that to be considered. On 26 April the Recorder again replied in a response suggesting that the application was 'frivolous'. Later Collins J gave leave as it was arguable that the recorder made a legal error.

The recorder and magistrates were not impressed by some of the written evidence from Dr d'Sa. Irwin J commented that the defence failed to make 'an application to adjourn to get her oral evidence'.

Irwin J then noted a finding of the Crown Court: 'Whilst it is right to say that the Appellant suggested that Kelly could stay indefinitely at the animal sanctuary, the Court had no power under the Act to direct that the dog remain at a particular venue for the remainder of its life, or until such time as it no longer presented a danger to the public.'

Irwin J said: 'That was, in my judgment, an error of law. It is an error of law which is conceded by Mr Boyd, appearing for the Crown Prosecution Service.

'The Dangerous Dogs Act 1991 … gives the court power to suspend a destruction order based on specific conditions. Under section 4A an order for destruction may be contingent on measures for its control specified by the Court "whether by muzzling, keeping it on a lead, excluding it from specified places, or otherwise." [underlined by court] There is an open-ended potential for making such conditions because the Act in effect says that any conditions can be imposed.

'Even if Mr Housego had remained an owner, the Court had power to make such a contingent destruction order. In fact the sensible outcome of this case was so to do … The appropriate order sought is that the dog will remain for life in the Lord Whisky Sanctuary; that if the dog is ever taken from the grounds of the sanctuary that should only be when she is accompanied by Mrs Todd or a member of staff of the sanctuary; that Kelly should be kept on a lead at all times and should be muzzled at all times when she is removed outside the premises.

The Recorder failed to grasp that such an order was available to him. That was a material error.'

This case is a signpost of guidance by the High Court to the lower courts. It points to the principle that the court has a duty to consider a practical solution where it is feasible as opposed to an immediate sentence of destruction. That is a sea change. Too often in the past what should be a last resort for the court has been the first one. *Housego v. Canterbury Crown Court* holds up a mirror to that error.

11.3   Nature

When a person is convicted of an aggravated offence, the court may order that the dog is destroyed 'unless the owner keeps it under proper control'. The onus is on the owner to follow the order which:

(a)   may specify the measures to be taken whether by muzzling the dog or keeping it on a lead or excluding it from specified places or otherwise; and

(b)   may, if it appears a male dog would be less dangerous if neutered, make a condition that it is neutered.

The power could exclude the dog from 'specified places' including a hospital, a nursery, a school or any place that may place a child or adult at risk. It could take account of vulnerable adults, which is consistent with the revised accent on sentencing by the SC from 1 July 2016. As for '*otherwise*', that could include exclusion from public parks where the dog could become excited and attack other dogs.

There is a growing problem of 'dangerous' dogs attacking guide dogs. Trained guide dogs are often Labradors of a gentle disposition that do not respond to their attackers. There were more than 70 such attacks in 2011 without a single prosecution. In June 2012 it was reported to be running at the rate of eight a month. In 2014 it was even higher at the rate of ten a month. However, the negative effects of these attacks extend beyond the trauma to the dog as they result in a psychological effect on the blind person, who becomes a dual victim: he can hear his dog being attacked and yet is helpless to act plus is immediately at risk himself. That is the precise reason the protection afforded to people who are attacked by an out of control dangerous dog has been extended by the ABCPA to include attacks on 'assistance dogs'. [See: **17.4**]

Adding to the victims' misery, The Guide Dog charity is concerned that many of its members are discriminated against by taxi drivers who refuse to carry their 'assistance' dogs. The fines imposed on such drivers are so paltry they are not a deterrent to that blatant discrimination. Consequently 100 guide dog owners visited Parliament in 2016 in a bid to change the law.

Dudu Miah is a newsagent in Limehouse in London. In 2016 James McCafferty, an 11-year-old, entered his shop. James, who is autistic, was accompanied by his mother, Katy, and his assistance dog. When Miah saw them he shouted: 'Get out … no dogs in my shop.' and threw them all out. Miah was ordered to pay £22,000 in compensation and costs for disability discrimination.

A dog that is not aggressive often becomes 'dangerous' by the deliberate acts of a violent owner. Such an owner can change his dog's character to become vicious to match his own. Collins J pin-pointed that precise position with arrow-like accuracy in *R (Sandhu) v. Isleworth Crown Court*: 'The section which deals with dangerous dogs, or dogs which have behaved in such a way as is clearly dangerous, notwithstanding the dog itself is not regarded as one which is inherently likely to be dangerous. Frequently, of course, section 3 offences depend upon the dog having been treated by its owner so as to exhibit dangerous tendencies …

'Clearly a dog, which has been badly treated by his owner may, as a result, not be able to shed the characteristics which apply to dogs, the subject of section 1, namely that they are likely to be inherently dangerous. So the treatment that the dog may have undergone is clearly relevant to that issue.'

The court confirmed the importance of whether the owner is *'a fit and proper person'* to own his dog may be material in the future. Fortunately that criterion and reasoning has shaped the form and spirit of the ABCPA.

That analysis has to be contrasted with *R. v. Donnelly* [2007] EWCA 2548. Ian Donnelly was convicted at Manchester Crown Court. His dog, Zak, a German Shepherd, had escaped from his front door on three separate occasions in 2004, 2005 and 2006. On each occasion Zak had bitten the respective person who went to Donnelly's door. Donnelly was subject to an Anti-Social Behaviour Order [ASBO] in relation to the incident in 2004. HHJ Khokhar sentenced Donnelly to a suspended sentence of imprisonment. He ordered the destruction of Zak.

In the Court of Appeal, Hedley J said: 'The learned judge heard evidence from an experienced person of veterinary qualifications, Miss Sarah Heath, to the effect that, although Zak was likely to bite, the reasons for his doing so were not inherent to him, but because of the way in which he was kept, and therefore it would be wrong in the circumstances to order the destruction of the dog on the basis that it related to the care the dog had received rather than its inherent nature … [the judge] took the view that he had to look at the position as it actually was. He had to consider whether Zak, in the condition in which he was and having regard to the circumstances in which he lived, constituted a danger to the public safety. He concluded that it had not been shown that the dog would not constitute a danger to the public safety. In our judgment that was a conclusion to which not only was he was entitled to come, but was clearly right to come in all the circumstances that we have set out.'

The decision to uphold the destruction order does not bear scrutiny. The problem with that solution is Zak was killed because of the *'care'* visited upon him by Donnelly rather than his *'inherent nature'*. It would have been better legally and socially to transfer the dog to another owner, such as ordered in *Housego* and *Devon*. That would have the advantage of allowing the dog an opportunity to be retrained by an expert to regain his 'natural' character. That would be a positive approach, providing the opportunity to remove the negative change caused by Donnelly, rather than using his crimes to condemn his dog. By confirming the sentence of death in the face of expert evidence the court made Zak a victim. Donnelly should have been imprisoned while Zak should have been reprieved. *R. v. Flack* was decided three months later and is the leading authority. More than merely a bad decision, *Donnelly* is irreconcilable with the ethos of the ABCPA.

The court used the bad behaviour of Donnelly to destroy his dog. That is the opposite position of one that should be adopted to ensure 'fair' treatment for a dog under our law.

There is no reason why Zak should be denied the opportunity of rehabilitation, especially as it was not his nature that made him dangerous, but his nurture by Donnelly. [See: **10.9**]

Nevertheless, the High Court repeated that erroneous reasoning in *Hooker* for the owner's lack of action in failing to 'get the dog muzzled and trained'. The court solved the problem by punishing Hooker by confirming his dog's destruction. If that reoccurred the defence should appeal as the court's failure to consider the expert report is contrary to the interests of justice. [See: **9.2**]

Neither *Donnelly* nor *Hooker* should be followed in the future. Each is irreconcilable with the ABCPA, which places a duty on the court to consider the character of the dog and the owner. In discharging that duty the court '*may* consider any other relevant circumstance'. The 'may' should be 'must' as there are few matters that would be more 'relevant' than the fact a dog has had its 'character' changed by an irresponsible owner. When it is deciding whether the dog should live or die it has a relevance that is not anthropomorphic, but consistent with the animal's right to life and the interests of justice. That is part of the continuing duty on the court to ensure the dog has a 'fair trial'. Zak should have been saved. Denying that act detracts from the purpose of law. [See: **7.3**]

11.4   Index

The Index of Exempted Dogs can be checked to prove that any dog in question is or is not legally exempt. A breach of a condition results in the dog losing the legal exemption. Just as an irresponsible owner can cause his death, so a responsible owner can save his dog's life.

The exemption under the Dangerous Dogs Exemption Schemes (England and Wales) Order 2015 is subject to several conditions, all of which must be complied with before the dog can be placed on the Index. Those conditions include that:

(a)   All the details of the dog have been reported to the Agency monitoring the Index.

(b)   The dog has been neutered and has a permanent identification by micro-chipping.

(c)   Third Party Insurance is in place in respect of the dog.
(d)   The Fee is paid to the Agency.
(e)   A Certificate of Exemption is issued and in force.
(f)   All the requirements specified in the Certificate are complied with by the owner.

The conditions cover everything about the animal from notifying the Agency to the change of address and insurance. It is a complete file that details everything about the dog from the moment of birth up to and including his death. A certificate is a log of the life of the dog. [See: **11.1**]

Besides the stringent conditions, lest they are not sufficient, the Agency has power to include 'additional requirements' they may 'reasonably require' for compliance with the Index. In *R (Sandhu) v. Isleworth Crown Court* Collins J said: 'No doubt any additional requirement could relate to ensuring that the dog was kept in sufficiently secure conditions. As it seems to me, it could also require that the dog was kept at a particular address, if that was something which was material in the circumstances of any given case.'

Once a person is granted a certificate he has to produce it if requested within five days. A responsible owner would know if he fails to produce the certificate he cannot show his dog has the right to live.

The High Court in *Sandhu* considered the use of exemption certificates in some depth. It was an application for judicial review of a decision of the Isleworth Crown Court, whereby the court made a contingent destruction order in relation to two dogs of a pit bull type, Bullet and Cuddles. Sandhu argued the judge was wrong in failing to consider the circumstances in which the dog was to be kept following the court's decision.

Collins J said: 'There was evidence from a veterinary surgeon that these two dogs were not dangerous. That evidence was not disputed by the prosecution and so the court had before it the evidence, which was accepted, and so made a finding of fact, which on the evidence was an inevitable finding of fact, that the dogs would not constitute a danger to public safety. Defra has been joined as a Defendant to this claim because it has a real interest in knowing what the extent of the court's powers are in making orders under

... the Act, and further what its obligations as being responsible for the carrying out of the requirements of the order are.'

The court advanced the legal position of a dog's fate by considering and using pending Sentencing Guidelines, which were not due [at the time] to come into force until 20 August 2012. That is a vital development because the court has to consider: *'The circumstances in which the dog has been treated ...'* That goes to the root of whether it is fair and just to kill the dog or make a contingent destruction order. For the court now has to consider the character of the dog in relation to the character of the owner.

Collins J said: 'Is the owner a fit and proper person to own this particular dog? ... So the treatment that the dog may have undergone is clearly relevant to that issue.'

After considering that question he said: 'All that the court can do, and should do, if satisfied that the dog in question would not constitute a danger to public safety, because it does not have the inherently dangerous characteristics that pit bull type dogs are believed to have, is make a contingent destruction order if asked to do so, so that attempts can be made to obtain a certificate of exemption. After all, that would not be altogether surprising because a dog is not to be regarded as a danger to the public, then it is *prima facie* wrong that the dog's life should be brought to an end.' [See: **17.10**]

The court concluded a certificate of exemption should be granted. Then the court considered the application for the certificate as it was made by Sandhu's cousin as he was unavailable. Sandhu was 'sentenced to substantial periods of imprisonment for offences other than those relating to the dogs. He will be in prison apparently for at least two years and possibly somewhat longer. Accordingly it is necessary, if these dogs are not to be destroyed, that they are looked after by someone else in the meantime. There is no question of transferring ownership. It is simply making the cousin the keeper of the dogs, or transferring possession of the dogs to the cousin for the period during which the Claimant remains unable to look after them because, in this case, he is in prison.'

Sandhu was an excellent example of a judicial interpretation of the DDA to give a positive effect to what could have been an obvious defect and injustice. However, this new Index attempts to overturn part of that judgment as it does not clarify who the 'owner' or 'keeper' is and how that status changes. It will be illuminating to see what light the court sheds on this aspect of the Index when it has to decide the wisdom of Defra's decision. That point has been made in case after case: after a fair trial, the court alone decides the dog's destiny. [See: **8.2**]

In 2010 there were about 800 dogs registered on the Index of Exempted Dogs. By August 2014 that figure had more than trebled to 2,658 dogs. Of those, the figure for 'pit bull-type' dogs is 2,652. It is clear that more responsible owners are gaining knowledge of the application and procedure involved in obtaining an exemption. [See: **12.3**]

A consequence of that increase is that as the certificate has gained in prominence and use it has the potential to become an important evidential document in any proceedings. It will be a dog's record of his 'good' and 'bad' behaviour, which is a criterion under the ABCPA. Further it will reflect the 'good' and 'bad' behaviour of the owner too. Each aspect independently and cumulatively could show a dangerous dog that is out of control in the hands of an irresponsible owner or a well-behaved dog with a responsible owner, plus everything in between. The record is relevant evidence that could be used by the court to determine whether the owner should be disqualified or the dog should live or die. [See: **17.12**]

Once a dog has been registered the conditions prevail until he dies. If the owner breaches any of the conditions attached to the registration then it is a criminal offence which carries a maximum sentence of six months' imprisonment. By virtue of the reason for the registration, namely that the dog is a 'banned' breed, it is presumed that the recalcitrance of the defendant will lead to the dog's death by law. However, that presumption is not as clear-cut as is often assumed, even after the primary issue was resolved by the High Court. What is definite is that the decision is for the court and only the court.

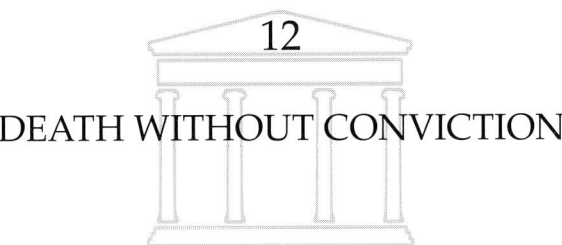

12

DEATH WITHOUT CONVICTION

12.1 Dangerous Dogs Act 1991 s.4B

(1) Where a dog is seized under section 5(1) or (2) below and it appears to a justice of the peace:

    (a) that no person has been or is to be prosecuted for an offence under this Act or an order under section 2 in respect of that dog (whether because the owner cannot be found or for any other reason); or

    (b) that the dog cannot be released into the custody or possession of its owner without the owner contravening the prohibition in section 1(3) above, he may order the destruction of the dog and, subject to subsection 2 below, shall do so if it is one to which section 1 applies.

This power allows a court to kill a dog even though there has not been a conviction. It arises where a dog has been seized by a constable or an officer under section 5. Then if it appears to a justice of the peace that:

    (a) no person has been or is to be prosecuted for an offence or an order under section 2 or

    (b) the dog cannot be released to his owner as he is a prohibited type, he may order the destruction of the dog. [See: **12.2**]

The power of destruction is clarified by confirming that if the dog is a prohibited type, the court '*shall*' order his death. However, the justice of the peace is not bound to order the destruction if satisfied the dog would 'not' constitute a danger to 'public safety'.

Providing the defence prepares the case professionally, an expert report would provide evidence that could be supported by lay persons and referees consistent with the principles set out in *R. v. Flack*. Yet often the prosecution report from a vet is the only expert evidence available. That position will increase as legal aid for defendants continues to disappear with each passing year. A related problem is that the owner may not be found. Indeed, he may have made himself scarce in order to avoid a potential prosecution. Certainly it is to the dog's disadvantage and welfare that he has no one to represent his interests, including the chance of staying alive.

The justice of the peace shall order that, unless the dog is 'exempt' from the prohibition within the 'requisite' period, the dog 'shall' be destroyed. So the onus is on someone to ensure an application for exemption is made. It is unclear who is responsible for making such an application if the owner is unavailable through illness, incarceration or otherwise.

The requisite period is two months. The period could be extended by the court. That is discretionary as it is a condition precedent to avoid destruction. So the court would have to be satisfied the owner had a good reason for his inaction. [See: **11.4**]

Although there is no conviction, if there is a destruction order that can be appealed to the Crown Court. However, where the owner cannot be found, who will appeal on behalf of the ownerless dog? Why would anyone wish to do so? If the unchallenged evidence of the prosecution is accepted because no one knows or cares, how is that reconcilable with the adversarial system? What if that unchallenged evidence is inaccurate, unreliable or untrue? Does it remain unchallenged while the dog is seized and killed? As there is no legal voice for the dog the likelihood is his own would soon be stilled.

Even if the owner is found he may disown the dog. Then his disposition could determine the dog's destiny. If that is the case the court ought to be under an inherent or statutory duty to appoint an *amicus* or 'friend' as the dog's legal voice. [See: 7.3]

12.2   Discontinue

The High Court in *R. v. Haringey Magistrates' ex parte Cragg* [1996] EWHC 162 is instructive for the bold analysis of the issue and the fair decision on the facts. Jeanette Cragg was the owner of a dog, Kizzie. Alan Bailey, her friend, was seen in a public place in north London with Kizzie in 1992. Bailey was charged with an allegation that Kizzie was a pit bull terrier. The trial started in May 1993 and was adjourned part-heard. Maurice Kay J said: 'The sole issue in the case was whether Kizzie is of the type of dog known as a pit bull terrier, and that was a matter for expert evidence.' [See: 9.2]

The trial was scheduled for January 1994. However, in December 1993, the CPS decided 'not to proceed'. It wrote to Bailey indicating it had sent a notice to the magistrates' clerk 'discontinuing' the case because 'it is not in the public interest to proceed'.

The CPS underestimated Bailey's character; he was a man of some mettle and insisted on the matter being brought back to court. It was listed in January 1994. The CPS offered 'no evidence' so the charge was dismissed. Maurice Kay J said: 'It is akin to a verdict of "not guilty" by direction in the Crown Court.'

Kizzie was not then 'unreservedly returned' to either Bailey or Cragg. Instead, on 10 February 1994, Kizzie was handed over, but immediately re-seized. The judge knew the reason. Maurice Kay J said: 'That in my judgment, was most probably because the police officers were unhappy with the decision that had been taken by the Crown Prosecution Service to discontinue the prosecution of Mr Bailey … an application was made to Haringey Justices by a police officer …'

Expert evidence was called on both sides. Indeed, four experts were called on behalf of Cragg. The Stipendiary Magistrate found the complaint proved, which meant [at that time] he was bound to make a destruction order for Kizzie. So he did.

Meanwhile, four years had passed after the initial seizure when the application came before the High Court. Cragg claimed the action of the CPS was an abuse of process.

Maurice Kay J specified the reasons: 'The first is that in the present case there was, in effect, an acquittal in the first proceedings and not just a discontinuance … the change in parties – that is to say, the Commissioner rather than the Crown Prosecution Service and the applicant rather than Mr Bailey … is not, in my judgment, so fatal when one takes a broader look at the facts … the second proceedings, that is to say the ones against the applicant, involved the same dog which had remained in the same ownership throughout. In my judgment, in these circumstances, it was wholly inappropriate and wrong for the Commissioner to take the second proceedings against this applicant, and the application which was made to the Stipendiary Magistrate to stop those proceedings as an abuse ought to have succeeded …'

That critical reasoning led to the right decision. *Cragg's Case* rested on a decision that was flawed in fact and law as the court considered that death for the dog was the best choice. Maurice Kay J injected fairness in the proceedings for both the owner and his dog by judging death to be the worst choice.

12.3   Declaration

The misconception by the police of the power they possessed was considered when they seized and killed the 22 pet dogs in Liverpool in 2014. Chief Inspector Chris Gibson, of the Matrix Serious Organised Crime Uniformed Services Wing, said the reason was: 'The action taken across Merseyside … today is solely in relation to banned breeds, which have been given exemption by the courts. When the courts grant these exemptions there are nine conditions imposed by the courts, which the owner must abide by … The owners of the dogs seized by the officers today were issued with a Contingent Destruction Order by the courts and the dog was placed on the Dangerous Dogs Index and the owners were sent a letter by DEFRA … advising them of the terms and conditions that were in place and that their dog may be destroyed if they breached the conditions. DEFRA monitors whether the owners have maintained the insurance required and remind owners when the insurance is due to expire. And if they fail to renew the insurance the relevant police force is advised and appropriate enforcement action can then be taken ... The dogs seized by the police today will be humanely destroyed.' All the 22 dogs were killed by the police without a court order. The action of the police was subject to judicial review by ten of the owners whose dogs were destroyed. [See: **8.2**]

In *Ali v. Chief Constable of Merseyside Police*, King J confirmed that the contingent destruction order 'only applies until such time as the dog is exempted'. [2014] EWHC 4772 (Admin)

The police claimed that if a dog ceased to be exempt, an earlier order for destruction could be automatically revived. The judge was clear and direct. He said their action was wrong and the authority they relied upon to kill the dogs was 'misconceived'. King J said if their claim was right, it would become 'a continuing order for destruction which can be executed at any time without recourse to any judicial authority, once the dog as a matter of fact has ceased to be exempted'. Moreover, if the owner was in a dispute with the police as to any exemption he would be denied due process of the law. The result of that claim would have meant that the police could seize any dog at any time whose owner may or may not have breached a condition and summarily kill it.

Therefore, once the dog is exempt the contingent element ceases. It could not be read into the DDA that a failure to comply with a condition would permit the destruction of the dog. King J said: 'Regard must be paid to the principle of due process.' There was nothing in the DDA that permits such destruction, nor is there any provision in the Exemption Scheme that spells that out as a consequence of failure to comply with any condition of the exemption.

Therefore, the police had acted unlawfully in seizing and destroying the dogs; a declaration was granted to that effect by the court. Although that could not affect the unlawful deaths it could save other dogs from 'misconceived' acts by the police. Indeed, it beggars belief why they thought they could kill all the dogs anyway without a court order, especially as the Inspector of the Merseyside police 'frankly' admitted in his witness statement that there were no pro-visions in the DDA to cover the position.

The unanswered question is: 'Was any other dog killed before this declaratory judgment?' Such an arbitrary act, whether by the police or any other body, is unlawful. [See: **4.3**]

13

SEARCHING AND SEIZING

13.1   Dangerous Dogs Act 1991 s.5

(1) A constable or an officer of a local authority authorised by it to exercise the powers conferred by this section may seize:
  (a) any dog which appears to him to be a dog to which section 1 above applies and which is in any place
    (i) after the time when possession or custody of it has become unlawful by virtue of that section; or
    (ii) before that time, without being muzzled and kept on lead;
  (b) any dog in any place which appears to him to be a dog to which an order under section 2 above applies and in respect of which an offence against the order has been or is being committed; and
  (c) any dog in any public place (whether or not one to which that section applies) which appears to him to be dangerously out of control.

This is the most controversial aspect of a bad Act because it raises a *'presumption'* the dog is of a 'type' it is illegal to possess unless the owner proves otherwise. That leads to the seizure of dogs who are then subject to the rigours of the law owing to their appearance and conduct. The officers enforcing this law rely on a total of 54 characteristics of a pit bull terrier. Many dogs are seized purely on their apparent resemblance to a known type. Then after an assessment to confirm the appearance, the burden shifts to the owner to disprove that view or face the penalty that follows.

In *Tyson's Case* he was identified by 57 characteristics. Even assuming that was right, the decision of destruction by the authorities was wrong as a matter of law. [See: **17.9**]

Some police forces have a Dog Legislation Officer [DLO] who is trained on dog-related legislation. In time, such officers, especially if they are dog handlers too, may acquire the status of experts. Yet identification of a family pet as a pit bull terrier remains contentious as once he is deemed to be one, that label may lead inexorably to his death.

Now a constable or an officer of a local authority may seize *'any dog'* that *'appears to him'* to be a prohibited dog which is in *'any place'*. Two conditions relate to that power before it can be exercised, namely (a) after the time when possession or custody of the dog has become unlawful or (b) before that time, it is not muzzled and kept on a lead.

This applies to the four 'designated' dogs under section 1. The officer has to be authorised by the local authority to exercise those powers. So it is strange, given the powers and consequences of exercising them, that neither an 'officer' nor a 'local authority' is defined anywhere within the DDA.

These powers have been extended by the ABCPA to apply to all dogs in all places. Apart from the four 'designated dogs', this allows seizure of one that is a 'specially dangerous dog' under section 2. Consequently, as it applies to all owners, there could be 'restrictions' placed upon their dogs, plus the ultimate restriction of their destruction.

A constable or officer could also seize *any* dog, regardless of any breach of any section or order, which appears to be 'dangerously out of control'. That enables the seizure if it is in any place and for whatever reason the dog is an actual or potential threat to people. As it is a subjective view, 'which appears to him', all that matters is his opinion is reasonable. Thereafter, the consequences for the owner and the dog can be detrimental to both of them.

13.2   Enter

A constable can apply for a warrant to enter premises to gain further evidence. If the justice of the peace is satisfied, by information on oath, there are 'reasonable grounds' for believing (a) an offence is being or has been committed or (b) evidence of the commission of any such offence is to be found on any premises, he may issue a warrant.

This additional power would be relevant if he saw a dog that 'appeared' to him to be or acting contrary to the DDA and he wanted to enter the premises of the owner. With a warrant he can enter, using reasonable force to gain entry if it is locked. He could seize any dog or *'other thing'* found there as evidence of the commission of such an offence.

The 'dog or thing' seized must relate to the past or present. It would not be the 'commission' of an offence that is arranged to happen in the future. As dangerous dogs and drug dealers are sometimes wedded together like thieves and handlers, the power is enhanced for the police by PACE, especially as that applies to the AWA. If there was evidence relating to an offence in the future, it could be charged as an 'attempt' or a 'conspiracy'. [See: **4.5**]

It is unsatisfactory that the term 'premises' is not defined accurately. It is potentially problematic as premises would usually exclude the private living area, which is the precise place where the evidence is likely to be found.

As a warrant is an invasion of a person's privacy it is closely monitored by the court. Therefore, if there is a breach of the strict conditions attached to it the evidence may be inadmissible. As a result, even if there is evidence of an alleged offence, the case may fail. [See: **4.3**]

13.3 Burden

Once the prosecution alleges a dog is within section 1, or section 2 applies, it shall be *presumed* he is such a dog. The burden of proof then immediately shifts to the defendant, who has to prove the contrary by 'such evidence as the court considers sufficient'. Where the defendant intends to adduce evidence to meet that burden he will not be permitted to do so unless he gives the prosecution 14 days notice of his intention. That allows the prosecution time to either accept it or obtain its own evidence, which is likely to be from an expert. [See: **7.2**]

That raises an 'evidential' burden on the defendant. It would not be sufficient for the defence to simply say via the defendant and his friends and neighbours: 'He's a lovely dog. He's great with children. He's just a pussycat.' The defendant would need to produce evidence that proves his defence and shifts the legal burden back on to the prosecution. He must adduce evidence that, if it does not destroy the presumption, raises a doubt as to whether the presumption is true. Then the court could decide in his favour on the *civil* burden of proof. Therefore, the defence would need evidence from an expert, be it a vet or animal behaviourist.

If he failed to adduce evidence the court considers *'sufficient'* he would fail to discharge the evidential burden. Then his dog would be branded as being 'dangerous' or of that 'type'. Such a potential result underlines the essential need for a defence expert. [See: **12.2**]

13.4 Aid

Legal aid is now limited for most standard criminal cases of a summary jurisdiction. Certainly it has disappeared for many cases within the DDA. Although with the increased sentences by the ABCPA many cases will be tried in the Crown Court, legal aid is often not available for an expert, without whose opinion it is impossible to prepare and present a proper defence. Many defendants now represent themselves or, worse, simply fail to attend court.

When there is limited legal aid available and the defendant is poor, there is a premium on him having a fair trial. The position was brought into sharp focus in *Knightsbridge Crown Court v. The*

Commissioner of Police for Metropolitan Police. This was an application for judicial review involving a dog called Elsa who was alleged to be a pit bull terrier. The Stipendiary Magistrate decided that as Elsa was a pit bull terrier she should be destroyed. That was a *civil* claim, which was then an easy procedure for the police to initiate and prove. Now the ABCPA makes it even easier for the authorities to seize any dog from any place at any time. [See: **12.1**]

McCowan LJ was concerned about there being a 'fair trial' for the dog. Leslie Crabbe sought an order quashing the decision of the Stipendiary Magistrate. Crabbe had the dog 'dumped on him by his girlfriend'. She had not bothered to get the dog registered.

The commissioner sought the destruction order as he had expert evidence Elsa was a pit bull terrier. His action in seeking the court's approval was the correct course, as McCowan LJ confirmed: 'After all it is for the court to decide whether the dog should be destroyed and not the Crown Prosecution Service.'

Crabbe wanted Elsa to be examined by an expert, Dr Roger Mugford, an animal behaviourist. McCowan LJ said: 'He is an expert on how dogs behave, and apparently it has become clear that how a dog behaves is a very important part of the test of whether it falls within the prohibited description in section 1.' [See: **9.2**]

However, when Crabbe tried to have the dog examined by Dr Mugford the police said he could only do so at Teddington Police Station. In that event McCowan LJ said he, 'would have to pay £300 towards the administrative costs … The Applicant did not have the means to pay this, as was made plain to the first Respondent [the Commissioner].'

Crabbe appealed to the Crown Court. Meanwhile, facilities were in fact granted so Dr Mugford and a vet, Dr Larkin, on behalf of Crabbe could examine Elsa. They both concluded she was not a pit bull terrier. Although Crabbe had expert evidence that could save her life, death awaited Elsa as the order remained in place.

McCowan LJ delivered a classic guide to the ultimate purpose of due process: 'It is important, in my judgment, that if the application were to be made, no steps should be taken which would prevent the dog having a fair trial. The relevant facts were that the applicant had no legal aid, no right of appeal to the Crown Court and no means to pay the £300 ... As it was, by insisting on a figure of £300 contribution to be made by the Applicant, the Commissioner made it well near impossible for the Applicant to get a fair trial for his dog.

In view of the combination of factors ... there was not, in the result, a fair trial.'

Elsa's destruction order was quashed.

Collins J endorsed the criterion: 'It seems to me that it is all the more important that the Magistrate, before whom the matter comes, ensures that there is a fair trial.' [See: **7.3**]

As legal aid continues to be unavailable in many cases, the opportunity to adduce expert evidence will be affected. Given the power following seizure, there is a balance between money and a dog's life where justice depends on hearing a sound as loud as a dog whistle.

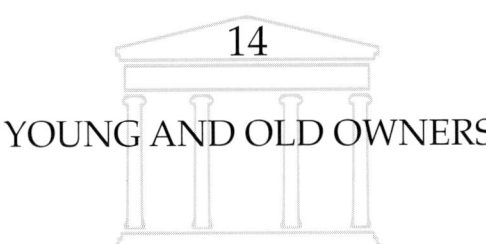

14

YOUNG AND OLD OWNERS

14.1   Dangerous Dogs Act 1991 s.6

Where a dog is owned by a person who is less than sixteen years old any reference to its owner in section 1(2)(d) or (e) or 3 above shall include a reference to the head of the household, if any, of which that person is a member or, in Scotland, to the person who has his actual care and control.

It used to be a common excuse for a young person to say the dog in question did not belong to him. That claim became a defence by a child that the dog belonged to his father or mother. This section was introduced to meet such an excuse or truth as now both the child and parent could be liable.

When a dog is 'owned' by a person under 16 years old any reference to the owner in section 1 or 3 '*shall*' include a reference to the head of the household. As there are more children in care now than in the past, the head of the care home would be equally liable for the behaviour of the dog. A better phrase to describe the relationship and cover different social situations is the one used in Scotland, 'actual care and control'.

There also used to be problems as to who is a 'keeper' of animals. Nowadays with the rise of feminism, gay marriage, one parent families and multiple marriages, the head of the household cannot be assumed to be the husband or father of the child. The 'head of the household' remains liable if the owner is under 16 years old as it 'shall' be that person.

14.2   Welfare

While the primary legislation that governs the criminal aspect of dangerous dogs and their owners is the DDA, the AWA also has relevance in relation to all domestic animals. As the object of the law is to ensure that animals are in the custody and control of responsible keepers, the age of the person in charge is important. Where dogs and especially dangerous dogs are concerned, the age of the keeper is relevant within the DDA and the AWA. Although the AWA is concerned with the welfare of the respective animal, nevertheless a negligent owner who breaches their 'duty of care' by failing to properly feed and water their dogs can create a dangerous situation that leads to horrific consequences. One of the worst examples and result is the case of Clifford Clarke, a 79-year-old man who was, according to the HHJ Mark Brown, 'literally eaten alive' by the two defendants' dog. Both defendants failed to discharge their duty of care under the AWA as well as allowing their dogs to escape contrary to the DDA. Their dogs escaped and one of them attacked Mr Clarke. [See: **19.1**]

14.3   Responsibility

The effect of the AWA on the DDA is to introduce an element of protection for the dog that is otherwise overlooked or ignored. The AWA is advantageous for prosecutors and abused animals. An onus is now placed on courts by the ABCPA as a mandatory duty to 'consider' the dog means they 'must' approach his fate knowing their decision will affect his future, including whether he has one. [See: **17.12**]

Regardless of the 'presumption' and identity of a type of dog, once he is seized by the police or a warden, the AWA bites so his welfare must be taken into account by them. That includes the 'five freedoms' as a bare minimum. [See: **2.2**]

15

LEAD AND MUZZLE

15.1 Dangerous Dogs Act 1991 s.7

(1) In this Act
   (a) references to a dog being muzzled are to its being securely fitted with a muzzle sufficient to prevent it biting any person; and
   (b) references to its being kept on a lead are to its being securely held on a lead by a person who is not less than sixteen years old.

A theme throughout the DDA is that a dog deemed to be dangerous must be muzzled. Similarly there is the need for a lead to keep such a dog at arm's length. Together they ensure the owner is in control as the lead and muzzle prevents potential dog bites and protects the public. When a contingent destruction order is imposed either in the Magistrates' Court or usually on appeal, the courts have consistently ordered a dog to be muzzled. A condition precedent means it must be done within a given period, normally 56 days. That should concentrate the owner's mind as his failure to do so can mean his dog will be killed. [See: **10.2**]

A muzzle has to be *'securely fitted'* and *'sufficient'* to prevent the dog being able to bite any person. It is not enough merely to be muzzled. When the dog is on a lead he must be 'securely held' by a person who must be at least 16 years old. Consequently, if the person in charge of the dog cannot hold him on the lead because the dog is too strong or he is too weak, if the dog bites someone the liability would follow.

The strength and weakness of that public policy can be seen in a sharp and blunt focus in *R. v. Fanneran*. Fanneran's nephew pleaded guilty to being in charge of a pit bull terrier in a public place without a muzzle as he had removed it in order to allow the dog to be sick. At that moment he was guilty. The strict interpretation can be seen by the fact 'necessity' is not available as a defence. A good example of a bad decision is *Cichon v. DPP* where Cichon had removed the muzzle because the dog had kennel cough, so he felt it was cruel to keep it on whilst the dog was coughing. Cichon was instantly guilty. [See: **8.4**]

The onus is on the owner to ensure any person in charge of his dog is over 16 years old and capable of controlling him. He must ensure the muzzle and lead are secure. It is a breach of this section, notwithstanding the dog is on a lead, if the person is not in control of his or her dog. It could be they are too weak to hold him, are untrained or even inattentive because they are talking to another person. [See: **9.2**]

In *R. v. Trafford Magistrates' Court ex parte Riley*, without Riley's knowledge, her friend took the dog to a nearby car park. Although the dog was on a leash, as her friend was unable to control him he bit a police officer. A summons was issued against her friend. She pleaded guilty and the magistrates ordered the destruction of the dog. Riley applied for judicial review of that decision. [See: **9.6**].

The Secretary of State may prescribe the kind of muzzle or lead to be used to comply in the case of a dog within sections 1 or 2. The regulation prescribing a muzzle and lead would relate to a dog of 'any' type. So far there have not been any relevant regulations.

Therefore, if the muzzle or lead is cheap and breaks under the strain, or is badly fitting and allows the dog to escape, the owner would be liable. The poor quality would be the equivalent of an insecure gate allowing a dog to be at large. Usually a dog would be without a lead or muzzle in the back garden of his home. A dog enforcement officer said the main reason that dogs escape is 'poorly maintained fences' between neighbours. The failure of an irresponsible owner to maintain their fence puts the public at risk of injury and death. They put their pets in the same position. [See: **7.2**]

If the muzzle is badly fitted and not merely insecure, it could be too tight and affect the dog's ability to breathe properly. That could affect the welfare of the dog and so would be contrary to the owner's duty under the AWA. If it was too loose it could slip and permit a badly muzzled dog to commit an offence by inducing fear or even biting someone. Either way, if it is not 'fit for purpose' the owner would commit an offence and his dog could be destroyed. [See: **9.2**]

15.2   Wife

A dog may need to be trained to accept a muzzle whether for a visit to the vet or for a walk in the park. An expert advises that: 'It is vital that your dog perceives the muzzle as a positive experience.' [See: www.doglistener.co.uk]

The importance of such wise advice was illustrated in *R. v. Shallow* [2012] 1 Cr. App. R. (S) 33 where the defendant's dog, a Staffordshire bull terrier, ran out in front of a nine year old girl who was riding her bicycle in the street in Dunstable. As a result she fell off and while she was on the ground the dog 'bit her on the thigh and held on for about 30 seconds'. A member of the public grabbed the harness and pulled the dog away.

The girl suffered a nasty gash, puncture wounds, scarring and needed hospital treatment.

In the Court of Appeal, Beatson J said: 'Shallow claimed that his dog was normally muzzled and it was muzzled at the time of the incident but the muzzle allowed it to drink and open its jaw to a degree.'

Shallow admitted he had second thoughts about the 'tempera-ment' of the dog and had sought unsuccessfully to get a refund of the price he paid to the previous owner. He also explained: 'Local teenagers had tormented the dog in the past. This had affected its temperament when it was outside the house. The dog did not react well to people cycling past on bikes and had chased him when he cycled to work.'

The court reduced the sentence from twelve weeks to six weeks' imprisonment suspended for a year and disqualification from owning a dog for ten years. However, that was not the reason for Shallow's appeal. His lawyer said what he really wanted was the disqualification to be reduced or ideally removed. She told the court the sort of muzzle available 'on the High street was not suitable for this dog because of the shape of its jaw'. So Shallow had obtained one from the internet that was 'delivered the day after the incident'. [Why did he not get one earlier?]

The court asked the lawyer several questions about the dog, including how long Shallow had him before he decided to obtain a muzzle and when it was ordered. Beatson J observed about her: 'She was unable to give [the court] any assistance.'

Why was the defence lawyer unable to give 'any assistance' on the precise point of the appeal? Why did she not seek an adjournment to obtain the evidence?

The court concluded: 'In any event the key issue is the nature of the obligation to which owners of dogs are to those who might be affected. It was the failure to have an adequate muzzle in place which, in our judgment, justified the disqualification order notwithstanding his previous good record.'

The appeal failed on that point because the muzzle was not an adequate form of protection. Shallow was concerned about the disqualification because his wife had a dog that would 'also have to go'. So her blameless dog would have to be rehomed because of Shallow's choice of an insecure muzzle.

The point remains, like the link in a chain securing a dog that breaks under the strain, is it a defence if the muzzle is badly manufactured? Why would it be right to sell a muzzle that is not fit for its purpose? Yet the owner voluntarily chose the muzzle and the offence is one of 'strict' liability. [See: **11.1**]

In the circumstances there was no destruction order for his dog. Indeed, there was no need as it became infected with a virus that, before the appeal, caused its death.

15.3   Owner

In *R. v. Rogers* the Crown Court judge 'found that it was a wholly inappropriate type of lead for an untrained dog especially one which was known to have behavioural issues, as Georgina Rogers accepted was the case in respect of both her dogs. The dog should have been on a short lead.' Lord Thomas CJ, in the Court of Appeal, added: '[she] lacked the strength or training to manage them, if they became involved in an incident such as this … using a retractable lead for one of them. Inevitably something would go wrong, as it did.' In the circumstances it was a foregone conclusion that her dog would be destroyed. [See: **9.2**]

15.4   Protection

The ABCPA now allows an application to be made to control irresponsible dog owners by a Community Protection Notice [CPN]. That has two immediate advantages, namely (a) a breach of the CPN is a criminal offence; (b) if a CPN is ignored by the dog owner the agency will carry out the work, which could include buying a muzzle that would then be claimed from the perpetrator. [See: **18.5**; **18.8**]

Ken Clarke, the brother of attack victim Clifford, said, 'The simplest thing in the world is to get a muzzle. If you can afford a tin of dog food for £1 you can afford a muzzle.' A responsible owner would not balk at the same sum to keep the public safe. Indeed, it is yet another reason why a licence should be introduced. [See: **17.11**; **19.1**]

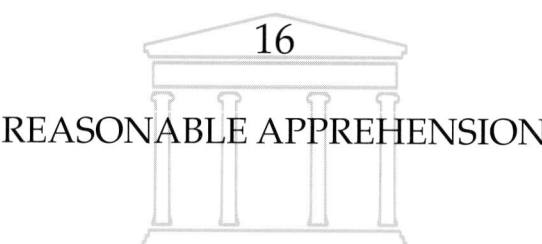

16

REASONABLE APPREHENSION

16.1   Dangerous Dogs Act 1991 s.10

(3) For the purposes of this Act a dog shall be regarded as dangerously out of control on any occasion on which there are grounds for reasonable apprehension that it will injure any person, whether or not it actually does so, but references to a dog injuring a person or there being grounds for reasonable apprehension that it will do so do not include references to any case in which the dog is being used for a lawful purpose by a constable or a person in the service of the Crown.

The changes by the ABCPA have radically altered the liability of all dog owners; from 'public place' to the amended definition of *'any place'*, has extended the owner's liability. Attacks by dangerous dogs whose owners are irresponsible are the reason for the DDA. There is a link between those problems as a dog is usually dangerous because of the feckless owner.

16.2   Attack

The DDA concentrates on a dog being 'dangerously out of control', which is defined as:

A dog shall be regarded as being out of control on any occasion on which there are grounds for reasonable apprehension that it will injure any person, whether or not it actually does so.

Therefore it is purely the potential effect of the dog's behaviour. No injury is necessary. All a dog has to do is merely act in a manner that persons in his vicinity feel the fear: the *'reasonable apprehension'* induced can be for their personal well-being or another's safety. That would apply to a parent fearing for a child or a nurse for her charge. It could be where a dog attacks a guide dog and the blind person has a 'reasonable apprehension' he would be attacked too.

The police use specially trained dogs, particularly Alsatians, to control crowds. They are exempt from this section and the consequences of their dogs being out of control if they are being used for a 'lawful purpose'. Similarly, it applies to prison officers using their dogs to aid their search of visitors for drugs and smuggled goods.

16.3 Stick

While there are many bad decisions under the DDA, *Regina v. Bezzina* is amongst the worst. Kennedy LJ justified his conclusion saying: 'It is urged that an owner may have no realisation that his dog is liable to behave in a way which will cause injury to anyone until, for example, a child pokes the dog with a stick and the dog reacts. That, indeed, may be the case. But it seems to us that Parliament was entitled to do what in this piece of legislation we find that it has done, namely to put the onus on the owner to ensure, if that is likely to happen, to take steps which are effective to ensure that it does not, either by keeping the dog on a lead or keeping the child away from the dog or whatever may be appropriate in the circumstances.'

How can a 'reasonable apprehension' be known and hence guarded against by an owner if he has no idea his dog is going to be poked in the eye by a child with a spiky stick? Moreover, if instead of a stick it is a knife or a vicious kick by a passing drunken thug? If this principle is right then the owner should act before it happens because he somehow knows it will happen. [See: **9.5**]

A gloss was put on this subject by the Civil Division of the Court of Appeal in *Criminal Injuries Compensation Authority v. First-tier Tribunal (Social Entitlement Chamber) and TS* [2014] EWCA Civ 65. TS, a 14-year-old boy, was riding a bicycle when a small dog, which had escaped from her owner's garden, rushed up to him barking in an aggressive manner. TS instinctively swerved away from the dog on to the road and into the path of a car. He was seriously injured. He spent four months in hospital and is now quite severely disabled. The owner of the dog was aware he was aggressive towards strangers [although it had apparently never bitten anyone] and had in the past frightened them by barking at them. She was aware her dog would try to escape from the garden where he was normally confined.

The defendant was charged with an offence under the DDA. However, the prosecution was 'discontinued' after she relinquished ownership of the dog, so there was no conviction.

Initially TS was awarded almost £500,000 compensation. The award was based on the fact the injuries suffered by TS were 'directly attributable to a crime of violence'. The appellant claimed the offence committed by the dog's owner was not 'a crime of violence'.

The court referred to *Bezzina* and Moore-Bick LJ said: 'If a dog is behaving aggressively towards a person there will almost always be grounds for reasonable apprehension that it will injure him.' The offence may therefore be committed without any violence on the part of the owner or even on the part of the dog. On the crucial question the court was not satisfied as 'I find it difficult to accept that negligently to allow a dog to escape, even a dog known to be aggressive, constitutes a crime of violence, giving that expression its ordinary meaning.'

So the appeal was allowed.

The point for the purpose of the DDA is the reason that if a dog is behaving aggressively towards a person, there 'will almost always be grounds for reasonable apprehension that it will injure him'. The key is the qualifying term *'almost'*. That term makes it feasible to reconcile a strict liability, but one that is not absolute. Hence it points in the direction of the reasoning in *Robinson-Pierre v. Regina* [2013] EWCA Crim 2396. [See: **16.6**]

16.4   Will

After *Bezzina* the High Court had another opportunity to interpret section 10 in *Rafiq v DPP* [1997] 161 JP R 412. Karen Rafiq was the owner of a dog, a German shepherd, called Venom. In December 1995 Jane Rusen visited Rafiq's garage in Souldrop, Bedfordshire. Rusen parked her car and went into the garage to buy a Christmas tree. Venom was loose on the forecourt. Then 'with the oral permission of the owner's daughter she let Venom into the shop'. Rusen bought some items and was handing back over the counter a knife she had borrowed. As she was passing the knife over Venom jumped up and bit her on the thigh. The Crown Court found that prior to jumping up and biting Rusen, Venom had 'given no indication at all of his intention to do so'.

Rafiq was convicted at the Magistrates' Court. Her appeal to the Crown Court was dismissed.

In the High Court Popplewell J referred to *Bezzina* and said: 'If there is a bite without a reasonable apprehension immediately before that, the use of the word 'any occasion' is sufficient to impose a liability because there are grounds thereafter for reasonable apprehension that it will injure some other person.'

Auld LJ referred to *Bezzina* and said: 'The act of a dog causing injury, a bite or otherwise, is itself capable of being conduct giving grounds for reasonable apprehension of injury.'

Each judge fudged the issue. This section is concerned with something happening which '*will*' confirm the reasonable apprehension of the owner. It is a present situation that causes the owner to be aware that his dog 'will injure any person or assistance dog'. That is an immediate warning of an impending risk; it is not dealing with a present position that is a contingency in the future. The problem for the court was that the attempt to uphold *Bezzina* meant it had to bend words out of shape to give the section a meaning that was neither stated nor intended. Where an injury occurs there may have been, immediately before, a reasonable apprehension that it would occur. It is not relating to 'some other person' at all. Something about the present position has to be indicative that an injury will immediately result. Liability should not automatically follow if the injury is unknown and unforeseen by the owner. [See: **9.5**]

16.5 Ruling

The reasoning of the Court of Appeal in *Robinson-Pierre v. Regina* has introduced a reasonable appreciation the law will allow for and follow a sense of how people act and react.

Bradshaw underlines an empirical point that should be taken into account by any court dealing with a case of a dog biting a child who has provoked that response: 'Dogs that were never exposed to children during puppyhood can be very wary of them when they first meet them as adults, although being dogs they can easily be trained to overcome this initial reluctance. On the other hand, if their first encounter with a child involves the pulling of their tails and ears, such dogs can easily become irritable and snappy with other children.'[*In Defence of Dogs* (2012)] That action by a child is exactly what cannot be expected by an owner when the parent is in charge of and in control of their child; conversely the reaction is what might or will happen if their dog is suddenly provoked without cause or teased without reason. Provocation of the dog must be relevant to their reaction. [See: **10.7**]

16.6   Trafalgar

Robinson-Pierre v. Regina was heard at the Inner London Crown Court before HHJ Bishop and a jury. That case changed the face of our law. Symieon Robinson-Pierre was charged with four counts involving five victims during a single incident. The charges were that the defendant was the owner of a dog that caused injury while out of control in a public place. All the victims were police officers who were at the defendant's home to execute a warrant. The defendant's pit bull terrier, Poison, was living there and locked in a room.

When the police arrived the event happened fast, really fast, as 'almost immediately after the officers entered through the front door a pit bull terrier belonging to the appellant descended the stairs from the first floor and attacked PC Corderoy as he was retreating towards the doorway. Other officers succeeded in freeing PC Corderoy from the dog's grip by inserting an asp into the dog's mouth and twisting it.'

Then the dog attacked PC Merritt, PC Bush and PC Garrard, and finally PC Bones. All five officers were injured. The 4½ stone dog clamped his jaws on an officer's thigh inside the house while another officer hit the animal on the head with a metal battering ram. The dog went on to bite officers who were in the garden and the street.

Sam Brown, the prosecutor, said: 'If you need a useful image of the aftermath of this event, imagine the sickbay after the Battle of Trafalgar and that will give you an idea – carnage.

This case concerns a horrifying episode in central London this year borne out of a criminal failure by a dog owner to firstly realise the risk his animal posed and secondly to be in a position because of that failure to properly restrain it.

During the incident the appellant and another male appeared. PC Bush and DC Clarke urged them to call off Poison. One of the two men said: 'We can't mate, there's nothing we can do.' The other said: 'You should have knocked. Why didn't you knock?'

Finally armed officers were called to the scene and caught Poison.

On arrest the appellant said: 'It's not the dog's fault. You should have knocked. I would have let you in.'

The prosecutor said: 'Through no fault of the animal's, its natural instincts manifested themselves in a terrifying display causing injury. No allegation is made that this defendant set his dog on these officers otherwise he would be facing very different charges.'

During the trial the judge directed the jury on the meaning of the law: 'Parliament, no doubt, thought that if you are the owner of such a dog you must ensure that the dog does not get out into a public place and be dangerously out of control in any circumstances. If it does get out and does go into a public place and behave like that, whether through the owner's fault or failure *or through no fault of the owner but through the inaction or action of somebody else*, it simply does not matter, if it is your dog and it is dangerously out of control in a public place then you are criminally responsible for that.' [Emphasis added by the Court.]

Count 1 was dismissed as there was no case to answer. The appellant was convicted of counts 2 to 4. The issue on appeal was: to what extent is liability for the section 3 offence *'strict'*?

Pitchford LJ set the case in context saying this was 'the first time' that issue was considered by the Court since *R. v. Bezzina* in 1994. The appellant relied on *Bezzina* as supporting the idea that whilst it was accepted there was a strict liability, it envisaged a situation where the owner was in fact in charge of the dog and thus able to take effective steps to keep the dog under control. That led to the question the court had to grasp and resolve, namely: What if the intervention of a third person was entirely outside reasonably foreseeable events?

Analysing that position it means that a person would be liable regardless of how the 'state of affairs' that gave rise to the offence occurred. Conversely, if the owner had done everything to reasonably prevent the 'state of affairs' from arising he would have a defence. Pitchford LJ classed those submissions with a laconic legalese as possessing 'a logical inconsistency'.

The submissions of the prosecution and defence were polar opposites in form and effect. The CPS argued 'the "guillotine comes down" whenever a dog behaves dangerously in public, regardless of how or why it got there.' The polar point raised by the defence was 'that the attacks were possible only because police officers released Poison into a public place'.

Pitchford LJ concluded that, given the judge's direction, the appellant elected not to give evidence. Hence he was not able to 'meet the assertion that by his act or omission after the escape from the house he caused or contributed to the prohibited state of affairs. We cannot in these circumstances be sure that the verdicts of the jury were safe'.

All the convictions were quashed.

While the incident was described by the prosecutor as akin to Trafalgar, however, rather than a Nelsonian triumph the truth is it was a Pyrrhic victory. It was of little solace to Robinson-Pierre, who was sentenced to 22 months' imprisonment, as by the time of his appeal he had served his sentence. Further, given the number of times the marksman fired a hail of bullets at his dog, with the final one to 'his head', Poison was dead.

16.7   Fault

The *Robinson-Pierre Case* deals with the real issue on a practical basis. The analysis of the previous judgments and the conclusion that the strict liability was not absolute is right. The court allows an owner to raise a defence if he is without fault for the situation that led to the result. If he did not create the circumstances that caused the injury there is no reason why the owner should be deemed to be criminally liable with the personal risk of imprisonment and death for his dog. The reasoning confirmed the law will allow for a sense of the action and reaction of people, which equally applies to children and to dogs. The previous decisions expect too much of the owner and demand too little of a careless parent. It excuses the latter whilst demanding the former is blessed with canine telepathy. Such a situation should not create a liability if any injury caused was not the 'fault' of the owner or his dog.

Perhaps unwittingly, yet no less true for that reason, the prosecutor alighted on what a court should consider when dealing with a dog that reacts to provocation, when he said: 'Through no fault of the animal's, its natural instincts manifested themselves …' That point was accurately made on his arrest when the appellant said: 'It's not the dog's fault …'

16.8   Provocation

While the Court of Appeal in *Regina v. Bezzina* has been the leading authority cn the DDA being absolute in its effect, it has now been interpreted and distinguished on an important point of law. The judgment in *Robinson-Pierre v. Regina* is a common sense conclusion that takes account of the fact the culpability for the actions of a third party, whosoever he is, has to be resolved in a logical manner. The result, even allowing for a 'strict liability', is nevertheless not absolute. The court in *Robinson-Pierre* injected a delayed sense of justice in this area. That principle should be followed in the future. [See: **9.5**]

Plainly the prosecution realised the impact of the decision in *Robinson-Pierre v. Regina*. That judgment has finally set the law on an even keel. Given the repercussions for the whole of the 'reasonable apprehension' aspect of the DDA, the prosecution sought to lodge an appeal to our highest court. In 2014 its application was refused by the Supreme Court.

This case has introduced a balance of fairness in this area of law that was sorely needed. Now there is good reason to believe that the blameless will no longer be denied a defence.

A poke in the eye with a sharp stick should not be excused because it results in being bitten. Instinct is borne of our most basic feeling. Failing to respond would be unnatural whether the eye belonged to a man or his dog.

The new SC Guideline states under the 'Culpability' category one of the factors that demonstrates a 'lesser' culpability: Provocation of the dog without the fault of the owner. That confirms it is mitigation. There is no reason why it could also be relevant to a defence, as if the circumstances show the dog was provoked neither the owner nor the dog, being without fault, should be denied a defence. [See: **19.4**]

Anti-social Behaviour,
Crime and Policing Act 2014

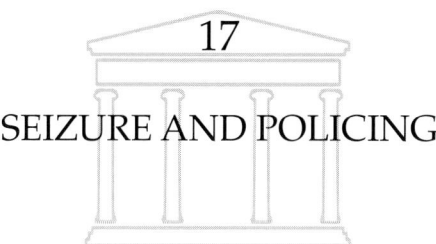

17

SEIZURE AND POLICING

17.1   Anti-social Behaviour, Crime and Policing Act 2014 s.106

(1) The Dangerous Dogs Act 1991 is amended as follows.

(2) In section 3 (keeping dogs under proper control)
   (a) in subsection (1)
      (i)   for 'a public place' there is substituted 'any place in England or Wales (whether or not a public place)';
      (ii) after 'injures any person' there is inserted 'or assistance dog'.
   (b) after subsection (1) there is inserted '(1A) A person ("D") is not guilty of an offence under subsection (1) in a case which is a householder case.

(1B) For the purposes of subsection (1A) 'a householder case' is a case where
   (a) the dog is dangerously out of control while in or partly in a building, or part of a building, that is a dwelling or is forces accommodation (or is both), and
   (b) at that time
      (i)   the person in relation to whom the dog is dangerously out of control ('V') is in, or is entering, the building or part as a trespasser, or
      (ii) D (if present at that time) believed V to be in, or entering, the building or part as a trespasser …

17.2   Amendment

The amendments by the ABCPA on 13 May 2014 are the most signif-icant in the history of the DDA. While the DDA has been amended over the past 25 years, most of those have been piecemeal and polit-ical. These core changes are the result of consultations with various interested bodies and members of the public.

The key areas those amendments changed are:

1.   Section 3 of the DDA has been extended so it now applies to *all* places.
2.   Section 3 of the DDA has been extended so it now applies to *assistance* dogs.
3.   Seizure of dogs by the authorities has been extended to apply to *all* dogs.
4.   Sentencing has been increased to a maximum of *14* years' imprisonment.
5.   The court has additional powers when *assessing* whether a dog is a danger to public safety
6.   There are *civil* proceedings that can be used against dogs and their owners.
7.   The court has a duty and a power to assess the *character* of the dog and the dog's owner.
8.   A court can order any dog to be destroyed even though the dog or the owner has not been *convicted* of any offence.

17.3   Places

The catalytic reason leading to the change was that since 2005 the fatalities comprised ten children and eight adults who have died as a result of being attacked by a dog, 16 of which took place on 'private' property. Many were high profile cases where a pros-ecution was not possible, despite death or serious injury, because the attack was on private property. Now it extends to '*any place in England or Wales whether or not a public place*'.

In the past decade the number of people requiring hospital treat-ment after a dog attack has increased by 76%. The Health and Social Care Information Centre stated the number of hospital admissions rose from 4,110 to 7,227. The most commonly attacked victims were children under nine years old.

As there is no limitation on the definition, it applies to any and every private place a person can be attacked. It applies whether the owner is with or without his dog. He may be absent from his home while his dog is present. Then, if his dog attacks a *lawful* visitor the absent owner can be liable for any potential and actual injury. An owner can now be liable if his dog commits an offence any-where at all, domestic or otherwise. The Communication Workers Union [CWU] campaigned for years for a change in the law to protect their members, who include postmen. The Royal Mail has confirmed that there were 2,660 attacks on postal workers in 2015. Of those, 1,888 attacks happened at the front door of a house. The Annual Dog Awareness Week [2015] by the Royal Mail states 27% of dog owners admit their pets have been loose when an exterior door is open. A postman delivering letters is now protected if he is attacked while retreating down the footpath using his bag as a shield or if while pushing the post through the letterbox, he loses a finger from a snapping dog inside the house. [See: **7.2**]

A charity collector confirmed the schoolboy chestnut, who blames his dog for eating his homework: 'An envelope was whipped from my fingers as I posted it through the letter box, following thumps as a large dog hurled itself at the door.' If the charity worker was bitten or even feared she would be, an offence would be committed.

In 2016 Mark Tipping was fined after his dog bit off the fingertips of Claire Offord, a post woman, at his home in Essex. Offord needed plastic surgery after the attack. Tipping was ordered to pay a total of £8,793 including £2,764 compensation. A contingent destruction order was imposed on his dog.

The changes alter the potential liability of every dog owner in his home. If his dog attacks a lawful visitor the owner now faces a prison sentence while his dog faces death. This extension to private property means prison for the owner and death for his dog is feasible, even if it is an unlawful visitor. [See: **17.5**]

These changes place the onus on every owner to ensure all visi-tors to his property are safe when in the vicinity of his dog. Each visitor, whether it is under a licence such as the delivery driver, a community nurse or one invited to enjoy a midsummer cucumber sandwich tea, is entitled to be safe from an attack by the owner's dog. The burden is now on the solicitous owner regarding his resident dog rather than on the casual or perhaps careless visitor. That might even mean muzzling the dog indoors while the visitor is present or locking him away until the visitor departs.

No time was lost by the police in charging a man for an incident that happened in his home on 13 May 2014. The first prosecution of an owner on *'private'* property was initiated the following day. A 54-year-old woman was attacked shortly after 2 a.m. by a bull mastiff in the home of Gary Deegan in Lancaster. The woman suffered a broken arm and severe cuts, and required hospital treatment. Deegan appeared at Preston Crown Court and pleaded guilty. The difference the ABCPA has made can be seen as a day either way meant he faced a maximum sentence of two years' or five years' imprisonment. [See: **19.1**]

17.4   Assistance

Groups representing people who use *'assistance dogs'* have campaigned for years for a change in the law to protect such dogs and their owners. Finally that change has been made.

The number of attacks on assistance dogs by other dogs has steadily increased over the years. Between March 2011 and February 2013 there were 240 attacks on guide dogs alone. Notwithstanding that statistic, there are more shocking facts that lie behind the bare number:

1.   Almost a quarter of those victims had been attacked before and of those 28% had been attacked before by the same dog.
2.   The attacking dogs were without their owners on 22% of those occasions.
3.   The attacking dogs were without a lead on 42% of those occasions.

When an assistance dog is attacked and injured or killed by another dog it is traumatic for the owner too. The owner feels an acute helplessness in being unable to assist his dog, followed by a deep psychological stress at having to witness the start and end of the attack.

That is exacerbated by the effect on the owner, especially if he is blind. Then perhaps by hearing alone he knows his dog is being attacked. That effect can lead to traumatic stress for the dog and the owner at the time and thereafter.

The guide dogs rarely respond when they are attacked as they are deliberately chosen because of their non-aggressive temperament. Indeed, their docility and disposition is enhanced by the training. Moreover, the person might instinctively intervene to try and rescue or defend his dog. In doing so, particularly if he is blind, he risks further injury to himself and his dog.

The economic and social repercussions of an attack cannot be discounted. If the assistance dog is injured, depending on the nature and severity, the dog will have to recuperate and may have to be withdrawn from the service. That has a further impact on the mental and physical capacity of the assisted person as well as their sense of safety and security. The financial cost of training an assistance dog often means that those whose dogs are 'retired' face a long wait for another dog. That limits their ability to live independently.

The meaning of an 'assistance dog' is specified by the Equality Act 2010, namely:

(a) a dog which has been trained to guide a blind person;

(b) a dog which has been trained to assist a deaf person;

(c) a dog which has been trained by a prescribed charity to assist a disabled person who has a disability that consists of epilepsy or otherwise affects the person's mobility, manual dexterity, physical co-ordination or ability to lift, carry or otherwise move everyday objects; a dog of a prescribed category which has been trained;

(d) to assist a disabled person who has a disability (other than one falling within paragraph (c)) of a prescribed kind.

A dog will be dangerously out of control where there are grounds for a 'reasonable apprehension' that it will injure any assistance dog, whether or not it actually does so.

As the DDA includes 'or assistance dog' the result is the same test applies as to a person and with the same consequence. Neither a person nor an assistance dog has to be the victim of an actual bite for an offence to be committed. All that is necessary is that an element of fear was engendered because of the pending attack. That is the 'reasonable apprehension' felt by the victim. There could be a lot of growling and snarling and bared teeth, resulting in fear without any injury to a person or dog. In that event the offence is committed. [See: **16.2**]

If the assistance dog is actually injured, then an *aggravated* offence is committed. That is more serious in form and result, regardless of whether the victim dog lives or dies. The simple offence is still summary and subject to a six months' maximum prison sentence. For the aggravated offence the owner faces a maximum of three years' imprisonment while his dog could be killed by a court order. Tina Delaney, the Newham animal welfare manager, said succinctly when she seized a pet dog that she believed was a banned breed because it 'appeared' to her to be a pit bull-type: 'Ultimately the DDA is difficult legislation to enforce as it is the dog that pays with its life.' [See: Animal Saints and Sinners: BBC 1: 11/8/14]

The British Veterinary Association [BVA] and the RSPCA campaigned to change the law to protect all dogs that were victims of an attack by another dog. The ABCPA did not include all dogs, as the purpose of the DDA is to protect the public rather than animal welfare, which is covered by the AWA. That omission was and remains another mistake.

Regardless of that deliberate omission, if a dog threatens or attacks any animal, be it a cat, a dog or horse, that has an immediate impact on a person who is riding, playing with their cat or walking their dog. Then, if the person has a 'reasonable apprehension' the attacking dog will injure him or her, an offence is committed. Whether or not the attacking dog actually injures the other animal or the person is irrelevant. The fear engendered of an impending attack amounts to an offence. Indeed, a case more than three centuries old equally applies to the DDA. In *Dodwell v. Burford* [1669] 1 Mod. 24 the defendant struck a horse, causing the rider to be thrown off. Although that was an assault, if a dog caused a horse to bolt making the rider frightened for his safety, it would be an offence under the DDA. Both animal and owner could be spooked by the same act.

New preventative powers granted to the police and local authorities enable them to send owners to dog training classes and require them to muzzle their dogs in public. Both are positive methods of educating an owner to act responsibly to prevent avoidable injury to other people and making them feel safer around him and his dog. It might prevent a serious offence happening. The power allows the authorities the means to tackle irresponsible owners by changing their behaviour while saving their dogs from destruction. [See: **18.1**]

17.5 'Householder case'

The extension of criminal liability to 'any place' is seemingly extreme as it would potentially make every householder liable for any injury by their dog to every visitor to their home at any time. That would not matter whether it was a welcome visit, such as by your esteemed mother-in-law, or a midnight break-in by the incorrigible village burglar.

Most householders would consider a burglar takes the risk of a bite on the buttocks as an occupational hazard, the backside of his illicit trade. To that end the DDA allows a defence in *'a householder case'*. If and when their dog attacks an intruder, there is an exemption for householders in the event of that person being a *'trespasser'*. That is an essential exemption for householders as most would feel there is little point in having a dog that does not sink his teeth deep into a burglar's bulging buttocks as he climbs in or out of their house. Protecting his owner and his home is part of the purpose of having a dog. Most law-abiding citizens would consider being bitten is a risk a burglar should be deemed to accept before any entry. The burglar as a victim would elicit little, if any, sympathy from the average judge or jury.

An interesting Irish incident involving John Purcell and burglars is a tale worth the telling from 1811. Purcell woke in the early hours to hear an armed gang of nine breaking into the room next door. Purcell picked up a knife and when the first burglar burst in he stabbed him to death. The gunman fired but missed, so Purcell stabbed and wounded him. The swordsman attacked him but Purcell defended himself and stabbed him to death. Purcell grabbed the sword. All the burglars departed with their two dead accomplices. [See: W. Leitch: [1967] 18 NILQ 322] While it may be apocryphal it is claimed that Purcell was knighted for his endeavour.

A quarter of people in Britain have been burgled. As a result almost half of those victims have moved home. Therefore it is manifest many householders live in fear of being burgled. In terms of their personal security, 10% of people said 'they had bought a dog to deter burglars'. In London that figure increased to 15%. From January 2015 to June 2016 there were more than 70,000 residential burglaries in London. Those statistics, coupled with the rise in the number of Neighbourhood Watch groups formed because of the poor police response to burglaries, speaks loudly of the need for dogs as a means of citizen protection. It is compounded by the fact the police now expect people to have a DIY approach to crime and be their own detectives. Yet on the basis of the ABCPA the resident dog must somehow distinguish between whether (i) he is in the garden or (ii) leaving the house or (iii) is still acting *'as a trespasser'*. [See: **17.8**]

The ABCPA puts beyond doubt that a defence is available to house-holders against intruders: *A person is not guilty of an offence … in a case which is a householder case.*

Yet this is an unnecessarily complex area that provides that defence. The defence is available in 'a householder case', which is subject to two alternative conditions that denote different situations, namely:

1. A 'householder case' is when the dog is 'dangerously out of control while in or partly in a building, or part of a building, that is a dwelling or forces accommodation, or both.'

2. Then the defence is applicable if *'at that time'*:
    (a) the person in relation to whom the dog is dangerously out of control 'is in, or is entering, the building or part as a trespasser'; or

    (b) the owner of the dog is present and 'believed the person to be in, or entering, the building or part as a trespasser'.

17.6   Areas

The three key areas of the 'householder defence' relate to (i) what is a 'building', (ii) what is a 'dwelling' and (iii) what and who is a 'trespasser'?

A 'building' was defined by Byles J in *Stevens v. Gourley* [1859] 1 QB 264 as 'a structure of considerable size and intended to be permanent, or at least to endure for a considerable time.' The judge correctly observed it was impossible to define the word with accuracy.

As the point is a person lives in a 'structure', that is a reason why it should apply to a tent. Alan Bennett, the droll author, allowed an eccentric lady to live in a van on his drive for many years. That was her abode, no less than the tramp with a tent. No different to the ordinary householder, burglary and robbery plus companion dogs make homeless people potential vulnerable victims too. Equally, a homeless person should not be denied protection.

Burglary and theft are committed from tents at music festivals. Even though it is contrary to the conditions of entry, except for guide dogs, people do manage to bring dogs on to the campsite. In June 2014 a woman somehow managed to bring her dog on to the site and when she left somehow 'forgot' she had brought a dog there so when the Glastonbury Festival finished she left the site and somehow left it behind. The dog was found alone, cowering in the corner of her tent. The dog was named Dolly by her rescuer, the staff at the local RSPCA, after the great star-spangled Miss Parton, who had earlier wowed the crowd. Somehow the massive publicity revived the owner's memory so Dolly was reclaimed by her. If Dolly had not been reclaimed, but had attacked a man entering the tent, what would have been her fate? Apart from Miss Parton's offer to rehome Dolly, the likelihood is she would have been 'put down' as an abandoned stray. [See: **8.5**]

The protection given to the householder by the ABCPA relates to the house and only the house as a 'building'. The reason behind that limit appears to be that it allows for a child to collect his stray ball and a neighbour dropping off a case of wine as compared to a burglar entering as a malignant trespasser. It only applies to a property that is the 'place of residence'.

17.7   Dwelling

As the exemption relates to a building where a person lives, whether it is a 'dwelling' is a question of *fact*. That will be determined by the particular court hearing the particular case. Consequently, it does not apply to the private land around a dwelling or any non-domestic property such as a barn. Similarly, it does not include a garden or a path or a shed.

Is a *'dwelling'* only where someone lives or sleeps, or occasionally visits? What if it is one of several properties owned by a politician; the one where he spends time while in London, his other home in his constituency and his weekend country mansion? Are they all his 'dwelling' or only when he actually sleeps in a particular place?

A building such as a block of flats may contain many dwellings. A hotel room is not normally a dwelling but may be for some people who live there. Premises do not cease to be a dwelling because of a temporary absence of the inhabitants, providing they intend to return. Recreational vehicles are becoming popular with our ever-increasing elderly snowbirds. The vehicle is a home for a family living in it, which could be during a holiday, but equally could be their permanent residence. A camper van beloved of ageing and new-age hippies as they head towards Stonehenge and Glastonbury Tor serves the same purpose. Are they all excluded from relying on the 'householder defence'? Was it intended that a mobile gap year lawyer and his trusty Rottweiler would be denied a legal defence?

The same principle applies to a communal laundry room used by the tenants in a block of flats. If the householder and his dog attacked a burglar on a common landing or the laundry room in a block of flats, neither of them could rely on this limited definition and defence. Indeed, the landing or the laundry room are the precise places a burglar would use to gain entry and then to escape. This 'defence' should protect the homeowner and his dog, rather than a burglar.

17.8   Trespasser

What and who is a 'trespasser' in law is at the root of the 'householder case' as it will affect the owner and his dog directly. However, the definition of a trespasser is laden with doubt and blurred by an unwelcome hawker or a nosy neighbour. Trespass is a civil concept rooted in tort [a civil wrong]. A person entering 'as a trespasser' for the purpose of burglary was defined by Edmund Davies LJ in *R. v.*

Collins [1972] 2 All E R 1105 as one who '… does so knowing that he is a trespasser and nevertheless deliberately enters, or, at the very least, is reckless as to whether or not he is entering the premises of another without the other party's consent.'

So in 'householder cases' where the victim of the dog's aggression either (a) was a trespasser or (b) was believed to be one by the owner, no offence will be committed under this section. As with all aspects of this Act, these amendments are riddled with a certain uncertainty.

Without doubt the position is different and better if the owner is *present* at the time. Then it does not matter whether the person actually was a trespasser. If the owner is in the building when his dog becomes out of control and he *believed* that the person was a trespasser that is sufficient to raise and rely upon the defence. As it is the personal belief of the householder who confronts, hears or is aware of the intruder in his home, it must be a subjective rather than an objective test. There is no reason why an unreasonable belief, providing it is honestly held, should deprive a person of a defence in the case of a trespasser. That approach allows for various types of residents, from the fearless ex-soldier who confronts the intruder to the frightened elderly disabled widow who has a heart attack at the sound of the shattered glass as the burglar breaks into her bedroom. In each case their belief is subjective and their dog may be a lifeline. Both the soldier and the widow may need the assistance of their dog against an intruder who is likely to be armed and definitely perceived to be dangerous.

There is unnecessary confusion caused by the conditions created by the 'householder cases'. If the owner is *absent* then it depends exactly where the person is in relation to the resident dog as to whether he is or is not a 'trespasser'. If the person is 'in' or is 'entering' a property then all is well providing he is in fact a trespasser. The section specifies that the person is present *'as a trespasser'*. Therefore if the intruder is still in the garden while casing the place, the defence does not apply. Then a single bite could mean the dog would die.

In these days of advanced technology it is possible for a person to scan his house in Llandudno while he is in Las Vegas. In doing so he might catch sight of a burglar in action. Why should he be denied a defence if his dog attacks the burglar as he is not 'in or entering' the house, but can be seen on the screen leaving with a swag bag full of the family silver? Why should he have to be present?

Moreover, with such advanced technology the householder might give a signal to his dog to actually attack the burglar: He might order the dog, recognising his master's voice, to 'Go get him, Genghis!' His absence or presence in his own home is irrelevant to his knowledge his home is being burgled and that his dog is at risk of being injured. The defence should not depend on the absence or presence of the owner. It is not fanciful to speculate on the status of an intruder 'as a trespasser' in relation to a dog if his owner is absent. The Court of Appeal in *Jaggard v. Dickinson* [1981] 72 Cr. App. R. 33 proves the problem for the dog. Beverley Jaggard was a drunken defendant who claimed she mistakenly but honestly believed the house she was breaking into belonged to her friend. While her friend lived at 67 Carnach Green, Jaggard broke into 35 Carnach Green, which was 'a house of identical outward appearance'. She was charged with criminal damage and convicted by the Essex justices. Mustill J in the High Court said: 'The justices found that the defendant did believe that she was in the property of Mr Heyfron [her friend], but that this mistake was induced by a state of self-induced intoxication.' Drunkenness was a defence resulting in her conviction being quashed. It was quashed because she *believed* she had the owner's consent, not because she was drunk. The question remains as to whether Jaggard would be entering 'as a trespasser' in relation to the resident dog. If she is not a trespasser and the dog is alone when he bites her, an offence could be committed by the householder.

Lest that seems extreme, it is mirrored by a scene reminiscent of the Three Bears by Freddy Shelby, who was arrested in New Mexico in Albuquerque. The police were called by a couple who returned home and found 'the naked intruder sleeping in their bed …' Shelby broke into their home, drank a Sprite from their fridge and ended up in their bedroom. The couple found 'Shelby in a deep sleep'. On arrest Shelby told the officers 'he thought he was at his girlfriend's house'.

Any person who legitimately enters property must be protected from a ferocious dog. A person exercising a legal power such as a police officer with a warrant or a bailiff with a court order will not enter 'as a trespasser', whether or not the occupier grants or refuses his consent. If the owner is present he might control his dog. However, if he is absent it can be problematic. For if the dog is alone and attacks such a lawful visitor, is the householder defence available? It seems it is not, yet what does the dog do except act on behalf of his owner. Is the person entering on red alert that a dog is or may be in the property? [See: **16.6**]

A lawful visitor may unwittingly cause the resident dog to escape from his home. He might attack a visitor or not, in the garden. Then it would be the visitor's action rather than the dog's reaction that determines the liability and the availability of a defence.

There should be a defence where a dog was provoked into action by someone or he is acting in self-defence to protect his owner, his pups or himself. Self-defence is available to a person charged with an offence, including murder. There is no reason why it should be denied to a dog, especially as against a burglar whether he is in the garden or the house. [See: **16.8**]

17.9   Seizure

As the ABCPA amended the DDA from 'one' to '*a* dog' the authorities can seize *all* dogs in private places. The enforcement officer can seize any dog from any place at any time:

'A constable or an officer of a local authority authorised by it to exercise the powers conferred by this subsection may seize any dog in a place in England or Wales which is not a public place if the dog appears to the constable or officer to be dangerously out of control.'

An enforcement officer, namely a local dog warden or police officer, can enter any public and private place and if it '*appears*' to the officer that any dog is dangerously out of control he can simply seize him. Such a subjective view is subject to too much variation. The one certain aspect it brings to this area is uncertainty. The subjective view of what 'appears' to the enforcement officer is too prone to human error. When the DDA was introduced a lot of dogs that merely 'looked like a pit bull' were seized and killed after an amateur assessment by the local bobby. It should be based on an expert opinion of a vet followed, if necessary, by an application to the court where his evidence can be tested under cross-examination.

The case of Tyson, the 'sniffer' police dog, illuminates precisely what is wrong with the present position. Tyson was a dog owned by the RSPCA in Somerset, but seconded to the police to help them sniff out illicit items. Over a considerable period they had assessed and trained Tyson, and had the opportunity to examine his appearance and behaviour. No one at the RSPCA or in the police force considered any point against Tyson in appearance or behaviour in relation to public safety. He even featured on a television show, *Dog Rescuers*. Then suddenly two officers believed he was 'a pit bull type'. As a result of their view, Tyson was returned to the RSPCA as his owner. It seems that everyone 'understood' they had no other legal option. They were wrong. So Tyson was killed. Even assuming the officers were right as to 'type', it is somewhat surprising that an application was not made to the court consistent with the principle in *Housego v. Canterbury Crown Court and CPS*. The decision is disappointing and wrong as Housego was guilty of three offences. Tyson had not committed any offence, except perhaps being born.

More surprising is the fact none of the parties seemed to be aware they could apply to the court on the authority of *Sandhu*. Ultimately it was his face that determined his fate as his appearance alone killed Tyson.

The power to enter private property or to seize a dog from private property, whether it is your home, garden or allotment, without the need for expert evidence is wrong. It is too wide that the dog merely has to *appear* to be dangerously out of control. Therefore any procedure regarding the dog's welfare and future should be subject to an examination by an expert. A dog should not be killed unless there is a court order as, notwithstanding any expert, if the opinion is wrong, death cannot be reversed. It is a telltale sign that such a simple test followed by the correct procedure could have saved Tyson's life.

Similarly, the Merseyside Police saw fit to kill 22 dogs without legal notice to the owners so they were not able to appeal against any proposed action. They acted unilaterally without a court order. That action was unlawful. [See: **12.3**]

17.10   Rehome

A concealed side-effect of seizure is what happens to the dogs once they have been seized. The report, *Breed Specific Legislation – A Dog's Dinner* [2016], by the RSPCA is a splendid and sterling analysis of all that is wrong with the DDA. Throughout the analysis pinpoints the inadequate way we treat dogs that are deemed to be 'dangerous' with the result they are often destined to die at our hands and by a court order.

However, notwithstanding the report's many positive features, there is one aspect of it that is unsatisfactory in terms of the idea and interpretation, namely: 'The Dangerous Dogs Exemption Scheme Order 2015 imposes severe restrictions on change of keepership of the exempted dog, despite a court previously being satisfied that the dog did not constitute a danger to public safety enabling its initial access to the register of exempted dogs. Under s. 12 of the Order, the only circumstances in which a new person may apply to the court to be substituted as the person in charge of the dog is in the event of death or serious illness of the current keeper. Given that there is no other legal means of moving a dog to another keeper, this is clearly a negative move, particularly for organisations such as the RSPCA who cannot transfer ownership once the dog is in their care and ownership. The same downside applies to any owner of a dog who is in good health but whose circumstances change and who wants to transfer ownership. It is clearly possible that this law change may increase the euthanasia of s.1 dogs.'

That view was endorsed by Dr Samantha Gaines of the RSPCA, who said: 'The police, the RSPCA … have to deal with the consequences of this flawed law by euthanising hundreds of dogs because legislation is forcing us to, due to the way they look, despite being suitable for rehoming.'

That view of, and hence consequent action by, the RSPCA, though it may be well-intentioned is misguided and more importantly, given the result, simply misconceived as a matter of law. The Dangerous Dogs Exemption Scheme Order 2015 by Defra states a prohibited dog can only be transferred if the conditions for substitution of a person in charge is unable to continue to be in charge of the dog by reason of:

1. The death of that person; or
2. Serious illness rendering that person unable to be in charge of the dog.

That is neither logical nor reasonable and does not appear to properly reflect the law. These are provisional legal problems with Defra's index:

1. If a person is sent to prison his dog cannot be rehomed.

2. If a homeless person's new home has a 'no pets policy' his dog cannot be rehomed.

3. If a person is divorced the court cannot order custody of his dog to his ex-wife.

There are numerous cases of dogs being rehomed by the courts. They have made such decisions in the interests of the owner and dog as often the choice was between being rehomed or destroyed:

1. In *R. Devon* [2011] the High Court was faced with the present owner being incapable of looking after the dog. It decided the dog should be subject to a contingent destruction order on the basis that the dog is rehomed. The alternative was immediate death. [See: **10.2**]

2. Collins J said in *Sandhu* [2012]: 'All that the court can do, and should do, if satisfied that the dog in question would not constitute a danger to public safety, because it does not have the inherently dangerous characteristics that pit bull-type dogs are believed to have, is make a contingent destruction order if asked to do so, so that attempts can be made to obtain a certificate of exemption.' Sandhu was in prison at the time. [See: **11.4**]

3. In *Housego* [2012] the police seized Kelly and placed her into the care of the Lord Whisky Animal Sanctuary. Housego renounced ownership and applied for Kelly to be permitted to stay there. The court confirmed the change of ownership. [See: **11.2**]

4. In *R. v. Hastie* [2016] at Exeter Crown Court the judge confirmed the change of ownership of Stella the pit bull terrier to Carolyne Pharaoh. HHJ Cottle said: 'We have to be sure Stella doesn't

pose a risk to public safety. Carolyne Pharaoh said she will take ownership of the dog and apply for an exemption certificate.' He confirmed the transfer. [See: **7.3**]

If Defra is right then all those judges are wrong. Significantly, the Devon and Cornwall Police, who supported the 'transfer' of Stella, said: 'The force has already put forward a report to the Defra Select Committee inquiry into the welfare of seized domestic animals.'

The index cannot stand within the principles considered and adopted with those authorities. Defra has ignored the principles within those cases: a dog is entitled to a fair trial and providing public safety is satisfied should be rehomed with a fit and proper person. The court, not Defra, decides the law.

17.11   Licence

While these increases in sentence are timely, they are dealing with the result rather than prevention. The stark reality is there are numerous irresponsible owners who should not be allowed to possess a dog, let alone have the opportunity to train one to fight or parade him as a trophy. That is why a licence should be reintroduced with a fee of £300 per dog per year. Allowances can be made for 'special cases' by granting exemptions for charities and professional breeders as well as on grounds of personal exceptional hardship and need. Save for those special cases that can properly be taken into account to allow for a reduced fee, if a person cannot pay less than £1 a day they cannot afford to own a dog. A responsible owner would not baulk at that sum to keep the public safe. [See: **15.1; 19.1**]

A licence would also still illegal breeders who sell dangerous dogs and breed litters year-on-year as if they were so much detritus. Each fee would raise revenue, which could be used to promote the welfare of ill-treated dogs and employ officers to enforce the law. Considering the dog population is about nine million, annually it would raise around £2.7 billion. Such a sum could also be used to pay for accommodation, behaviour therapy, sanctuaries, veterinary treatment and all the attendant expenses relating to the offence. Allied to that the revenue could be used to appoint and pay for an Animals' Ombudswoman to legally represent dogs in and out of court as their advocate.

In 2015–16 more than 3,000 stray dogs were destroyed by local authorities. More than 37,000 stray dogs remain unclaimed. As owners fail to update the microchip details, 12 dogs a day are at risk of being killed as strays.

The cost of lost and stolen dogs for the taxpayer and welfare charities is £33 million per year. That is one reason all dogs now have to be microchipped. Breeders have to microchip their puppies before they sell or give them to a new owner. Breeders have to register their details and those are recorded against the microchip number for the life of that dog. Microchipping will have the effect of allowing the police to identify a dog that is involved in crime, anything and everything from assault to murder. Even after April 2016 when it became compulsory, with a £500 fine, a million owners have failed to microchip their dog.

A licence would curb the ever-growing problem of irresponsible owners whose dogs attack children, adults and other animals. The time for it to be a legal requirement has passed.

Whether a dog is a danger to public safety

17.12   Anti-social Behaviour, Crime and Policing Act 2014 s.107

(1) The Dangerous Dogs Act 1991 is amended as follows.
(2) In section 1 (dogs bred for fighting) after subsection (6) there is inserted
  '(6A) A scheme under subsection (3) or (5) may in particular include provision requiring a court to consider whether a person is a fit and proper person to be in charge of a dog.'
(3) In section 4 (destruction and disqualification orders) after section (1A) there is inserted
  '(1B) For the purposes of subsection (1A)(a), when deciding whether a dog would constitute a danger to public safety, the court
  (a) must consider
    (i)   the temperament of the dog and its past behaviour, and
    (ii) whether the owner of the dog, or the person for the time being in charge of it, is a fit and proper person to be in charge of the dog, and
  (b) may consider any other relevant circumstances.'

17.13   Scheme

The court has power to make the defendant, subject to his means, pay for his dog to be killed. It may allow him to register for an exemption as opposed to the destruction. Alternatively he may apply for an exemption by gaining a certificate and complying with the strict conditions. [See: **11.4**]

The ABCPA amendment has developed that application by making the condition relevant to the owner's character: in section 1 a scheme may in particular include provision requiring a court to consider whether a person is a fit and proper person to be in charge of a dog.

That he must be a *'fit and proper person'* is a positive addition to the conditions that pertain to dog ownership. The court can assess whether that person is worthy of owning that dog. As it refers to simple possession as opposed to actual ownership, he must comply with the condition even to be in 'charge' of a dog.

Lord Alverstone CJ said in *R. v. Hyde JJ* [1912] LT 152: 'The prima facie meaning of the words "fit and proper person" [in the Licensing Act 1920] is that the applicant must be a fit and proper person to hold a licence and carry on the business of the licence-holder.'

It is why several of the Asian–Pakistani taxi drivers in Rotherham who were involved in multiple abuse of underage white school girls were refused licences. They were not 'fit and proper persons' to hold the licence. Similar to an irresponsible owner of a dog, the criterion was the safety of the public and public policy.

This condition takes into account the character of the owner as applicant or defendant, and hence assesses whether he will look after the dog in terms of the necessary care and welfare. That would relate to his duty and responsibility under the AWA too. So it is assessing *'the'* owner in terms of his antecedents. That questions whether he is the right person to be in charge of *'the'* dog now and in the future. A defendant with a bad character would be balanced against a dog with a good character. The answer would be to deprive the owner and save the dog. That would be a judicial desert.

17.14   Safety

Following *Sandhu v. Isleworth Crown Court* it was essential the revised DDA took into account the points raised by the court. That judgment concentrates on the character of the defendant as owner and the character of his dog. The ABCPA makes the court concentrate on those aspects when deciding whether a dog is a danger to public safety as that affects his future and right to live.

Now there is a rigorous test to apply by the court *before* deciding to issue a destruction order:

When deciding whether a dog would constitute a danger to public safety, the court:

(a)   must consider the temperament of the dog and its past behaviour and whether the owner of the dog or the person in charge is a fit and proper person to be in charge of the dog, and

(b)   may consider any other relevant circumstances.

The positive aspect of the test is the court must consider the *temperament* of the dog and his *past behaviour* in order to decide his fate. Therefore, a well-behaved and properly trained dog should not be condemned to die at this stage. As the court considers that fate first it can be independent of the owner's character. While the dog may benefit from having an owner with a good character, the dog should not automatically suffer because the owner has a bad character. Now, as the decision determines the dog's death, it is a balancing exercise rather than as has been the case in the past, a rubber stamp result confirming destruction as the first and final choice. [See: **9.2**]

Then, in a related test, the court must consider the character of the owner and whether he is a 'fit and proper person' to be in charge of the dog. The bad character of the defendant is significant as a person with a penchant for violence can change his dog to reflect his own. Collins J noted the point in *Sandhu*: 'Frequently, of course, section three offences depend upon the dog having been treated by its owner so as to exhibit dangerous tendencies ...'

There is no reason why a dog should suffer as otherwise any ill-treatment by the defendant as his owner is thereby revisited on him by the court. The better course is to consider a contingent destruction order and allow expert behaviour therapy for the dog in the future. Otherwise the dog suffers twice, when he was ill-treated and again when he bites someone and is deemed to die because he is be a danger to public safety. That would be using the cruelty inflicted by a bad owner as a base to order the dog's destruction. Such a result ending in the dog's death would solely show the court being cruel to be cruel.

If a person is found guilty of owning a 'prohibited type' of dog the court will continue to have two options, namely (a) to order exemption that the dog is added to the Index of Exempted Dogs within two months or (b) to issue a destruction order. Nevertheless, the court must now make an assessment of suitability as part of the process of deciding whether the person should be allowed to keep his or her dog with an exemption. The advantageous aspect of that test is it puts the 'welfare' of the dog ahead of the 'ownership' of the defendant. So it places a value on the dog's life and future.

Though the court '*must*' take into account certain points, the court '*may*' consider any 'other relevant circumstances'. That seems an afterthought that is negative in form and effect. If it is 'relevant', whether it touches the dog or the owner or otherwise, it should be 'must' rather than 'may' in each case. What is the value of a 'relevant' circumstance the court can ignore? A court could find a matter to be relevant yet decide not to take it into account. Failing to take it into account by killing the dog might then be the option. Such a result defies law and logic and proves that, where dogs are concerned, the law is an ass.

17.15   Dangerous

The court will consider such an exemption based on a number of factors, including an assessment by dog legislation officers as to whether the dog is aggressive. That is inadequate, as the tale of Tyson's life and death is its own testament. There should be an *independent* expert to advise the court. [See: **17.9**]

Besides those factors the court will consider making an assessment of the owner whether he can provide suitable accommodation for the dog and abide by the restrictions required by the court. At the heart of the assessment the court will assess his character. Now that is even more important than it was before as the court has a duty to investigate it. To that end perhaps the peremptory decisions of many courts hitherto to destroy a dog may lessen in the future. [See: **17.12**]

17.16   Civil

The position of a dog seized under this amendment is now more perilous as civil proceedings can be brought 'in exercise of a power of seizure conferred by any other enactment'.

That will allow the authorities to rescue an abandoned dog left when people move house, gypsies move on to a new site or when situations arise such as Dolly's owner absent-mindedly leaving her at the Glastonbury Festival. It will allow them to kill a dog at will. The power is so wide it applies to any dog that the authorities happen to seize, be it a stray or abandoned or otherwise. They may at best keep the dog for seven days before deciding on his demise. Who then represents the legal interests of the seized dog?

17.17   Repeal

These amendments by the ABCPA are a missed opportunity to finally repeal the failed DDA. It should be replaced with a bold non-breed specific Act that would enhance the protection of the public and responsible owners alike. As a consequence, it should not protect a burglar as against a resident dog protecting his home, regardless of whether his master is present or whether the burglar is in the house or leaving. [See: **17.8**]

This law has failed to address the crucial issues. It should be changed to protect us and dogs. That is reason we need a licence and an Animals' Ombudswoman. [See: **17.11**]

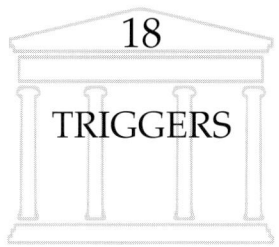

18

TRIGGERS

18.1 Anti-social Behaviour, Crime and Policing Act 2014 s.104

(1) In a case where a person has made a complaint about anti-social behaviour in a particular local government area, the relevant bodies in that area must carry out a review of the response to that behaviour (an 'ASB case review)' if:
  (a) that person, or any other person, makes an application for such a review, and
  (b) the relevant bodies decide that the threshold for a review is met.

After extensive consultation with various animal welfare bodies and local councils and the police, the Home Office published a report of its findings, *Reform of Anti-social behaviour Powers*, in July 2014. The theme of that report was adopted from an earlier report which expressed the aim in its title, a mantra that was repeated throughout the White Paper, *Putting Victims First: more effective responses to anti-social behaviour* [2012].

18.2   Remedy

It heralded a new approach to crime, policing and community powers based on a shift from bureaucracy to a proposed democracy.

It places an emphasis on local problems and local solutions rather than the latter emanating from Westminster. The approach is on solving local issues as they affect a particular victim. Such a shift towards the victim has an implicit advantage in allowing a person to seek a remedy to counter anti-social behaviour that threatens his 'quality of life'.

To reflect the concern of people in the community, but guard against the busybody and the professional complainer, there has to be a 'community trigger' to set the complaint in motion. Then there is no undue delay in dragging cases through the courts in a long drawn out process. It is intended to provide a quick 'community remedy'.

The process involves the victims and the perpetrators following a set of rules to find a swift solution to their problem. That involves a series of actions taken towards a remedy according to the serious-ness of the complaint in respect of the solution sought now and in the future. The action taken involves an analysis of the problem and the remedy, namely:

1. The community trigger;
2. community protection notices;
3. public spaces protection orders;
4. civil injunctions.

They can be used, separately or together, to protect the victim from 'anti-social behaviour'. That is defined as 'behaviour causing harassment, alarm or distress to members or any member of the public'.

It covers aspects of everyday living and matters that detract from the quality of ordinary life. For one man's indulgence is another man's irritation, one man's noise is another man's music, be it the sound of hip hop at midnight or the bellowing of a bulldog during daylight hours.

Dogs are targeted to tackle the continued alarm felt by the public. It is aimed at irresponsible devil-may-care owners who wilfully cause others a problem by failing to control their dogs.

18.3   Triggers

The process gives victims and communities the right to request a review of the issue causing them a problem. A *'trigger'* ignites the complaint by a request of a 'review' by the relevant agencies to find a solution. The agencies, be it the local authorities and councils and police, liaise on behalf of the victim. Together they should seek and secure a solution.

To warrant an investigation the complaint has to pass a 'threshold'. That is defined by the local agencies. However, the threshold cannot be set too high as otherwise it will defeat the very purpose of their duty to help the victims. The threshold cannot demand more than 'at least three' complaints in the 'previous six-month period'.

To ensure the complaint is a valid one rather than some petty whinge, the threshold may also take account of various factors that reflect upon the seriousness of the issue. The agencies can consider the 'persistence' of the anti-social behaviour and the resulting 'harm or potential harm' caused by that behaviour. It may be the case that the victim has already brought the matter to the attention of the perpetrator. Then the perpetrator has ignored his request or not dealt with it in a satisfactory manner. Hence the agencies can take into account the adequacy of the perpetrator's response to the victim's request.

The victim is informed of the result of the review, therefore if further action is necessary an action plan will be made. That too will be discussed with the victim. As delay may cause yet further frustration to a victim, the method and time taken will also be discussed with him.

18.4   Voice

Sometimes it might be a vulnerable person, be it for a mental or physical reason or otherwise, who is a victim of anti-social behaviour. While that person could raise the issue personally, if he is inhibited from acting or unable to do so, he is not prevented from having another person raise it. So the Community Trigger can be raised by another person acting on behalf of the victim, such as a carer, a member of his family or a relative.

It is feasible and might be appropriate in the event of a conflict between neighbours and the consequent embarrassment or harassment, for a Member of Parliament to raise the complaint. While the victim can and perhaps usually would be an individual, equally it could be a company or a community group. The crucial point is that the victim's voice is heard and acted upon by an agency that has the power to make a change to the quality of their life.

Community Protection Notice

18.5   Anti-social Behaviour, Crime and Policing Act 2014 s.43

(1)   An authorised person may issue a community protection notice to an individual aged 16 or over, or a body, if satisfied on reasonable grounds that
   (a)   the conduct of the individual or body is having a detrimental effect, of a persistent or continuing nature, on the quality of life of those in the locality, and
   (b)   the conduct is unreasonable.

The purpose of a community protection notice [CPN] is to stop a person aged 16 or over, a business or an organisation committing anti-social behaviour that detrimentally affects people within their community. That type of behaviour actually does or has a tendency to spoil the community's quality of life. After all, a community is a cohesive unit that is formed and feeds off the positive energy of individuals. They are entitled to enjoy a quality of life that is consistent with the quiet enjoyment of their home and garden rather than have their eardrums assaulted or be attacked by snarling out of control dogs and barking neighbours. That extends to the streets in the neighbourhood.

The CPN is a practical measure in approach and scope. It can include a requirement that the perpetrator stops the negative conduct or starts some positive action and takes reasonable steps to avoid further anti-social behaviour in the future. So it could instruct the owner to ensure his fence is in good condition and prevent his three dogs from constantly entering the High Street and frightening people at the Saturday market and at the local car boot sale. The advantage of issuing a CPN is the power that flows from it and follows if the perpetrator ignores the request. Then the council could carry out any necessary works in default on behalf of the perpetrator. The expense would be due to him as it is a debt for which the council could claim the 'amount' in the Magistrates' Court under the ABCPA.

It is of practical value to victims that a breach of the CPN is a criminal offence. In September 2016 a man allowed his 'four dogs to attack other pets in a Bristol park'. The council issued a CPN with the 'warning' to him that: 'If steps are not taken to ensure the animals are not a threat to other local people and animals, the council will pursue enforcement action.'

An alleged perpetrator may dispute the nature of the complaint or the issue itself. There could be a challenge to the terms of the CPN. A dog owner might dispute that it relates to his dog or the volume of noise created by barking or an escape from his garden. He can lodge an appeal under the ABCPA regarding the terms of the CPN within 21 days of it being issued.

If a CPN is ignored by the dog owner the agency can and will carry out the work, perhaps securing a gate, mending a fence or even buying a muzzle. As the council or police could undertake the work and charge the perpetrator, the sum claimed from him could be quite high. The perpetrator can challenge the agency if he believes the cost is disproportionate.

Once a CPN is issued, that is not the end of the matter as the CPN can include requirements of the perpetrator to ensure that the problems are rectified and that he takes steps to prevent the anti-social behaviour occurring again. If he fails to do so then, as it is of a continuing nature, it could be used as 'evidence' in any proceedings against him. His behaviour could also be relevant, if it should arise, to show he is not 'a fit and proper person' to own his dog. [See: **17.12**]

Public spaces protection order

18.6   Anti-social Behaviour, Crime and Policing Act 2014 s.59

(1) A local authority may make a public spaces protection order if satisfied on reasonable grounds that two conditions are met.

The *first* condition is that (a) activities carried on in a public place within the authority's area have had a detrimental effect on the quality of life of those in the locality, or (b) it is likely that activities will be carried on in a public place within that area and that they will have such an effect.

The *second* condition is that the effect, or likely effect, of the activities (a) is, or is likely to be, of a persistent or continuing nature, (b) is, or is likely to be, such as to make the activities unreasonable, and (c) justifies the restrictions imposed by the notice.

The purpose of a Public Spaces Protection Order [PSPO] is to stop individuals or groups committing anti-social behaviour in a public space. A public space is precisely that and intended to be enjoyed by members of the public rather than them feeling threatened by a marauding mob of unleashed dogs while the multiple-studded sleepy keeper supposedly in charge of them idly rolls an illicit cigarette while slurping from a flagon of cheap scrumpy. Such behaviour disturbs the right of the public to enjoy a lazy Sunday afternoon in the park. That type of owner cares little for his fellow citizens and less for his dogs, given that their twin fates are dependent on his actions.

As this is a more serious form of a community order it requires consultation before any action is taken. A PSPO is issued by a council. Before it does so it must consult with the relevant bodies, including the police and the police and crime commissioner.

Before a PSPO can be issued the complaint has to pass a test. To do so the behaviour has to (a) have a detrimental effect on the 'quality of life' of those in the locality. Additionally, the behaviour has to be (b) both of a continuous or persistent nature and (c) be unreasonable. That approach is to ensure that the behaviour is indeed anti-social and not merely one of the myriad irritations of ordinary life. Dogs are now part of the landscape of England. One in four households own one and there are about nine million. However, that does not mean that owners can do what they want when they want, regardless of the feelings of others who share the same space as them and their dogs but have different views.

The PSPO can be enforced by council officers and a police officer and a PCSO. Similar to the CPN, it is of value to victims as a breach of a PSPO is a criminal offence.

The important changes introduced by the PSPO mean that more than one restriction can be added to the same PSPO, so a single PSPO can deal with a wider range of behaviours than the order it replaces. The important changes introduced by the PSPO mean that it can now deal with a wider range of behaviours that trouble others during their daily lives. A council has to have an open mind to review a complaint from a member of the community about his fear resulting from a feckless owner and his unruly dogs and their joint actions in an open public space.

Civil injunction

18.7 Anti-social Behaviour, Crime and Policing Act 2014 s.1

(1) A court may grant an injunction under this section against a person aged ten or over ('the respondent') if two conditions are met.

The first condition is that the court is satisfied, on the balance of probabilities, that the respondent has engaged, or threatens to engage, in anti-social behaviour.

The second condition is that the court considers it just and convenient to grant the injunction for the purpose of preventing the respondent from engaging in anti-social behaviour.

With the other amendments to the DDA, this makes radical changes to the legislation, specifically in relation to actions by recalcitrant dog owners in their community.

An injunction is a useful tool to tackle bad behaviour before it escalates into something more serious. The purpose of it is to stop a person acting in a way that affects others negatively or positively preventing him from even starting an intended activity. An injunction can prevent a dog owner from engaging in anti-social behaviour before it starts or can stop him immediately after it becomes a problem. The benefit of it is the speed with which it can be applied for and granted. An injunction should and would only be granted where a dog owner disregards the rights of others who share the same local space as them and their dogs.

Where an injunction is applied for varies according to the age of the alleged perpetrator of the offending behaviour. If he is over 18 years old it is issued by the county court and the High Court. If he is under 18 years old it is issued by the youth court. An advantage of an injunction is it can include negative and positive points that the perpetrator must address and change. While it will generally include a prohibition on his activity it can also include positive requirements that the perpetrator has to address that are the underlying causes of his anti-social behaviour. Where the perpetrator is under 18 years old the agencies must consult with the youth offending teams when an application is made. That is a practical remedy as youths are on every high street every day with barely controlled dogs as they struggle to hold the chains of their snarling charges towards passing strangers and their dogs.

An injunction has legal repercussions which can land a person within the criminal justice system. While a breach of the injunction is not a criminal offence, nevertheless any breach must be proved to the criminal standard of 'beyond reasonable doubt'. The reason is the penalties for the perpetrator are quite severe. Where someone is over 18 years old any proven breach is a civil 'contempt of court' which has a maximum sentence of an unlimited fine or up to two years' imprisonment. The penalty for those under 18 years old is a supervision order or a civil detention order up to a maximum of three months' detention.

Given those penalties, especially detention and imprisonment for what is not a criminal offence, an appeal is essential. Hence someone who is over 18 years old can appeal to the High Court. A person under 18 years old can appeal to the Crown Court.

Although an injunction is a serious action, it has several advantages over the present position. An important change is it is available to a wider range of agencies than the form of injunction it replaced. It can be sought on a civil burden of proof, unlike the old anti-social behaviour orders [ASBO]. Further, unlike an ASBO, there is no need to prove 'necessity' as the test is whether the dog owner is behaving in an anti-social manner that is affecting the 'quality of life' of his neighbours. While it is usually a form preventing some action, an injunction has the scope to impose positive requirements on a perpetrator to focus on long-term solutions. That has the advantage of a resolution for the dog owner, his neighbour and his dog.

18.8 Practical

The new powers are designed to allow the authorities to take action before a dog bites another person or another animal.

The CPN extends an existing power where a dog is a nuisance by barking too loudly or too often, or both, especially at strangers and/or throughout the day and night. Often there is an 'associated' problem. It is not an isolated effect. The test is whether the dog's behaviour is having a persistent and unreasonable detrimental effect on the quality of life of those in the locality. Some people have a peculiar habit of bagging their dog's excrement and hanging it on trees as a substitute Christmas gift no one desires.

These practical examples serve to show what differences the changes can make to the safety and quality of life of those who are or might be affected by reckless dog owners:

1. The owner has a dog on a lead that snarls at people and children outside a school. The parents and the children are frightened. It happens on a daily basis. The owner could be banned from bringing his dog to the school gates at all and/ or forced to muzzle his dog.

2. The owner allows his dog to escape from a hole in the fence and stray from his home into the neighbouring streets. The dog is aggressive to passers-by and other animals. The owner could be forced to secure his garden and mend his fence so the danger is fended off in future.

3. A group of residents complain that some owners fail to clean up after their pets on a popular grassed area or park. They hang the faeces in plastic bags on the bushes and trees. If dog faeces are touched by a child they can cause toxocariasis, which can lead to blindness. The owners could be banned from exercising their dogs in that area at present and in the future.

4. An owner of a large dog attends a hospital for treatment. He has obviously been drinking and is unsteady on his feet. He is abusive to the staff and his dog is barking and jumping up at other patients and visitors. The owner would be prevented from visiting the hospital unless he was sober and without his

dog, unless he was on a leash and muzzled. He could be forced to undergo training and education classes for his dog as well so both were well-behaved on future occasions.

18.9   Habit

These changes are not aimed at responsible dog owners who respect other people and their animals. They are aimed at irresponsible dog owners who disregard the right of other people and their children and animals to be safe and untroubled by their dogs being out of control. The resultant fear or injury could and should be avoided; with these prohibitions there is an opportunity for that aim to be achieved.

The sanction of detention and prison remains where the perpetrator fails to fulfil his duty. Notwithstanding that sanction, it is infinitely better to solve the problem by conciliation and compromise. So the alternative action of a CPN or a PSPO forcing an owner to attend a training and behavioural class, use a lead, have his dog microchipped, use a muzzle, have his dog neutered or prevent him and his dog from visiting a place, is always the better choice. Then it nips the problem in the bud before the smell of the flower has time to go sour, let alone bloom. The balance is between ensuring the quality of life of those who are genuinely troubled by badly behaved dogs as compared to the pettiness of the querulous quidnunc. If that balance is achieved then the spirit of these changes will ensure the enjoyment and safety of those affected in their own home and neighbourhood.

Significantly, a PSPO can last for a period of up to three years. That power was not available within the previous legislation. Given that timescale it allows the agencies to monitor the dog owner to ensure he complies with the particular order as there is always the chance that any change is only temporary. This period enables the agency to ensure he does not revert to the bad habitual behaviour it has sought to negate.

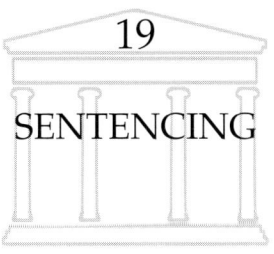

19

SENTENCING

19.1 Sentence

The Sentencing Council [SC] issued the first Guidelines on the DDA on 20 August 2012. Until then the courts treated defendants with undue leniency while killing dogs as a perfunctory sentence. The SC recommended increased sentencing powers for the courts according to the various offences. In aim it was an aid to the courts. Nevertheless, it had an inherent weakness in that the proposed sentences remained too lenient. It was also overtaken by the prescient ideas of the High Court in *Sandhu* in 2012. Therefore the SC amended the Guidelines on 1 July 2016. [See: **11.4**]

The approach of the SC is extended by the ABCPA. It has increased from seven-fold from a maximum of two years' imprisonment to 14 years' imprisonment for the most serious offence where the victim is killed. It also has introduced new offences in relation to an attack and injury to a person or an assistance dog. Now the maximum sentence is:

(a) 14 years if a person dies as result of being injured;
(b) five years in any other case where a person is injured;
(c) three years in any case where an assistance dog is injured whether or not the dog dies.

An instructive case happened in Liverpool in 2013. Clifford Clarke, a 79 year old man, was a retired hospital porter preparing his midday meal at his home. He opened his kitchen door to air the room where he was preparing a pan of Scouse [a type of stew]. He was immediately attacked by a huge dog, who overcame him.

The dog, Charlie, was a Presa Canario that had escaped through a wooden panel from the owners' home. Charlie was owned by Hayley Sulley and Della Woods. Both Sulley and Woods went to a barbeque, leaving Charlie at home alone. Charlie had been neglected and had not been fed or watered for 45 hours. He was 'left to swelter without shade on one of the hottest days of the year'. Charlie was 'so hungry he was seen in the hours before attacking Mr Clarke attempting to devour a plastic bowl, bird food and cigarette butts'.

With regard to Mr Clarke's injuries, at Liverpool Crown Court it was said that the dog 'amputated' his left arm and left his right arm 'hanging by a thread'. Judge Mark Brown said: 'I am satisfied this dreadful and forceful attack on Mr Clarke was entirely avoidable … Mr Clarke was literally eaten alive by Charlie when large amounts of tissue were ingested by the dog and that is a very shocking, appalling and tragic event.' A police marksman shot Charlie twice and he died at the scene.

Sulley and Woods were each sentenced to 12 months' imprisonment. They would serve half that term at most. Given the present prison overcrowding they would have been eligible for release on licence after three months. At the time the maximum sentence was two years' imprisonment. Such a case would now warrant a much longer sentence. After a guilty plea it should proportionately be at least seven years. It should be much longer, ten to 12 years', if a conviction was after a trial.

Dogs can be used as a weapon by crooks and drug dealers to attack 'unwelcome' visitors, be they police or other gang members. The new sentences will reflect the higher maximum. Hence, as they are now hybrid offences, many more will be sentenced in the Crown Court.

19.2   Severe

The combination of the SC Guidelines and the ABCPA will result in more severe sentences. There will be no reason for hand-wringing frustration from judges like Butterfield J in *R. v. Murphy* [2013] 2 Cr.

App. R. (S) 70: 'If [Murphy] did not recognise her propensity to go for other dogs during that time when he was exercising her, then he was blind to the obvious.'

More cases will be tried in the Crown Court before a jury. The courts must pay more respect to where the true liability for the canine criminality lies. They must distinguish between the behaviour of an irascible dog compared to the delinquency of an irascible owner.

These sentences show how the courts have treated the owners and their dogs:

In *R. v. Cox* [2004] 2 Cr. App. R. (S) 54 Jacqueline Cox pleaded guilty to an aggravated offence of keeping a dog that was dangerously out of control and attacked a seven-year-old boy. Her sentence was reduced to three months custody. All seven dogs were destroyed.

In *R. v. Donnelly* [2007] EWCA Crim 2548 the defendant was subject to an ASBO in relation to the same dog. This was his third appearance with the same dog. The Court of Appeal reduced his suspended sentence to 35 weeks. His dog was destroyed.

In *R. v. Baballa* [2011] 1 Cr. App. R. (S) 50 four dogs belonging to Moses Baballa attacked and injured Jalal Dawad. Baballa pleaded guilty to an aggravated offence in respect of a mongrel and a simple offence for the other three pit bull terriers. Baballa received a suspended sentence. The court ordered the mongrel to be killed.

19.3   Approach

The guidelines specify '*8 Steps*' that have to be taken by the court in relation to an offence. The guideline deals with all aspects of the offences, particularly the *character of the owner*. Allied to that position, it has to take into account the *character of the dog*. Both aspects are welcome as part of the sentencing process because prior to it the courts seemed intent on disregarding any references for the owner and equally for the dog.

The guideline has been published following a consultation that received responses from members of the public, judges and magistrates, the police, and animal welfare organisations. Those responses shaped the approach:

(a) The guideline widened the definition of 'vulnerable victims' so it applies to children and the elderly, disabled and blind or visually impaired people.

(b) The guideline was extended to include injuries to other animals as an aggravating factor in the offence of allowing a dog to be out of control and causing injury. This was supported by many responses, including the CPS and the Association of Chief Police Officers.

(c) The problem of dog fighting was taken into account in the offence as training or possessing paraphernalia for dog fighting is a factor increasing the seriousness of this offence. This follows concerns from the Police Federation about this issue.

19.4   Steps

The new SC Guideline is effective from 1 July 2016. It applies to all offenders over the age of 18 years, regardless of the date of the offence.

The offences are split into five sections that reflect the various degrees of seriousness. Those sections are:

1. Dog dangerously out of control where a person is injured and death results.

2. Dog dangerously out of control where a person is injured.

3. Dog dangerously out of control where an assistance dog is killed or injured.

4. Dog dangerously out of control.

5. Possession of a prohibited dog and breeding, selling, exchanging or advertising a prohibited dog.

The eight steps have to be followed in order by the court. Step 1 requires the court to determine to which of the three categories the offence applies.

Step 1: Determining the offence category:

Culpability:

When determining the offender's culpability, the court has to refer to the factors indicating that culpability outlined in the specific section. Those factors in turn comprise the main factual elements of the offence. Those indicators include these:

Higher culpability:

Dog used as a weapon or to intimidate people.
Dog trained to be aggressive.
Training and/or possession of paraphernalia for dog fighting.

Medium culpability:

Failure to respond to warnings or concerns expressed by others about the dog's behaviour.
Failure to intervene in the incident [where it would have been reasonable to do so.]
Ill-treatment or failure to ensure welfare needs of the dog [where connected to the offence and where not charged separately.]

Lower culpability:

Attempts made to regain control of the dog and/or intervene.
Provocation of the dog without fault of the offender.
Incident could not have reasonably been foreseen by the offender.

Step 2: Starting point and category range:

After determining the relevant category of Step 1 the court should use the appropriate starting point to reach a sentence by proceeding to Step 2. The starting point applies to all offenders, regardless of the plea or their antecedents. The court then has to further consider adjusting the position according to a list of aggravating or mitigating features set out in each of the specific sections.

Each one contains a list, which is not exclusive, of additional factual elements relating directly to both the offence and the offender. They are used throughout the Guideline and include:

Aggravating factors:

Statutory aggravating factors

Previous convictions, having regard to (a) the nature of the offence to which the conviction relates and its relevance to the current offence and (b) the time that has elapsed since the conviction.

Offence committed whilst on bail.

Offence motivated by or demonstrating hostility based on any of the following characteristics or presumed characteristics of the victim: religion, race, disability, sexual orientation or transgender identity.

Other aggravating factors

Victim is a child or otherwise vulnerable because of personal circumstances.

Sustained or repeated attack.

Lack or loss of control of the dog due to influence of alcohol or drugs.

Factors reducing or reflecting personal mitigation

No previous convictions or no relevant/recent convictions.

No previous complaints against the dog.

Evidence of responsible ownership.

When the court has considered all the relevant factors, it might decide it is appropriate to move from the identified category range. At that point the court can take into account an offender's previous convictions. The court then moves to steps 3 to 8, which includes a credit for a guilty plea, the question of compensation, disqualification and destruction of or a contingent destruction order for the dog.

The aim of it is to provide guidance so there is a consistent approach to sentencing and appropriate sentences are given to owners of dangerous dogs. It will help courts use their power so irresponsible owners who put the public at risk can be imprisoned and banned from keeping dogs in the future.

The guideline is aimed at offenders and victims, for the father is a victim if he has witnessed an attack on his family and thereafter has to share in the sheer trauma caused by that out of control dog. Now that can be taken into account as it is an 'other aggravating factor' if there is a *'significant continuing effect on witnesses to the attack'*. Then there is the real culprit, namely the feckless owner who is reckless with regard to the lives of other people as well as the fate of his dog. At present the DDA has failed the man and his family by being too lenient with those typical owners. To merely keep killing the dogs as happens at present does not begin to address the problem at all. You end up with a pile of dead dogs matched by irresponsible owners who will in due course just go to a shelter and get another 'rescued' dog. To be effective this Guideline needs a delivery to match its promise. It has to show the public that its legal teeth will bite the criminal owner. At present the victim is barely and rarely compensated and the dog is often routinely destroyed. This Guideline should target those responsible as a matter of fact yet who often escape from the fate they deserve, while the victim and the dog continue to reap the whirlwind of the actions of every irresponsible owner.

A common criticism of the SC is that the sentences are too low. That criticism is well-founded. The expected change has not been realised. Considering the worst case scenario of the death of the victim, the SC considers within the 'higher' and 'medium' and 'lower' culpability range to be six to 14 years and two to seven years' and high level community order to two years' custody respectively.

Those are all too low as the 'starting point' in each case is eight years', four years' and 12 months' custody respectively. So where death results it could be a community order or 12 months' custody, which would be reduced by a plea of guilty to eight months' and further reduced by the CJA so the defendant would serve half his sentence. He would be eligible for release on licence after two months.

Even in the 'high' culpability range it could be six years' custody, which would be reduced by a plea of guilty to four years' and further reduced by the CJA so the defendant would serve half his sentence. He would be eligible for release on licence after 12 months. Meanwhile the victim is dead.

19.5   Grandmother

Bruiser was an American pit bull who was kept in a 'flimsy' cage, which he escaped from 'without apparent difficulty'. Molly-Mae Wotherspoon was a six-month-old baby. Her grandmother, Susan Aucott, was 'in charge' while Molly-Mae's mother Claire Riley went for 'a night out'. Riley knew Bruiser was 'aggressive and jealous of her baby'. Aucott was an alcoholic who 'had had a glass of wine'. Bruiser escaped from the cage in the kitchen and opened the door of the lounge where Molly-Mae was on the floor. He attacked her, causing severe injuries. Molly-Mae died at the scene at 11.08 p.m. Bruiser was destroyed at the scene.

In 2016 Aucott and Riley were sentenced to two years' imprisonment. Carr J said: 'Bruiser was a large, strong and aggressive dog. He should never have been couped up in a small house with a new baby, and the two of them should never have been left alone by Claire Riley in [the] charge of someone such as Susan Aucott.' Each will be released on licence after a year.

Craig Greve had a 'life-time ban' from keeping dogs in 2012. A police officer said Greve showed a 'complete disregard' for that ban. Greve had a bulldog, Solo, which attacked Rona Greve, his grandmother. Solo bit her 16 times. Rona Greve suffered a heart attack and later died from her injuries. Solo was destroyed at the scene.

Craig Greve had witnessed the attack. He lied about ownership of Solo and claimed his dog belonged to his grandmother. Later Greve admitted two charges, namely being in charge of Solo and possession of him while he was disqualified. In 2016 he was sentenced to 5½ years' imprisonment.

19.6   Conclusion

The public need protection from those who treat their dogs in such a way as to transmute their character. The dogs do too. Dangerous dogs are not born that way but created by dangerous owners. It is that type of owner rather than the type of dog that should be restrained by the law.

The increased sentences affect the offences as we now have the means and the method. That needs to be marked by judicial action in favour of the public and the victims. The courts must move from their present approach of killing a dog while protecting their offending owner. So far we have failed in that aim and action.

20

ANIMALS DO NOT HAVE AN ARTIFICIAL PERSONALITY

20.1   Horse sense

On 11 August 2016 the politicians of New Zealand announced that they were taking action to destroy *all* the non-indigenous animals by 2050. Many of the creatures will be poisoned using sodium flouroacetate, which causes heart or respiratory failure in mammals. That positive measure for the people will cost $9 billion and be led by the Predator Free New Zealand. It was the Maoris, Norwegians and English that introduced the non-indigenous animals to their country. They were initially seen as an asset, now they are devalued as a liability.

That action adopts the universal view of animals given that each sacrificial step is an echo of the etymological origin and purpose of the ritual of our holocaust and scapegoating of them. If in the future it should prove to be viewed as necessary in New Zealand then they will kill the indigenous animals too. By that action and aim that country is no different than any other anywhere, including Britain.

Legally the animals' lives and future count for nothing. They are not even pawns in a political game. Animals are less than pawns because they are not part of our plan, which comprise of rules made by and for us. We decide who can share the benefit and who will bear the burden. We dictate the state of society's game plan so animals are bound by our ball and their chain.

The English jurist Blackstone stated in his *Commentaries* [1765] that: 'Natural persons are such as the God of nature formed us; artificial are such as are created and devised by human laws for the purposes of society and government; which are called corporations or bodies politic.' We have adopted that idea to categorise people and bodies that are either legal entities as *'natural'* or *'artificial'*. The essence of that status is it allows an entity to have rights and duties, to sue and be sued, to prosecute and defend. That status grants a body, whether belonging to a person or a company, a legal right of life.

Animals do not have that status in our society because we deny them what we possess: a legal *'personality'*. As a result they are our subjects and subject to our legal rules.

Yet certain 'things' of value are specifically chosen by us to have a legal status and consequent rights. The Whanganui River in New Zealand became a 'legal entity' and so was accorded a 'legal voice' in 2012. It was the first time a river had been granted a 'legal identity'. Under the agreement the river has been given a 'legal status' under the name Te Awa Tupua. Two guardians have been appointed with the role of 'protecting the river'. The New Zealand politicians thereby granted a status to the river that they have deliberately denied to animals. That denial applies to all animals, be they indigenous or otherwise.

In 2015 the New Zealand government amended the Animal Welfare Act 1999 by including a provision that *'animals are sentient'*. Whether that is a perverse anthropocentric status or a positive step towards a better future awaits the verdict of a future jury.

What is sure beyond reasonable doubt however is that the New Zealand approach mirrors English law as we do not recognise animals worthy of possessing an 'artificial personality'. Lacking that artificiality renders an animal's voice as valueless as a ventriloquist's dummy. Animals, being hamstrung without the use of a human tongue, are our artefacts.

That echoes the Founding Fathers of America, who declared their self-evident truth that 'all men are created equal' while excluding black people and every non-American not in their self-image. To them it was as natural as a master of slaves trading them as a sub-human species. Many signatories of the Declaration of Independence owned slaves. Those signatories saw slaves as 'property', just as we see animals without any legal rights.

It is why Moses Finley identified in *Ancient Slavery and Modern Ideology* [1980] the reason: 'When Roman lawyers defined a slave as someone who was in the *dominium* of another, they used the quintessential property term *dominium*. They were not dissuaded by the slave's human quality [not even when they used the word homo to refer to a slave, as they did frequently]. Nor were the millions of slave owners who bought and sold slaves, overworked them, beat and tortured them, and sometimes put them to death, precisely as millions of horse owners have done throughout history.'

Finley has pinpointed with precision how we have forged a relationship with animals much as we have done with slaves. Given the choice, we have chosen and continue to be parasitic rather than symbiotic. One moment we are willing to vivify them, next moment we are willing to kill them. Just as the Romans did, we morally and legally ignore the impure truth that one man's meat is another animal's life.

The principle we prefer not to dwell upon is that many members of our society are vulnerable because we deem them to be inferior. Our law then allows us to assume superiority over those in our clutches as by our conspiracy we gain control without any loss. When might is right we have the legal and moral benefit that the victim cannot resist our strength. Like Roman lawyers, though they are intertwined in all aspects of our society, animals are our underdogs' underdog. We can use them in commerce, religion, science, sport and war. Then whoever they are, the last act our victims will do when completing their duty to us is to die.

20.2   Principle

We can grasp what law is meant to be for and do by considering the reason we have a Human Rights Act yet only an Animal Welfare Act. That signifies the principle of our self-ordained superiority. Rights run with life itself and guarantees legal freedom.

Would we be content with a Human Welfare Act that granted state care during our life? Human rights are beyond price because without them people cannot live and die freely with dignity. Without them people are fettered by the chains of law and subjugation.

Racism is evil because it devalues and prejudges people without a valid cause. Those affected by racism who oppose it but do not support animal rights fail to understand the nature of and reason for racism.

Sexism is base as it discriminates against humans purely as a matter of biology. Women who oppose it but do not support animal rights fail to understand the foundation of and need for suffragettes.

Children and animals both need legal protection because they are vulnerable in similar ways. Both need others to ensure that they are not abused and used so as to cause them suffering. The only way they can be protected is for children and animals to be in a category where we apply the law with the respective victim in mind. In *RSPCA v. Chester Crown Court* [2006], Beatson J said: 'You are like the NSPCC in relation to children.' That was an astute observation because despite the common claim that 'it cares more about animals than children', the RSPCA was instrumental in forming the NSPCC.

20.3   Pus

Our relationship with animals is based on a cycle of suffering caused and controlled by us and sanctioned by law. Our benefit is balanced against their burden, so the animal usually loses. Consequently, the limited legal concessions animals possess are subject to our interests.

Modern legal suffering caused to animals tends to be committed by us for reasons of commerce, pleasure or science. It is valuable to consider how Swinfen Eady LJ viewed the legitimacy of a gift under a trust for animals: 'A gift for the benefit and protection of animals tends to promote and encourage kindness towards them, to discourage cruelty, and to ameliorate the condition of the brute creation, and thus to stimulate humane and generous sentiments in man towards the lower animals, and by these means promote feelings of humanity and morality generally, repress brutality, and thus elevate the human race.' [*Re Wedgewood* [1915] 1 Ch. 113]

The judge illuminated the reason that morality in our treatment of animals is the core issue. Yet a century later we have myriad forms of suffering now that are legally permissible that were not even within the imagination of the judiciary at that time. There was a time when our judges considered that morality and law coincided to obviate our innate penchant for cruelty.

The judges in *Ford v Wiley* recognised the repercussions of cruelty to animals and abhorred it in clear and certain terms. Wiley, a farmer, caused 32 oxen to have their horns sawn off close to their heads. He claimed this changed their 'character, made them quiet, they were fattened easily, more could be stored in the yard and in trucks, and increased the value of the animal from 30/- to £2.' Their horns were 'sawn off by Wiley's men with a common saw as close to the head as a flat saw could do it. They bled for five or six minutes and blood flowed from their horns every time the heart beat. His man was covered in blood ...' That man, a Mr Feek, was asked if the animals made a noise. He said: 'I should think they did – you might have heard them a mile off. I told Mr Wiley I would not do it again.'

Professor Walley, the Principal of the Royal Veterinary College in Edinburgh, testified that: 'Every tooth of the saw as it tears through the structure causes excruciating pain and the inflammation following the operation produces great and prolonged suffering. Cutting through the sinus is excessively painful and very cruel ... the pain caused by cutting the sensitive tissues is like cutting through the quick of a man's finger ... the pain continued for a fortnight and probably longer.'

Pus was still discharging from the sensitive membranes for almost a month. F. B. Lust, a vet, said alternative methods would prevent goring of other animals and workers. The actual method used 'caused extreme and prolonged pain, was cruel and absolutely unnecessary.'

After hearing that evidence anyone would be forgiven for considering the verdict to be a certainty. Anyone that is except the magistrates who heard that evidence: they acquitted Wiley. The magistrates considered that Wiley had no cruel intention. They believed he believed that the operation was for the benefit of the animals.

The divisional court rejected the reasoning of the magistrates and reversed their decision. Throughout the judgment the judges referred to the legal and moral aspects of the suffering and our collective duty as a community towards all animals.

Lord Coleridge CJ added this clincher: 'On the walls, higher than a man could reach, were marks of blood as if made by a syringe which had spurted out from the animals ... here sloughing and pus running down their cheeks after 25 days ... to put thousands of cows and oxen to the hideous torments described in this evidence in order to put a few pounds into the pockets of their owners is an instance of such utter disproportion between means and object, as to render the practice described here not only barbarous and inhuman, but I think clearly unlawful also. I am not afraid of the possible application of the principles to other practices which have not yet been attacked, but which may hereafter turn out to be prohibited by law. If the suffering is necessary ... it may be inflicted; if not, it is an 'unnecessary abuse of the animal' and we have neither the moral nor the legal right to inflict it, a conclusion not of sentimentalism but of good sense.'

The tenor of his judgment was endorsed by Hawkins J, who said: 'If the law were that any man or any body of men could in his or their own interest, or for his or their pecuniary benefit, cause torture and suffering to animals without legitimate reason, and could, when charged with cruelty, excuse himself or themselves upon the ground that he or they honestly believed the law justified them, though in fact it did not, it is difficult to see the limits to which such a principle might be pushed, and the creatures it is man's duty to protect from abuse, would often-times be suffering victims of gross ignorance and cupidity.'

Hawkins J made no attempt to camouflage his contempt for Wiley: 'Anyone who could read that description and reflect for a moment upon the agony of poor mutilated creatures without being painfully touched with commiseration must be devoid of all pity for the miseries and distresses of God's creations, unless under direct necessity, must indeed be cruel in heart, and insensible to every dictate of humanity.'

While both judges considered the relationship between money and the animal's suffering was insufficient to justify practices that were inhumane and unlawful, it has to be borne in mind that that was in 1889. Now we have many forms of animal abuse, including battery cages, circuses, experiments, factory farming, ritual slaughter and zoos that are legal.

Hawkins J raised a salient point: 'Many instances might be put in which, at the cost of extreme suffering to the animal, it might be rendered more serviceable for the use of man, by means of an operation which it is impossible to suppose that any Legislature would sanction. What would be said of a man who sewed up the eyelids of his sheep, or cut the hoofs of his cattle to the quick to keep them from moving about as nature dictated, in order that they should more quickly fatten in his field for his profit?'

The judge considered acts such as sewing eyelids of sheep were not reasonably necessary. Those examples were chosen to indicate extreme measures that were not legal on pure economic grounds. Now practices are legal that make them seem by no means extreme. When the Bristol University Division of Farm Animal Science investigated 'broiler chickens' they found that: 'The welfare implications of this study are profound. Worldwide approximately 20 billion broilers are reared within similar husbandry systems that are biased towards economics of production and detrimental to poultry welfare.'

In *State v. Newcomb* [2016] 359 Or 756 Linder SJ posed the quintessential juristic question: 'Here, the seized property was a living animal – Juno, the dog – not an inanimate object or other insentient physical item of some kind. Central to the issue that we must resolve is whether that distinctive fact makes a legal difference.' For a common law judge to even have to pose that question shows at once the problem that infects our legal system.

20.4   Slavery

When in 2016 Steven Wise, the American attorney, made the application for a writ of *habeas corpus* to attempt to gain '*personhood*' for Hercules and Leo, the imprisoned chimpanzees, he made a comparison with prisoners and slavery. However, the presiding judge in the New York State Supreme Court, Justice Jaffe, in *The Non Human Rights Project v. Stanley* [2015] Index No 152736/15, was visibly irritated by Wise during his application and tetchily asked him to refrain from constantly referring to '*slavery*' in describing the plight of animals. Although the judge was well-meaning she was wrong. The submissions of Wise relating to 'slavery' and a lack of rights are so inextricably linked from the time of the Greeks through Roman law to the present that his analogy was and remains valid.

A Spartan's priority shows how he categorised his slaves in comparison to his animals: 'Apart from land, his house, and his armour, a Spartan's most valuable possessions would normally have been his slaves, horses and dogs'. [*Spartan Law*: D. M. MacDowell: (1986)]

In that respect, when the Greeks enslaved people whom they conquered they called them a '*natural*' slave. Initially the word 'natural' was used to describe a female slave taken in war. That gave them the advantage that any children of the natural slave belonged to the master as children born of slaves were also slaves by birth and blood as a fact of 'nature'. To that extent the concept of slavery was a creature of law. Thereafter the ownership and trading of slaves meant they were as freely disposable as any inanimate chattel. Slaves were thus in every way treated and traded as merely being a different form of chattel, much like cattle and other animals. Slaves and animals were neither born free nor could be seen as other than property as a matter of law. The one thing a slave was not was a human being. Killing another person's slave was a criminal act equivalent to damaging his 'property'. That is the same as killing his animal under English law.

Slavery in America was so rife with injustice that in *Commonwealth v. Turner* 26 Va. (Rand) [1827] the court held that it had no jurisdiction to try a defendant slave master who 'cruelly', 'excessively' and 'violently' assaulted his slave as the victim did not die. The court held that while a 'private' assault would be excluded a 'public' beating could be prosecuted. However, the court made clear that that was not to protect the slave, but to avoid a breach of the peace. The reason was: 'The same would be the law, if a horse had been so beaten.'

Lawrence Friedman in *A History of American Law* [1973] captured the prejudice with stark accuracy: 'The exact origins of the legal meaning of slavery are obscure, though, clearly, developing custom guided the lawmaker's hand. Before the end of the 17th Century, slavery had become a definite legal status in both North and South; it was peculiarly associated with the Negro; it had become a terrible, timeless condition, inherited by children from their mothers. The legal status of the slave, as it took shape in the statute books, reflected and ratified social discrimination and the sense of race.'

That passage magnifies the gimlet eye of that 'timeless condition' that places the children of a slave mother in the same position as the progeny of all animals. Chattelism and cattle is connected by custom, history and law. For similar to slaves who do not feel the chains until they move, we choose when animals can move.

20.5   Personality

Animals have no soul. At least that is what we conceive to believe. Then, as a self-engendered superiority, we have decided that animals are so unlike us they are not deserving of rights. Although that hardly explains vivisection as we experiment on animals because they are so like us and can feel pain like us, that we prefer them rather than us to be the ones to suffer. We can conveniently overlook any idea of sentience, as we have historically in the case of slaves. Yet we have gone much further in our assessment of animals: by concluding that they have no souls we rely on that lame claim to deny that they are worthy of a legal *'personality'*.

Our problem in how to treat animals was immediately solved by Aristotle, who claimed that the 'intellectual or rational soul' was possessed by man alone. Later, that absurd notion was adopted by Descartes, who claimed that animals were mere automata without feelings. Their cries and howls if struck was not an indication of pain, but no different than the chime of a clock. That is such a crass idea you might as well say 'all animals except Frenchmen have souls'. Then if you substitute humans for 'Frenchmen' the Cartesian reasoning is the same.

The problem that stems from Aristotle and Descartes is that their belief is no more than that, a self-serving belief. They may be philosophers, but there is no proof at all that their belief is true. After all, Sir William Petty in *The Petty Papers* [1927] believed that humble bumble bees were special because 'their souls seem like the souls of men'.

Which of them is right and which is wrong is purely speculative. There is no evidence to support the idea that humans have souls and animals do not. Later the immoral and illogical idea percolated through to our legal system. In our social conspiracy we have assumed that it was so and elevated that idea to a presumption that we use as a substitute for proof.

Given the treatment meted out to slaves, women and animals, all considered to be 'inferior' by Aristotle, it proves that a community can use any legal ruse to justify any abuse of those who are vulnerable and under your control. As for the Cartesian concept, that made it permissible for humans to experiment on animals. The real reason was, as Descartes later confessed, it freed them from 'any suspicion of crime, however often they may eat or kill animals'.

Denying mortality to animals has granted us a legal right to treat them as we wish subject to limiting their suffering. We assume we have a soul, transfer that belief into a presumption and then adopt that presumption as proof. Then we adapt the same assumption to prove the reverse, namely that animals do not have a soul. It is a premise devoid of logic that leads to cant rather than a legal tenet. Moreover, the concept of who has and who has not a soul is irrelevant to justice. After all, if it was suggested that the only living creatures on the planet with a soul were animals, any attempt by us to show that that belief is false is beyond proof.

20.6 Justice

In 2016 it was advocated by the European Union Committee on Legal Affairs that as robots possess artificial intelligence they are deserving of legal rights, a recognition of an *'electronic personhood'*. In Europe, at least, the idea is getting some traction. Robots are playing an increasingly active role in Europe's economy and society, assembling machines, conducting surgeries and driving vehicles. It is seriously claimed that as robots possess 'cognitive features' and 'interact with their environment' they should have rights and responsibilities under the law.

Following a vote on regulating intelligent machines, the European Parliament has taken a step forward in the march to identify robots as 'electronic persons'. That will effectively grant robots a legal personality. Such a status is derived from the Members of the European Parliament [MEPs] who endorsed it during a debate on the strict rules of how humans interact with machines so that they can be held accountable for any harm they do. That would apply to self-driving cars. The MEPs showed political wisdom by supporting that status as they confirmed that robots also 'must have kill switches' as part of their role. There is also the reality and role of 'unethical robots' that possess the ability to pull a trigger on a weapon that could kill a person. Together all these factors pose a moral problem which can only be resolved by legislation. A serious suggestion by scientists seeking to grapple with this seemingly practical mechanical problem is to manufacture robots with an in-built morality. The concomitant of such a practice is to place artificial intelligence above an animal's consciousness: it measures morality by using a mirror that reflects our natural prejudice. [See: *The i*: 17/2/17; *The Rise of the Robots*: BBC R4: 21 February 2017]

Alan Winfield, the only Professor of Robotics in the world, is concerned that we should be aware that robots are only 'android, not humanoid.' For it would be unethical to 'assume they are human'. Winfield is concerned for us lest we are deceived by robots and led to believe that they 'have more feelings for you'. Dr Jim Al-Khalili, who was interviewing Winfield, alluded to the question whether robots are 'sentient or not'. That unanswered question is as piquant as a Colt 45 given that robots are now equipped with LAWS, a *'lethal autonomous weapons system'*. Hence a robot could be armed and dangerous with the ability to shoot to kill. That ability, along with the robotic driverless car that can kill other road users, is the reason they are driven to consider their legal status. [See: *The Life Scientific*: BBC R4: 21/2/17]

A society that denies a legal status to animals who are our kindred spirits in so many manifest ways while considering a mass of flashing lights, metal, plastic and wires is worthy of being granted an 'artificial personality' is one that misunderstands the meaning of morality. For like us, though unlike robots, animals bleed and breathe, have a heart and a pulse.

Our common law as an instrument of social change always strives towards fairness and equality as that is ingrained within its sinews. A valid legal system naturally aspires towards a sense of justice for the community, which then inspires those within it to follow as well as lead for the future. Hence a law that promotes equitable treatment for animals is a test of a society as it moves with time's arrow towards justice for all.

Law is the universal language of natural justice. Much as a slave needed to be freed from his owner, animals need a legal personality. For that status alone guarantees the quintessence of natural justice that rights run with life itself. In the *Somerset v. Stewart* KB [1772], involving a claim by the master for his runaway slave, the court had to determine whether slavery was legal in England. Lord Mansfield CJ laid the foundation stone of its abolition: 'The state of slavery is of such a nature, that it is incapable of being introduced on any reasons, moral or political; but only by positive law … It's so odious, that nothing can be suffered to support it, but positive law … I cannot say this case is allowed or approved by the law of England; and therefore the black must be discharged.'

Abraham Lincoln said: 'I am in favour of animal rights as well as human rights. That is the way of a whole human being.' As the US president and a practising lawyer, he saw the law as it was and as it should be.

Dovetailing their ideas with an unassailable truth, Darwin said: 'Animals, whom we have made our slaves, we do not like to consider our equal.' In 2016 Attenborough echoed his view. [See: **Introduction**]

When Salt's *magnum opus* was reviewed by a Victorian feminist, Edith Ward, she stated in *Shafts* [1892]: 'The case for the animal is the case of the woman.

'What [is] more likely to impress mankind with the necessity of justice for women than the awakening of the idea that justice was the right of even an ox or a sheep?'

Animals must have a legal personality. Without such a personality there can be no progress towards justice for animals. Isonomy has no meaning or purpose if equality applies to humans alone. Philosophical discussions about rights are as valueless as verbal smoke rings fading into thin air unless and until animals possess a defined legal status.

If it is right that we can assume a superior role over animals and then treat or ill-treat them accordingly, then the law is wrong. Animals are entitled by virtue of being alive and sentient to the mantle of law. It is not that they breathe the same air as us that matters, but that they breathe to have life. Justice for animals is rooted in their very existence.

Animals need an artificial personality precisely because like us they are not artificial. Animals deserve an artificial personality as a matter of law because like us they are real. Jurisprudentially, a legal system that fails to protect vulnerable victims promotes the letter and spirit of injustice.

INDEX